How
ONENESS
Changes
EVERYTHING

Empowering Business Through
9 Universal Laws

RATANJIT S. SONDHE

BALBOA
PRESS

A DIVISION OF HAY HOUSE

Balboa Press books may be ordered through booksellers or by contacting:

Balboa Press
A Division of Hay House
1663 Liberty Drive
Bloomington, IN 47403
www.balboapress.com
1 (877) 407-4847

Printed in the United States of America.

Cover design: Alison Holen

For ordering information, please visit www.discoverhelp.com or contact the publisher at business@discoverhelp.com.

ISBN: 978-1-4525-7914-6 (sc)
ISBN: 978-1-4525-7916-0 (hc)
ISBN: 978-1-4525-7915-3 (e)

Library of Congress Control Number: 2013917269

Balboa Press rev. date: 10/28/2013

Table of Contents

Acknowledgments vii

Introduction ix

Chapter 1   A Wake-Up Call 1

Chapter 2   My Journey in America Begins 7

Chapter 3   My First Job in America 15

Chapter 4   Launching My Own Business 29

Chapter 5   Bets That Paid Off 45

Chapter 6   Remembering My Roots 53

Chapter 7   Taking a New Direction 81

Chapter 8   Who Am I? 85

Chapter 9   Perception and Reality 97

Chapter 10   A Tabula Rasa 115

Chapter 11   Making Our Best Better 129

Chapter 12 Shattering Limitations 143

Chapter 13 Discovering True Freedom 153

Chapter 14 Forging a New Company 159

Chapter 15 Empowering the Real Boss..171

Chapter 16 Help from Uncle Sam 185

Chapter 17 Principles in Action 195

Chapter 18 A Second Awakening.. 215

Chapter 19 Life after POLY-CARB 247

Appendix A Life's Intrinsic Wisdom.. 257

Immutable and Intrinsic Wisdom for Success in Life 277

Appendix B A Little Indian History 281

About the Author.. 285

This book is dedicated to the three amazing women to whom I am eternally grateful for having so deeply shaped and enriched my life:

My Mother
Amrit Kaur
For her amazing insight into Divine wisdom
and her inspiring me to search for truth within.

My Wife
Dolly A. Sondhe
For her unconditional love and support in leading
me in our uncompromising quest
to continuously making our best better.

My Daughter
Nisha Sondhe
For her loving and honest reflection and suggestions in helping me
to understand unconditional gratefulness, thereby
elevating my thoughts, work and creations.

Acknowledgments

To my parents who made me understand Oneness by first practicing and living Oneness in their everyday activities and decisions.

To all my extended family and friends for their love and guidance not only during this book project, but throughout my life. I am especially indebted to my sister-in-law Kitty Bhasin, MD, who encouraged, guided, and supported this book project.

To the many individuals with whom I had the honor of working alongside at POLY-CARB, thank you for your patience, strength, and innovative endeavors that gave the principles and values revealed in this book extraordinary life, depth, and meaning. I am also grateful to all the customers, suppliers, and consulting engineers over the years for their continuous support and on-going challenges that encouraged me to continuously improve my best.

To the owner of WELW radio and my spiritual brother, Ray C. Somich, who has stayed with me since 1995 to challenge and nurture the Oneness thought process both on radio and television. Thank you for your unconditional love and unstinting faith in me.

I am deeply indebted to the founder and past owners of the AASTHA TV channel Kirit and Neena Mehta for believing in me, and giving me the opportunity to air my Oneness-based television programs in more than 150 countries for many years, which allowed this thought process to reach millions of viewers worldwide.

I am also indebted to Pennie Yograj, founder and CEO of JUS Broadcasting Corp., for airing my television shows focused on Oneness across the U.S. and Canada on her JUS-PUNJABI TV channel for so many years.

I am utterly humbled by and grateful to all my viewers around the globe for their undying support and feedback to let me know how these programs have made such huge differences in their lives.

To my thousands of Facebook fans for their support and comments on my daily postings based on Oneness.

To those who have been significant and integral contributors to Discoverhelp, Inc. in all its facets, thank you for assisting me in realizing my dream of bringing the concept of Oneness to the world stage. Thank you to the Discoverhelp team who helped me with all of my television, radio, public speaking, and product development endeavors. A special thank you to Paula DePasquale and Sunder Iyer for continuously challenging our team to upgrade our products and content, and for keeping me grounded—and especially to David Christel, my writing collaborator and editor for his wisdom, experience, skills, and insights.

I'd like to thank the many people over the last four years who provided their discerning comprehension and thoughtful perceptions in bringing this book to the world.

To every person who crossed my path: you inspired and challenged me to practice and live Oneness. Through you, I came to genuinely understand its true meaning, and thus, my life has been forever enhanced and enriched. I thank you with the utmost, heartfelt appreciation.

And my final and greatest thanks must go to the bigger ONE present in all of us unifying us all in ONENESS.

Introduction

A person experiences life as something separated from the rest—
a kind of optical delusion of consciousness.
Our task must be to free ourselves from this self-imposed prison,
and through compassion,
to find the reality of Oneness.

—Albert Einstein

When I look at America, I always feel that it should be seen as an experiment that the entire human race has undertaken. In this experiment, the world has sent its best and brightest sons and daughters here—as well as the most challenging and spoiled citizens and the most revered and spiritual souls—to see what our human race can accomplish under the circumstance where there is a minimum of baggage, where hard work and innovation are not only rewarded but also respected, where there are no hierarchies or caste systems, where anyone can dare to dream big in a land where dreams do come true. As a result, this nation has been able to build the richest country on the face of the Earth. However, in the midst of this glitz and glamour, it would be a tragedy if we did not understand and realize the true strength that blessed us with this hard-won status.

I feel that what made this country the greatest was not its industrial revolution, its technology, its vast natural resources, its domination in the number of patents granted each year, its nuclear arsenal, or even its leadership or political system. In my humble assessment, this country's greatest asset is its core value system of basic honesty, working hard, keeping promises made with a simple handshake, understanding what is fair and living by that fairness, believing in people and accepting everyone at his or her face value, helping the needy without expectations (the United States is the most charitable nation in the world), and, most importantly, measuring success by a person's character and contribution to society rather than just by wealth and/or fame. Banks and lending institutions used to evaluate risk via three Cs: Character, Collateral, and Capacity. In today's world, those Cs have changed to Credibility, Collateral, and Capacity. As a result of eliminating Character as a key criterion for evaluating their own management, as well as interacting with their customers, institutions have not only paid an incredibly high price, but also brought this great nation to its knees.

I came to this country in 1968 as a student at The University of Akron. I still remember an incident at a local grocery store near our campus. I brought my groceries to the checkout counter, and after the clerk presented the tally, I realized that I had forgotten my wallet. The grocery clerk looked at me and said, "Don't worry. I have seen you so many times that I trust you. Please take your groceries and pay me the next time you are here." Such trust and honesty have been the cornerstones of America.

When I started my business here, I did so not to become rich or famous, but to see if a business could be built on and driven by the core values of trust, honesty, and integrity. This book is the true story of my business life in America, and, as you will find, these values will not only help you survive, but also help you succeed against any and all odds stacked against you.

I thought that in this time of turmoil from corporate corruption, a depressed economy, and the depleted faith of the average American in the fairness of our current system, it would be refreshing to read my story of struggles and survival empowered and supported by these values in action. I feel that if we, as Americans, lose our core value system, we will lose everything regardless of our apparent wealth, power, and technology.

Ultimately, a values-based system is not for the world, not even for the success it provides. It's for one's inner harmony, peace and satisfaction, which will radiate outwardly to the rest of the world. Sustainable worldly success is merely a consequence or bonus. Therefore, the task for each of us as individuals is to incorporate the universal laws contained within these pages into the very core of our being in order to gift the world with the greatest expression of who we are—the Divine presence residing within all of us. In essence, it is oneness.

Oneness is not a religion, cult, philosophy, or mythology. It is a simple yet profound truth. It means that every being and everything around us is part of an integral, omnipresent single resource and power. Any decision that embraces this thought process can never be wrong. Not only is this truth always empowering and fulfilling, it is also the essential core of every sustainable relationship, endeavor, happiness, and success in life.

Oneness is at the crux of this entire book. Without understanding and aspiring to live in harmony with the profound truth of oneness, a value system is only partially effective, as its focus is on personal needs and desires. Oneness connects us to all of life so that we are no longer about our egos, but about the bigger picture. We are no longer interested in selfish agendas, but in striving to uplift all of life.

My wish for you is that you find resonance in oneness and that the nine laws found within these pages will speak to your heart and soul.

Our true wealth is reflected in our character.
Our strength is reflected in our kindness.
Our generosity is reflected in our gratefulness.
Our wisdom is reflected in our selflessness.
Truth is reflected when we see one in all and all in one.

Ratanjit

www.discoverhelp.com

Chapter 1

A Wake-Up Call

"We have good news, and we have bad news."

I sat looking at my accountant and lawyer, unblinking, my mind charging about in several directions, apprehensive as to what the news could be. I got that funny sensation in the pit of my stomach when it feels like the rug is about to be pulled out from under me.

"The bad news is that POLY-CARB, Inc. is broke—but the good news is that you live in America. You can file for protection under Chapter 11 bankruptcy and settle all your debts for pennies on the dollar. We can do it very quickly without you losing your name or the business or accounts," both men explained, trying to sound upbeat in the face of this dispiriting news.

It was 1980, and I sat thinking to myself that this couldn't be true—the company couldn't actually be broke. I'd been working like a fanatic for years, nurturing the company, developing products, marketing, spending weeks on the road, traveling around the country to garner clients, and building a polymers company to rival the leaders in the field. My associates and I were continually building our customer base and had long-standing clients. We were busy and had orders in our pipeline. How could we possibly be broke?

I listened to both men, thanked them for meeting with me, and then returned to my office, feeling set adrift—no longer tethered to my own company. What was I going to do? Declare bankruptcy? How could I possibly do such a thing?

More importantly, how could I possibly create the shift needed to turn the company around? I needed to get a clear picture of how POLY-CARB had arrived at these crossroads after we'd worked so hard for so many years.

That night, I discussed the meeting with my wife, Dolly, who also worked at POLY-CARB. She oversaw everything and everyone's welfare. There had to be another option besides bankruptcy.

From a business point of view, bankruptcy would seem to be the most logical solution, and it is certainly considered a viable and reasonable direction to pursue.

But it truly did not feel like the right thing to do. Aside from closing the company down and letting people go, it didn't feel right ethically. Bankruptcy was too easy a way out—a cop-out really. Could I just say, "Oh well, that's life," and walk away, turning my back?

I brought all of the accounts home with me that weekend and analyzed them from top to bottom. I was completely shocked to discover that 90 percent of the sales the company had generated were created by me. I had seven vice presidents and a number of sales managers and sales reps, but the majority of my time was spent helping or correcting their 10 percent of the sales. With all of their expertise and experience, why was I producing the lion's share?

When I'd first started putting POLY-CARB together, I'd followed the advice of business professionals who looked at me with my education—two master's degrees and PhD work—but couldn't see past my turban. They only saw me as a crazy scientist who had no understanding of business.

They told me, "Look, you're a scientist, not a marketer, and you don't understand business. You need to surround yourself with people who know what they're doing." I heard the same explanation from my accountant, banker, lawyers, and advisers. They all must have been members of the same club.

On the surface, they all appeared to be correct, explaining that I needed to hire people with lots of experience. So I did, hiring people with fifteen to twenty years of experience and résumés that listed amazing past successes and marketing feats. For their positions, they felt they needed titles, offices, personal cars, personal assistants, etc. As the saying goes, "You get what you pay for." So I complied.

For many years, I thought I'd been doing the right thing—and spending a lot of money doing it—and now the company was failing. What was I doing wrong? I followed the advice of experts and felt I was doing the right thing on the surface, but was I?

How was it that a person like me, with no background in marketing and business, was generating 90 percent of the sales? What was it in me that was making this happen?

The more I thought about it, the more I realized that the focus of my inner being was always on adding the highest value to whomever I dealt with—and I always had an inner conflict with the language and actions of the experienced people around me. They were purely about making money, whereas my soul was always saying, "Ratanjit, it's all about adding value, not making money. Your sole purpose in life is to add the highest value you can in all your endeavors."

> My soul was always saying, "Ratanjit, it's all about adding value, not making money."

My priority wasn't to make a sale, but to provide my customers the distinct advantage of achieving higher profitability, higher productivity, ease of operations, and an even better understanding of their own business. It was ironic that this practice was coming from a person with no business experience. Why weren't the experienced people I had hired doing this?

When I looked deeply into their habits and ways of working, I realized that they worked in silos: they didn't talk to each other, they were concerned only with their commissions, and no one wanted to help anyone else. Their number-one priority was generating higher commissions for themselves with no interest in helping or even knowing the customer.

On top of this, they often sold the wrong product with the excuse that they weren't chemical engineers and didn't know the difference in products. They were just salesmen, they said, and what they really needed was a technical-support person to accompany them.

Instead, I tried to train them and give them a basic understanding of chemistry, but it was like talking to a brick wall. Their pet response was that if they'd wanted to be a chemist, then they'd have gone to school to be one. But their interest was in being a salesperson; that was why I'd hired them. Consequently, I ended up spending a lot of my time and resources correcting their mistakes.

Right now, though, bankruptcy was staring me in the face. I thought long and hard about the company, disturbed by its financial situation and equally disturbed that my accountant and lawyer were advocating bankruptcy. This kind of thinking went completely against how I'd been raised and educated.

I didn't sleep for two days as I tried to find a way out of this predicament. What was I going to do? How could I lower my overhead? What could I do to retrain the staff?

Determining my course of action was going to take some deep contemplation and an examination of all the events over time that had landed me and POLY-CARB in this present quandary. Deep within me, I felt something quiet yet dynamic beginning to bubble up into my consciousness. I instinctively knew that within me were the keys to resolving my dilemma—keys that were more than just the usual steps to success in methodologies, technologies, and systems.

What I was sensing burgeoning up in me were understandings about life—fundamental, essential, immutable, and intrinsic wisdom—that applied across the board to any field and, actually, to every human endeavor and our very character and being. It dawned on me that life never operates in silos, but is an integrated one that encompasses our personal, business, social, and spiritual lives.

I began writing, trying to encapsulate this wisdom. I knew that codifying it would get not only me and POLY-CARB back on track, but also every other aspect of my life. Bankruptcy was not an option. There *was* a way out of this predicament; I just needed to regain a higher and more elemental perspective of reality and rediscover the *real* rules of the game. The tangled web I was caught in was merely a temporary state of confusion and illusion.

As I pondered my situation and studied the inner workings of life, work and how success is achieved in all human endeavors, I realized that there was, deep within my core being, a truth I'd lived with my entire life. But, as life has a way of doing, I'd let the demands and pressures of everyday survival and the so-called expertise of others overshadow that truth. That truth is that the foundation of this wisdom, which simply, yet comprehensively, encapsulates all of life, is sort of a Prime Directive:

"For true, sustainable, and stress-free success and happiness, every thought, word, action, and decision must be completely immersed in oneness."

This truth—the wisdom of oneness—was deeply imbedded in me, yet I had managed to let it fade into the background. The upshot was that in order to attain "true, sustainable, and stress-free success and happiness," I needed to jettison everything I'd done up to this point and embark on a path of re-awakening and grounding to this wisdom—and

I needed to enroll everyone in POLY-CARB, too. It was going to be a formidable task, yet it was the only option that would ensure success at every level of my life and for those around me.

Oneness is the voice of clarity to everything in life, yet I'd sidelined this mind-set in favor of other people's principles, methodologies, and philosophies. I needed to peel away all the layers of external, worldly diversions and return to the wellspring of life: oneness.

Oneness is a simple concept that integrates everything and every person in a gestalt of interconnectedness and intrasupport. It's a 360-degree perspective seeking only to add the highest value to all of life. It's not about ego and personal agendas, but about the big picture. Hmmm … wasn't this what I was already doing? Apparently not, so how was I going to get myself re-integrated and POLY-CARB immersed in the concept of oneness?

I decided that the best way to begin unraveling the snarled and intricate web I'd fashioned was to return to my roots, the square one of my life. I needed to journey back to when it all started for me here in America.

The year was 1968, the same year Richard Nixon ran for the presidency and won; the feminist movement was picking up momentum; students took over five buildings at Columbia University, protesting the university's participation in the Institute for Defense Analysis; the Democratic National Convention in Chicago was marred by police violence against demonstrators; women's lib groups and NOW (the National Organization for Women) targeted the Miss America Pageant in Atlantic City; President Johnson called for a total halt to the bombing of North Vietnam; Apollo 7 orbited the Earth 163 times; Apollo 8 orbited the Moon; and Martin Luther King, Jr., Andy Warhol, and Bobby Kennedy were all assassinated.

It was a tumultuous year in which to take my first steps in a new land. I was the proverbial stranger in a strange land, but when we're young, adventure calls. Little did I know what lay ahead of me.

Chapter 2

My Journey in America Begins

I had always wanted to come to America—ever since I was eight years old. I dreamt of launching my own business. What it would be, I had no idea.

In 1968, while studying for my PhD at the University of Bombay, I applied for admission to a PhD program at The University of Akron in Akron, Ohio, and was accepted. I was scheduled to join my PhD program in September 1968. I received an I-20 form from The University of Akron to help me get my student visa from the American consulate in Mumbai (called Bombay at that time). At the time, I realized that per restrictions imposed by the Reserve Bank of India, I could only get eight dollars in American exchange to come to the US (See appendix B for more on that story.)

So, armed with a few dollars and two master's degrees—one in organic chemistry and the other in polymer technology—and two years' worth of a PhD program at the University of Bombay, my plan was to attain a PhD in polymer chemistry from a prestigious American university, such as The University of Akron, which is known worldwide for its polymer chemistry program.

Though I had my student visa, I hadn't received confirmation as to whether I was to receive a fellowship or scholarship. So the first thing I did when I arrived in Akron was get a room at the local YMCA. Then I visited Professor Harwood, my PhD advisor, at The University of Akron.

When I checked into the YMCA, it had been only three days since I'd left India and Dolly. This was the first time Dolly and I had been away from each other for any length of time since getting married in 1966. I was already missing her and wasn't sure when circumstances would allow us to be together.

I went to The University of Akron's administrative offices, and they gave me three letters, all from Dolly. I immediately read them and could hear her melodious and comforting voice. I thought about when I'd heard her voice for the very first time and had fallen in love with her.

Dolly and I grew up in totally opposite environments a thousand miles apart. She went to sophisticated convent schools in Bombay, and I was born in a remote desert area of Bikaner, although I did go to college at Birla Institute of Technology and Science (BITS) Pilani, an internationally known and sophisticated college, now a university. But her aunt on her mother's side, who was married to my cousin, saw both of us grow from children into adults. In her mind, we were made for one another. She often mentioned this point even when we were little.

The truth is that we grew up rather disliking each other even without having seen or met each other. Because Dolly came from Bombay and a society that includes Bollywood and glitz, I had created an image in my mind of a flashy, trendy, and ultramodern girl. Conversely, in Dolly's mind, Bikaner, where I was from, was provincial.

Finally, we accidently met at a friend's wedding in Delhi. We were introduced at her uncle's home in Delhi. Suddenly, our dislike for each other vanished, and instead, curiosity set in. We still didn't know much about each other, except that she wasn't as glitzy as I'd thought and I wasn't as provincial as she'd thought.

Following that meeting, I was admitted to a PhD program at the University of Bombay, and Dolly's aunt gave me her father's name, address, and home phone number to contact them. She reminded me that Bombay could be a very unsettling place for newcomers and said I should not hesitate to contact them if I needed help.

It so happened that my room at the dorm at Bombay University wouldn't be available for two months. I needed temporary lodgings. I didn't know anyone in the jungle of Bombay's concrete and steel and millions of people. As a final resort, I called the phone number given to me, hoping to talk to Dolly's father—and guess who answered the phone? Dolly.

There was an amazing combination of grace, manners, sophistication, and melody in her voice. I'd never heard anyone speak so elegantly. It was as if I were listening to divine music. There was an amazing clarity and innocence, as if I were looking straight into her soul and how pure it was. I didn't know what love was, but that was the closest I'd come to falling in love.

I asked her many questions, which she answered without hesitation and with the utmost composure. Obviously, she hadn't recognized me yet. We talked for almost an hour. Then she was interrupted by a call from her grandmother. Ending our conversation, she gave me her father's work phone number.

When I called her father, he was thrilled to hear from me and asked me to come to his factory, which produced auto parts for Fiat. He brought me to his home later that day in his Studebaker. Everyone was surprised to see me. He insisted that I stay with them for the two months I would be waiting for my dorm room.

Apparently, Dolly still had some reservations about this guy named Ratanjit, whom everyone in her family was telling her she should marry. As meticulous as she was, she didn't want to marry anyone who wasn't organized. One day, when I was out of the house, she and her sister, Kitty, went into my bedroom and opened my suitcase. They examined it thoroughly. They were very impressed with how organized, neat, and clean everything was.

That must have done the trick, as we were married November 20, 1966. Now at The University of Akron reading her three letters, I found they were not only comforting, but also made me realize that everything would be all right going forward. I received a letter every day until Dolly arrived three months later.

Dolly's letters gave me the courage to see Dr. Harwood, my PhD advisor, and ask him, "What does it take to get a scholarship or fellowship for the PhD program or any kind of financial help?" He explained that I would need to have a master's degree first class, the equivalent of being a straight-A student. I replied that I had two master's degrees that met that criteria.

He then asked if I had any teaching or research experience, as that would be helpful. I explained that I had been working for two years on my PhD at Bombay University before coming to the States. Before that, I was teaching at BITS in the chemical engineering department as a lecturer. My research work had also been published in international technical journals.

Upon hearing this, he stood up and asked me to follow him. We immediately went to see the dean. In five minutes, we discovered that my application had been misplaced and therefore never brought to the attention of the dean. The outcome was that Professor Harwood was able to immediately get me a fellowship in the amount of $300 a month in addition to my tuition being waived.

Later on, I was introduced to other students in the department, and the Office of Foreign Student Administration helped me get my paperwork ready for an F-2 visa, which was required to bring one's spouse into the US. I was thrilled that with this paperwork, Dolly would be able to join me soon. We were reunited after a long gap of 105 days on January 5, 1969, a frigid winter day of five degrees Fahrenheit that somehow brought amazing warmth to my heart. The climate was a shock for Dolly, who grew up in the warm weather of Mumbai, and she has never forgiven me for subjecting her to this "torture chamber," as she calls it.

Her second shock was when we stepped into our new home in America. Within the budget of $300 per month, I could only financially handle the rent of an old house near the university campus. As Dolly walked into the house, she could hear screeching sounds from the wood floors and the old, outdated, and worn-out furniture. Tears started flowing from her eyes. She asked me where I had brought her. "Is this America—that land of gold, milk, and honey?"

I hugged her and said, "What counts most is that at least we are together." I looked into her eyes and said, "I assure you that this is not the end, but our beginning of a future that we're going to build together."

That brought a smile to her face, which made that screechy old home into a palace for us.

Want to make God laugh? Tell Him your plans.

Now that I had my goddess of moral and emotional support, Dolly, with me and my PhD plans scheduled, I thought I knew where I was going, what the master plan was, and that I was on schedule for getting my doctorate and eventually launching a business. As the old saying goes, "Want to make God laugh? Tell Him your plans."

I lasted two years and never attained my PhD, for the simple reason that I never submitted my doctoral thesis, even though I'd completed my coursework. And the reason I never submitted my doctoral thesis is for another simple reason: Dolly and I were expecting our first child.

With mounting medical bills, I needed to quickly find work, as I was not in a position to finance the upcoming hospital bills for our daughter's delivery based on the $300-a-month scholarship I had. I scoured the classifieds and sent my résumé to a number of companies to no avail. The job market was extremely depressed, and the economy was in a deep recession.

I decided to flip the job-search process and put an ad in the Cleveland *Plain Dealer*, stating the position I was seeking and my qualifications.

Almost immediately, I received inquiries from about sixteen companies, including several multinationals.

I had several interviews with Monsanto, Goodyear, Firestone, BFGoodrich, and others and received four job offers. But something inside me knew that these big companies weren't the right place for me. If they hired me, they'd put me in a cubicle and label me a research scientist for the rest of my life. My aspirations for being a business owner would always remain just that—aspirations.

Then I received a call from Harold Parks, the founder of ChemMasters. He explained that he wasn't sure he could offer a job to someone of my caliber, but he was looking for someone who could duplicate a specific product that other people he'd brought into the company weren't able to re-create. If nothing else, he'd take me to lunch in Chagrin Falls, the beautiful and picturesque town where he lived and the company was located.

I visited ChemMasters, which was in a five-thousand-square-foot shed. There wasn't even a corner set aside for a lab. Something inside me said, *Ratanjit, if you're going to learn something about business, this is the place. You will not only learn about developing a product and manufacturing and marketing it, but also learn about every facet of the company.* For me, this would be practical MBA training.

I told Hal I needed to talk to Dolly about it. I described ChemMasters to her, saying that it wouldn't pay half of what I'd receive with other companies and there was no job security, but I had a feeling that this is where I belonged. Dolly supported my decision without hesitation. "If this is where your heart is, then this is where you belong."

More and more, I was learning to rely on Dolly's innate sixth sense about life's issues, and I felt that if there were any problems in the future, Dolly would see them when I didn't.

More and more, I was learning to rely on Dolly's innate sixth sense about life's issues, and I felt that if there were any problems in the future, Dolly would see them when I didn't.

Dolly was a straight shooter and didn't mince words. She had enough confidence in me that she didn't worry about hurting my feelings or annoying me; she just clearly conveyed her thoughts, helping me to see what I often wasn't able to see myself. Her support took away any hesitation I had of moving forward. I felt my courage to pursue this opportunity was because of her unbiased, clean mind and well-grounded soul.

Before making a decision about the job with ChemMasters, Dolly and I had dinner with Hal and his wife, Janelle. Dolly was not only put at ease concerning Hal and ChemMasters, but felt the affection of a mother from Janelle.

When I went to see Hal the next day to accept his offer, I explained that I needed some money to complete some business at The University of Akron. He gave me $900, and that became my monthly salary. I was so excited about joining the company and the untapped opportunities it offered that I never bothered to negotiate my salary. One thing he offered was health insurance, which relieved me of a great burden.

I joined the company on January 1, 1970. On January 11, our daughter, Nisha, was born at Akron General Hospital. Since I left home at six o'clock in the morning and didn't get home from work until around seven or eight at night, I didn't get to visit Dolly and Nisha in the hospital for four days, as visiting hours were only during the day. Finally, an intern at the hospital, who was also from India, snuck me in to see them, with me wearing a doctor's gown as my disguise.

By the end of January, we'd moved to Chagrin Falls and were renting an apartment not far from ChemMasters, and thus began my business career.

Chapter 3

My First Job in America

The founder of ChemMasters, Harold Parks, offered me a position as the technical, marketing, and management director for the company. Accepting his offer, I began my first job in America as a jack-of-all-trades for this small company. It was perfect on-the-job training in a real-world setting. I was on my way.

My first assignment with ChemMasters was to re-create an existing product for a precast company, the largest in Ohio, George Rackle & Sons. Their main concrete design engineer

> I had so many job titles that Hal made business cards for each position I held. Depending on whom I was talking with, I'd hand them the appropriate card.

was David Hill. I explained to David that they really shouldn't reproduce the product, but instead create a product that would be the best on the market. In order to do that, I needed to know what their wish list was.

The product David wanted to re-create was a chemical retarder used in precast concrete structures where aggregate was exposed through the retarder. When I began to explore what David was looking for in a retarder, I realized that the sample given to me wasn't the right chemical retarder for his needs, as it was inconsistent, took too long to dry, and had several other drawbacks.

> ChemMasters produces specialty construction products specifically designed to improve, protect, repair, and beautify concrete and masonry.

I had to develop something from scratch.

I didn't open and study the containers I'd been given by Hal, as I didn't want to be influenced in any way. Within three months, we came up with a product that exceeded David's requirements, which he began to use. Hal gave me an amazing opportunity to travel around the country, promoting the product for ChemMasters, and also challenged me to develop several other systems and products for the company, which were used in the construction industry, bringing great success to the company.

In addition to developing many new products and product upgrades, I was also entrusted with overseeing the manufacturing process along with writing and designing the technical literature. I worked with the company's sales representatives located around the country to educate and market the new line of products. I found myself overseeing every aspect of the company's operations. It was a demanding job, and I had to work long hours, including weekends, but in hindsight, I am utterly grateful to Hal Parks and ChemMasters for providing me the perfect learning scenario.

It was astounding how I was pulled into and absorbed by my work. Looking back, I can say this was the best time of my life, and I also realized that all my success was a result of my total integration with the company, its products, its customers, and its team. In other words, I was totally immersed in oneness.

In less than two years, the company grew from annual revenues of over $200,000 to more than $2.5 million.

The first year and a half was hard yet intoxicating work, as I was once again in student mode—a significant aspect of the oneness paradigm that allows us to be more receptive and creative—but I was also entrusted to make executive decisions. During this period, my job had me traveling around the country and meeting people who'd never seen a man wearing a turban. I received a variety of responses, from very serious to uncomfortable to wondering why I'd wear a turban since I was living in America where I needn't hold onto my old customs.

I could have decided these people were being prejudiced, but instead thought that when someone doesn't have complete information about me and my customs, then it's up to me to upgrade his or her knowledge base. It's not prejudice, but lack of data. I always used my sense of humor to ease situations whenever I could. One such situation comes to mind that was quite humorous.

The incident occurred when ChemMasters was supplying chemical flooring to an army base in Charleston, South Carolina. I was there to oversee its application and was greeted by the base commander, who had never met someone wearing a turban.

Our initial discussion was strictly business. Finally, at lunch, I invited him to join me. He accepted. During lunch, I began the conversation by saying that he must be wondering why I wear this cloth on my head. In all seriousness, he responded saying it must be my religion.

His seriousness made me become impish, and I decided to lighten things up. "You're right. Sikhism, which developed in India, is a faith that's only five hundred years old. We all wear turbans like this not only as a way to distinguish ourselves, but also as a reminder of our true mission, which is to serve everyone we come across—unconditionally. However, in my case, I have another reason for wearing a turban.

"When I was moving to the US, I wanted to see some of Asia, so one of my stops was in Tokyo. The plane crashed as we attempted to land. There were only two survivors—myself and a little baby. The baby was completely unharmed, but I had a severe brain injury. The doctors determined that I was going to end up being a vegetable.

"My father was called in India. They asked his permission to install a computer chip. This was something that'd never been done before, and there was a remote chance I would die, but there was a very good chance that I could live a full life with this chip installed in my brain."

When I got to this point in the story, I had the commander touch the bump on my head, which was actually from my uncut hair tied in a knot under my turban, and told him the bump was the batteries for the computer chip. "Whenever I travel, I have to tell someone that in the event I start acting funny, they can either replace the batteries or call my wife, Dolly, and ask for her help."

I described, in detail, aspects of the operation to the commander, who was listening intently, and explained that I had actually technically died during the operation, but that the doctors were able to revive me, and the operation was a tremendous success.

"They warned me, though, that my brain doesn't have the capacity of the typical human mind to manipulate and lie. In the business world, where everyone manipulates and lies, I'm an anomaly. However," I explained, "it is this very quality that has brought tremendous rewards and success in my life."

The base commander was completely engrossed in my story. He asked with great seriousness, "What does your turban have to do with this?" I responded that I didn't want the batteries showing, so that's when I adopted this way of life and became a Sikh.

By the time I returned to Chagrin Falls, the commander had called Hal, exclaiming over my brain operation and my situation of having to use batteries. Hal laughingly explained to the commander that I'd been joking with him. Hal told me I'd been naughty, as the commander had actually believed my story.

The next day, I called the commander, who, by now, was chagrined and said that he had almost believed me, as I'd been so serious in relating the story. He asked if I'd told the story before. I said no, I'd come up with it right on the spot due to the seriousness of our conversation.

The commander and I became good friends, and every time he subsequently called me, he'd always ask if he was speaking to me or the computer chip.

My mother used to tell me that humor is powerful, but it can work both ways. She would explain, "The power of humor is extraordinary, as it can break down barriers, ease tense situations, and bring people together. Humor completely backfires, though, when the joke disparages others by making fun of them in some manner. The secret to humor is to make the joke about yourself. When you make fun of yourself, your customs and way of life, in a strange way, it reflects your inner confidence and comfort level with yourself." She would emphasize this reminder: "When we laugh at ourselves, the world laughs with us, but when we laugh at others, the world frowns on us."

I had learned growing up as the only Sikh student in my class with a turban on my head both in primary school and college that …

> The unique differences we have amongst us don't have to be barriers, but, instead, can be stepping stones to greater connectivity and the deepening of our relationships.

… our unique differences don't have to be barriers,
but, instead, can be stepping stones to greater
connectivity and the deepening of our relationships.

Every time we meet someone new, it's an opportunity to engage, learn from that person, and share. You never know whom you're going to meet, what his or her background is, and how you might enhance each other's lives. That's one of the beauties of life, which has so much to offer us.

That's how I felt about coming to America—the proverbial "land of opportunity," the land where dreams come true. I'd heard that hard work and chutzpah always worked out, and my experience so far led me to believe that I was definitely on the track to success.

Looking back on that exhilarating period, I was actually living the wisdom of oneness, though I was unconscious of the fact. I was so caught up with my work at ChemMasters, striving to push not only my personal envelope, but that of the company. I wanted us all to win. Amazingly, though, the core of my being—oneness—was always operating under the radar, gently nudging me along as I expanded and honed my skills.

I learned a lot from Hal Parks and my experience with ChemMasters, but I began to notice that Hal was not comfortable with the company's rapid growth. He felt he was losing control of the company and that I was taking over. Suddenly, my freedom, which had inspired me to grow and bring about the company's tremendous growth, was being continuously questioned and restricted. It was then I realized that I needed to find another avenue to nurture my ultimate mission in life of adding the highest value by cultivating my creativity and growth.

During that period, George Rackle & Sons was sold to a precast company in Houston, and they closed the Cleveland offices to consolidate in Houston. David Hill, the main concrete design engineer for George Rackle & Sons, didn't want to move from his extended family in Cleveland and asked me to meet with him. He brought with him Brian Hodgkinson, a six-foot-seven-inch tall, Canadian-born, local radio and television personality with whom I'd worked previously on many marketing campaigns to promote products I'd developed for ChemMasters.

We met at Rick's Café in Chagrin Falls, and David explained that the new owners of George Rackle & Sons were going to close one part of their business and were willing to sell us, for just pennies on the dollar, large steel molds to produce channel tiles, a technical term for large ten-by-twelve-foot-long and two-by-three-foot-wide precast channels. They are typically used by manufacturing plants as roof tiles to enhance fire-code ratings.

Brian jumped in and said, "David and I would like to have you as our partner in this new venture where we will start with manufacturing precast concrete and eventually make chemically modified concrete and other lightweight concrete structures for commercial buildings."

He pointed out that it's not easy to get into such a business without a tremendous investment to buy molds like the ones George Rackle & Sons were offering us for so little. David's expertise in designing the concrete, my knowledge of chemicals used in this industry, and Brian's contacts and marketing expertise would position us to launch a successful business. My immediate reaction was, "I can't just leave Hal and ChemMasters, who are so dependent on me. It would be very selfish of me, as everything I've learned and become is because of them."

Brian suggested I make the transition gradually, as we could start the manufacturing process at our new company in the evening, and then I could join them after working at ChemMasters during the day. At the same time, this would allow me to slowly transition, so they'd be less dependent on me. I could then become a consultant for them in the future. I said I would get back to them after discussing the idea with Dolly and that I might just stay with ChemMasters.

The next day at ChemMasters, Hal was very upset, saying some things that directly questioned my integrity and honesty. At that point, I realized that I'd overstayed my welcome and that I had to move on.

Now, in hindsight, I realize that I hadn't caught on that upholding the oneness principle is difficult to do when those around you know nothing about it and are operating strictly within man-made laws, whether sociocultural or governmental. We're all doing the best we can, yet without an understanding of the wisdom of oneness, we're like the Hindu fable about six blind men trying to describe an elephant. Concerning ChemMasters, I realized I'd gone as far as I could go with them and that new challenges were calling me.

By practicing oneness subconsciously, I could only make so much headway. Even though I'd expanded our bottom line to over $2.5 million, to continue to grow at that rate, I would have to bring my team members into the same thought process. Obviously, I had not had that opportunity at ChemMasters.

At that time, oneness was not as crystallized in my mind as it is today. It was simply in my subconscious, so to speak. I wasn't operating openly under the umbrella of oneness, but under the radar. I now realize that this wisdom only becomes immensely powerful once it is brought to light and clearly defined, understood, practiced, and shared.

So, I called David and Brian to arrange another meeting. We then formed HSH Enterprise, Inc. (Hill-Sondhe-Hodgkinson). The three of us would be equal partners. We located the company in a garage near the town of Parkman and started manufacturing roofing tiles, as Brian had already lined up orders with Chrysler Corporation. They were replacing some of their broken channel roof tiles that had been originally purchased from George Rackle & Sons.

For the next six months, I worked at ChemMasters from eight o'clock in the morning to five-thirty in the evening and then from six in the evening to two in the morning at HSH—long and grueling hours. Every evening, Dolly would bring my dinner and, as was her nature, would prepare enough food for all three of us. David and Brian were not used to spicy Indian food. Brian consequently drank a lot of water to handle the spiciness.

Luckily, Dolly had made some rice pudding for dessert. To neutralize the spices, both David and Brian gulped the pudding down. But Brian, who had a husky voice that required no loud speaker, came in the next evening, screaming, "You bloody swami! You almost killed me with those spices."

Without raising my voice, I said, "Brian, you have no idea what you've just done. The moment you called me a swami, you adopted me as your guru. You now have to touch my feet."

Brian had a big wrench in his hand and chased me around the garage, saying, "I'll touch your feet!"

David could not stop laughing, and from that day onward, both David and Brian called me Swami. When Dolly brought food that same evening, David and Brian ate the spicy food and shared the episode with her. Dolly said to Brian, "You have made a grave mistake by calling him Swami. Without knowing it, you have designated him to be your boss for the rest of your lives."

Brian said, "He's still an Indian, but I'm the chief."

David, Brian, and I poured all our efforts into our precast business, producing custom-formulated products based on market needs. Brian, who had a contact at Snaveley, Inc., a construction firm in Cleveland, came in one day and said excitedly, "Swami, put on your polymer-technologist turban because we have a unique opportunity. There's a major construction project going on in downtown Cleveland called Park Center."

He went on to explain that Snaveley was running behind schedule for completion of the high-rise. They'd been sold an epoxy adhesive to be used instead of mortar, but the adhesive would not cure at temperatures below fifty degrees Fahrenheit. Since it was already late autumn and temperatures were hitting below forty degrees, they couldn't use the adhesive. They were asking us to create an adhesive to meet their requirements.

We developed a product called Mark-8 in a couple of weeks that was capable of curing at temperatures below freezing. This concept in itself was revolutionary, as a concrete block wall could be built five times faster than with conventional mortar. In addition, the bond between the concrete blocks was stronger than the blocks themselves, which was not the case with typical mortar.

The product met all the fire-code ratings essential for mortar use in construction. In the entire twelve-story building, all the curtain walls made of concrete blocks were constructed with Mark-8. We also manufactured precast-concrete copings and windowsills for the building, which is now called the Renaissance Hotel.

Remarkably, as distracted as I was at the time by life's vicissitudes, oneness managed to percolate through my thinking and work. You might say I was asleep at the wheel, yet the universe was still watching over me, guiding silently with gentle nudges here and there.

We suddenly found ourselves in the chemical business and accumulated an inventory of many resins, hardeners, fillers, pigments, and many other chemicals. Our incredible enthusiasm to market Mark-8 nationwide was stopped in its tracks by the construction workers' labor union, which stepped in to quash further use of our epoxy. The fact that using the epoxy reduced the number of work hours required for construction by five times threatened their sense of gainful employment. HSH had to seek clients and markets elsewhere.

As a side note, this was a perfect example of people living and working without knowledge of oneness. I saw people who were not seeking to add the highest value because they thought they "owned" their jobs and territory, and they in no way felt gratitude for improvements that did not benefit themselves, even if those improvements benefited their customers and the public. They were only interested in ensuring job security. It was simply their narrow focus of thinking based on "What's in it for me?" and the idea of "protecting their own." This mind-set was the antithesis of the oneness principle. Imagine how different life would be if we thought and created within the immensity and inclusiveness of oneness.

But back to HSH. Before we even began the Snaveley project, Brian said it was time for me to move into working for HSH full time, as we couldn't avail ourselves of this opportunity with me just working evenings. Seeing that he was right, I went to Hal and explained my situation. I said to him, "I'm forever indebted to you, and you've been like a father to me, so I'm adopting you as my father. But as a child growing up needs to leave the nest, spread his wings and find new horizons, I'd like your blessing for me to do just that.

"From a business standpoint, you needn't worry about my stealing customers, duplicating your products or infringing on your technology, and I'll always be there if you should need technical support."

My words brought tears to Hal's eyes. He hugged me and said, "Well, I guess I'm losing a key employee, but gaining a son." My relationship with Hal remained intact until the day he passed away.

HSH's business was growing, and to meet client demand, we needed to expand our production shop. So, we moved our operation. Dick Ford, the county commissioner, and Jerry Munn, who had commercial land available, agreed to build a seven-thousand-square-foot building for us in nearby Newbury Township. We signed a ten-year lease. The building lot had a large yard where we could store our precast-concrete inventory, which left the rest of the building available for manufacturing and storing chemicals.

Brian, who was quite an accomplished carpenter, built the offices, as well as a small kitchen in the facility, along with benches in the kitchen for dining purposes. He asked me to apply an epoxy sealer on the new benches so that they wouldn't stain and deteriorate. At the end of one day, I applied the sealer to the benches. It would take about eighteen hours or more for the sealer to fully dry. What I didn't know is that David was scheduled to make a delivery to a customer in Buffalo, New York, the next morning. He always came in at four-thirty in the morning to load the truck with precast concrete to deliver to our customers.

The next morning, David came in at four-thirty, made himself some coffee, and sat on the benches, which were only semi-dry. He got up and realized that the benches weren't completely dry, as he had a little stickiness on the seat and legs of his pants. Annoyed, he got into the truck and drove to Buffalo to deliver the concrete. Due to his body heat and the heat in the truck, the epoxy cured to a dried state, and David found himself stuck to the seat. He tried harder and harder to get loose, eventually tearing his pants in the process. He had to go to Sears to buy a new pair of pants before delivering the product.

When he returned to Newbury, he was very angry. "You bloody Swami!" he yelled at me, and he went into a tirade. I couldn't understand a word he was saying; his ranting more a torrent of strung-together syllables than recognizable words. When I finally understood him, I burst out laughing.

Brian, with his dry Canadian humor, joined in. "David, this Swami and his epoxy surely created new openings for you."

David shrieked, "New openings, my foot! He tore my pants." Eventually, David saw the humor in it all and began laughing.

By that autumn, we'd completed a full year. Suddenly, our precast and chemical business came to a dead stop, as both were tied to the construction industry. We had three equal and large salaries to pay, and our overhead costs had risen. With little customer work, we needed to cut costs. We met to discuss the situation, and both David and Brian said, "You're the most qualified and hirable among the three of us. Why don't you find a temporary job during the winter, and that way, we'll only have to pay two salaries? Then, when the weather turns for the better, you can come back to HSH full time."

I realized that no one would hire someone of my position and skills for just for a few months. Importantly, I also realized that David and Brian's ambition and vision were not in total alignment with mine. I was feeling the type of constraint I'd felt at ChemMasters.

I offered a counter idea: How about I buy the $20,000 worth of inventory from them, start my own company, and, at the same time, allow them to market the products? They could continue running HSH, and I'd split all the profits from the chemical business on sales generated through HSH—essentially, I would be a silent partner. It was a win–win situation for HSH as well as for me.

In September 1973, I incorporated POLY-CARB and leased a vacant warehouse adjacent to HSH in Newbury. And that is how POLY-CARB, Inc. was born.

That was the beginning of my foray into business for myself. I had the drive, the imagination, technical know-how, and the vision. Now the rubber was going to hit the road, and I would see in just what direction my life was headed. Just what kind of trouble or success could I find for myself?

Chapter 4

Launching My Own Business

After incorporating POLY-CARB in 1973, I was able to generate business by selling a unique adhesive I'd developed to the Ohio Department of Transportation (ODOT) for old and new concrete, as the bond between old, cured concrete and fresh concrete is generally very poor. This application was best suited for bridge decks that had delaminated due to corrosion of the rebars coupled with the freeze-thaw cycle.

Typically, a new layer of two inches of concrete is laid after removing the older, delaminated concrete. This adhesive was specified by the ODOT to assure the proper bond between the two concretes.

I ended my first year of business in 1973 with close to $100,000 in sales and $64,000 in net profit. I was the sole employee of the company, and the burden of tending the shop, answering the phone, and handling the accounts fell to Dolly.

When business came to a screeching halt in the autumn, we reflected on the first few months of our first year of business. Dolly commented, "It's so boring just sitting and answering a few phone calls all day and staring at these concrete walls."

This gave me an idea: Why not take a front corner of the five-thousand-square-foot space and open a gift shop? Dolly had an innate sense for

> Dolly had an innate sense for elegance and beauty, which was perfect for selecting items of artistry, value, and grace.

elegance and beauty, which was perfect for selecting items of artistry, value, and grace.

We decided Dolly should take a trip back to India, not only to visit her family, whom she'd not seen in five years, but also to use her inherent talent to shop for unique and unusual merchandise that she could then sell in the gift shop.

While Dolly was in India, I created a dome ten feet in diameter made of polymer concrete and put it over the entryway of the shop, gluing gold flakes onto the top of the dome. The obvious name for the shop: The Golden Dome. The interior was decorated with murals I'd drawn using various colored epoxies and polymer concrete.

While Dolly was away shopping for merchandise in India, I spent my days garnering business for POLY-CARB and my nights building the Golden Dome, sometimes until the early morning hours.

Dolly finally returned the first week of December 1973 with her shipment of merchandise and was pleasantly surprised at what I had been able to build. With great enthusiasm, we started decorating the shop. Dolly also brought back her sister, Kitty, who had just finished attaining her medical degree, to help her with the shop and with our daughter, Nisha. Kitty had wanted a vacation, so had agreed to come help.

We became so engrossed in setting up the shop that when we finally finished labeling the merchandise and displaying it, there had been a major snowstorm and it was four o'clock in the morning. There must have been several feet of snow, as we couldn't distinguish where the road began or ended. That night, it took us six hours to reach our home, which was a little over six miles away.

The next day despite the snow, The Golden Dome was open for business, and the shop soon began bringing in significant revenues. In fact, it was doing so well we thought we should franchise the name and concept. It became a favorite hot spot among locals and tourists. The Cleveland *Plain Dealer* ran a story saying that Emperor Shah Jahan built the Taj Mahal for his love, Queen Mumtaz, and that Ratanjit built The Golden Dome for his love, Dolly.

The next year, The Golden Dome again generated substantial revenue. On the POLY-CARB side, however, we were directly impacted by the oil embargo of 1973–74.

OAPEC: Organization of Arab Petroleum Exporting Countries

The oil embargo was a response by AOPEC against the US in retaliation for the US re-supplying the Israeli military during the Yom Kippur War. Since epoxies are directly related to oil, the manufacturer immediately put POLY-CARB on a quota, meaning that they would supply only 75 percent of our purchases based on the previous year's purchases.

In mid-summer 1974, I received a new order that required over thirty thousand pounds of resin and hardener. When I called my supplier in New Jersey, he said, "Everyone is on allocation because of the oil embargo. We're only supplying seventy-five percent of purchases based on the previous year."

I then requested to speak to the president of the company.

When I was connected to him, I described the situation, saying that I'd just started POLY-CARB in 1973 and that this wasn't fair. My company would be put out of business before it really even got a chance to launch itself. The president said he couldn't do anything about it, as he needed to follow a uniform policy with every customer. He hung up the phone. That was Friday morning.

I explained the situation to Dolly, saying that we couldn't buy any more material. Being the forthright and clear-eyed person she is, Dolly said I had to go to the supplier and explain the situation in person. She immediately arranged a flight for me.

It dawned on me that if I went to the supplier and convinced him to sell me the material, he wouldn't extend me any credit under the current circumstances. He'd want me to pay in advance and would ask how I was going to pay for it. I didn't have that much cash and had no credit established with the bank. There was the possibility that I could get an advance payment from the customer who needed the product that next week.

I called the contractor and explained the oil embargo situation to him and the difficulty in purchasing materials only on a cash basis. He was sympathetic, but hesitant to advance me any money. He said, however, that he would write me a check once the product was delivered.

He was a reputable contractor, so I knew I could trust him. I could write a check and give it to the supplier, as I absolutely knew the check would be good on Monday when I brought the material back on Saturday, manufactured the product over the weekend, and delivered the product on Monday to the contractor, who would then pay me.

The supplier, though, when I presented him with the check, would likely want to know if the check was good. I feared that until he spoke with my banker to verify the check, he wouldn't release the material.

I immediately called my banker, Dwight Mathias, at Central National Bank, which today is known as Key Bank. Dwight agreed to meet with me.

I explained the situation to Dwight and showed him the purchase order from the contractor, whom he knew was reputable. I told him I was going to the supplier in New Jersey and that if I was able to convince him to sell me the material, I'd give him a check. The problem was that he'd want to know if the check was good. I suggested that I could give the supplier Dwight's name and phone number? That way, when the supplier called, Dwight wouldn't have to do anything except tell him the check would be good, which it would be.

Dwight said, looking directly into my eyes, "You know, Ratanjit, you're asking me to do something I shouldn't do."

I said, "All I'm asking you to do is help an honest, hardworking guy save his business from dying before it even begins, without adding any risk to you or the bank."

After a pause, he smiled and said, "Okay, go ahead. I'll support you."

I then caught my flight to New Jersey. When I finally entered the supplier's offices, I gave my card to the receptionist, who asked if I had an appointment with the president of the company. I earnestly said, "No, but I've traveled all the way from Cleveland, and it's very important that I see him." She said she'd give him my card.

The president, Tom, came out and said, "Didn't I explain the situation to you this morning?" I replied that he had, but I'd come all the way from Cleveland and would really appreciate him giving me five minutes. I then explained the entire situation from top to bottom. I told him about POLY-CARB, which wasn't even a year old. I said that I realized that thirty thousand pounds was small for a company like his, but that it was a matter of staying alive for a company like mine. And by helping me, he'd be creating a future customer, as the oil embargo was a temporary situation.

He paused for several minutes, thinking. He then picked up the phone and called his plant manager to ask if they had the amount of material I was requesting. He confirmed that they did. Turning to me, he asked how I was going to pay for the materials. I gave him the check, and as I had predicted, he asked if the check was good. I gave him Dwight's business card with his name, title, and phone number. Tom called, and Dwight replied that the check would be good. Tom said he'd have the material ready by five o'clock that afternoon and that I needed to arrange for a truck to transport it.

Very relieved, I called my friend Dr. Yadav, a professor of mathematics at a local college with whom I was staying, and asked him to contact local trucking companies for me. He reported back that no one would take on the job of driving the material to Cleveland on such short notice. I was in a bind. I needed the material delivered the next morning so that I could manufacture the product over the weekend and deliver it to the contractor on Monday, who would then give me a check that I could then take to the bank that same day.

Finally, as a last resort, I called Ryder Truck Rental asking them if they had a truck that could handle a thirty-thousand-pound load. They answered yes and gave me

Ryder took me over to the trailer truck I'd just leased. To my great surprise and dismay, it was an eighteen-wheeler, something I'd never driven in my entire life.

directions to where they were located. My friend took me there, and after signing the papers, Ryder took me over to the trailer truck I'd just leased. To my great surprise and dismay, it was an eighteen-wheeler, something I'd never driven in my entire life.

At my request, the Ryder Truck man showed me how the gear system worked. After receiving my short tutorial, I somehow managed to drive the eighteen-wheeler, following my professor friend back to the plant where the thirty thousand pounds of material were awaiting me for transport. I somehow managed to safely drive the truck to the plant and back it into the loading dock without running anyone over or damaging anything along the way. I was so nervous that I felt as if I'd driven a thousand miles.

While the men were loading the truck, I did some quick thinking and realized I'd kill myself driving the truck all the way to Cleveland. I needed to find someone else to do this. I asked the workers at the plant who were loading the truck if they knew of anyone with a chauffer's license who could drive the truck to Cleveland. I'd pay that person good money.

One of the guys said that his brother-in-law had that type of license and that he just happened to be in town. He called him. Now, my return flight to Cleveland was at seven-thirty that evening, and it was already six o'clock. When the brother-in-law showed up, he discovered that he'd managed to leave his driver's license at home.

Obviously, I couldn't give him the keys to the truck without seeing his driver's license. I asked my professor friend to wait for the driver's wife to bring his license, and after verification, he could give the driver the keys, as well as travel money. Meanwhile, I would go to the airport and call him just before my flight left to verify that he had the correct driver's license.

Five minutes before the flight was to leave and the doors to the plane were about to be closed, I received confirmation that the man had the license and that my friend had given him the keys and money to drive the truck to Cleveland.

The driver's plan, since he'd already slept all day, was to drive all night and reach POLY-CARB by about eight o'clock the next morning. He didn't arrive until eleven-thirty. Meanwhile, I'd been on pins and needles waiting for him since eight.

What had happened was that he'd experienced a lot of traffic and had grown drowsy, so had decided to pull off the highway and take a nap.

Once the material had been delivered, though, I was able to work all weekend to manufacture the product and deliver it Monday morning to the contractor. I then took the check I was given, deposited it in the bank, and POLY-CARB was saved from a quick demise.

Adventures like this were commonplace for us throughout POLY-CARB's history, though the challenges and stakes changed constantly. Oneness was always an integral part of my being and approach to everyday life. But just as with an onion, there are always layers of understanding to be peeled away or, in this case, unveiled. Unbeknownst to me, I was still actually rather unconscious of the depth and breadth of the oneness principle. That is, though, the journey of life, which is a process of discovery. The irony is that the truth of oneness has always existed, yet for each of us, it's a matter of forever being the explorer, extending our reach to find ever-greater truth. And so it was for me.

Dolly and I worked steadily on several fronts: expanding our customer base and fulfilling orders, consistently creating top-of-the-line products to meet customer needs and challenges, raising Nisha, and developing our markets and POLY-CARB team, which left little time for getting involved in the social fabric of Cleveland.

They were wonderful times full of tremendous creativity, innovation, and promise. One such innovation involved something most of us take for granted: pavement markers. Though the product I created exceeded the client's requirements, it brought to light a different issue for POLY-CARB.

In 1975 and '76, Ohio embarked on a new pavement-marker system, the signature safety program instituted by Governor James Rhodes. The markers are the little protuberances imbedded in roads that reflect car lights at night, illuminating traffic lanes. The purpose of the markers is to reduce car accidents and fatalities. Statistical analysis revealed that while only 25 percent of driving occurs at night, over 50 percent of all vehicular fatalities occur during the night.

The markers are designed to withstand being hit by snowplows. What they are is a metal casting with an imbedded reflector, all of which is designed to be glued to the roadway surface, which has grooves cut into it to fit the casting. A special, high-strength epoxy adhesive is required to hold the casting in place. The bond has to be stronger than the concrete or asphalt while also withstanding the impact of the snowplows.

What I did was formulate the Mark-29 product, which met all the requirements of the Ohio Department of Transportation when it was tested. I was then given the first order, which consisted of six hundred five-gallon buckets, each weighing over sixty pounds. I was able to manufacture the material and packaged it in five-gallon pails, which Dolly helped me label.

However, when the commercial trucking company arrived to load the material, I had a major problem: we didn't have a loading dock.

I ended up having to lift each bucket and hand it to the driver, whom I had to pay extra, as this was work outside the scope of his job. Typically, moving heavy material of this type is done by loading it onto pallets via a truck lift.

By the end of the day, after loading six hundred buckets—over thirty-six thousand pounds in total—I was unable to walk. Fortunately, since the loading had been done on a Friday, I was able to spend the weekend sitting in a bathtub of hot water to recuperate. It was then that I realized I would end up being in even hotter water if I didn't bring in some employees to share the workload.

Dolly had been right there beside us as we loaded the buckets. She had made sure that each bucket was absolutely spotless and polished so that it looked brand new. That standard was instilled throughout POLY-CARB over the years. She ensured that every product that went out the door was sparkling and pristine.

POLY-CARB was consistently bringing in orders, which required me to do a lot of traveling. I was finding that I couldn't travel as much as I needed to and manufacture product the rest of the time. So, I hired my first POLY-CARB employee, a close friend, Dr. Bipin C. Pant, who was my colleague and a professor at the Birla Institute of Technology and Science.

Dr. Pant had visited MIT in 1967 and is the person who encouraged me to come to the US. Toward the end of 1975, I asked him if he'd consider joining POLY-CARB. Although the company is based in polymer technology, I knew he was a creative and bright scientist. He accepted and became POLY-CARB's first employee. He took over the manufacturing and development aspect of the company, which gave me more time to generate business.

As an aside, I had to buy myself a radio-frequency mobile phone, paying close to $4,000. I would travel around in my car, wearing my turban, the phone in my hand, and people driving by would yell from their cars while I was on the phone, "Sheikh, sheikh! How many oil wells do you have?"

Besides hiring Dr. Pant, I hired two more local Newbury residents to work in production, as well as an administrative assistant. In early 1976, I hired another engineer and a marketer.

As for The Golden Dome, we had an interesting spectrum of clients, including the wives of executives and people with spare time. Dolly usually had cookies, cheese, fruit, nuts, and sometimes wine set out for her clients. With this inviting atmosphere filled with treasures, The Golden Dome soon became a regular meeting place for society's elite.

Interestingly, Dolly had difficulty when it came to pricing the merchandise. She was always worried about overcharging customers, especially on exotic and expensive items. For example, she'd brought from India a beautiful chess set made of hand-carved ivory. She had priced it at eighty dollars. People, seeing the price, would remark, "It so beautiful. Is it really ivory? How come it's so cheap?"

Dolly sitting on the Great Wall of China
contemplating the surrounding mountains

It just so happened that one weekend, I was watching the shop and doing paperwork while Dolly was at home caring for Nisha and preparing food for the week. While there, I added to the chess set's price tag a 3 in front of the $80, making it $380. That afternoon, a regular visitor, the owner of a small company in Newbury, came in. He had seen the chess set before and had always felt it must have been incorrectly priced. Seeing the new price of $380, he immediately bought it.

When I told Dolly what I'd done, she was very upset with me, as she thought that what I'd done was unethical. So, the next day, she called the gentleman and returned $300 to him, explaining that she couldn't charge him more than what the chess set was worth. I, in the meantime, was in hot water.

Dolly has always been the epitome of the oneness principle. No matter what she does or is involved in, she consistently seeks to raise the bar in quality and depth, and create a deeper connection through sharing and giving. She is resolute in ensuring people are well served in everything we do. At no time has anyone felt ignored, forgotten or slighted, only enveloped by her kindness, warmth, generosity, and gratitude—oneness.

Meanwhile, The Golden Dome was doing so well that I asked Dolly what we should do with the shop. We decided we could franchise the concept, catering to the wives of executives, as running a shop would give them something to do, and since the merchandise and physical golden dome were so unique, we could franchise the name, design, and merchandise.

As it turned out, we had three ladies who loved the shop so much that they mentioned we should open more shops. We told them about the franchising idea, and they responded enthusiastically, saying that they wanted to be franchisees. So, we already had three strong candidates.

But during that period, I received from the state of Indiana an approval for our sealer, which would allow me to bid on state projects. Having passed that hurdle, at the beginning of 1977, I secured a large order for epoxy sealer from the state of Indiana. It needed to be packed into three hundred fifty-five-gallon drums—that's 16,500 gallons of sealer. I didn't have the manufacturing capacity or a way to lift and load the material onto a truck.

So, I called a friend in the real estate business whom I knew through The Golden Dome. I told him that I needed to immediately find a building with a loading dock where a truck could back in and unload materials and load product. The plant needed to have between ten and fifteen thousand square feet and be zoned for light manufacturing.

He said he knew of just such a building in the town of Parkman; the company currently renting the building hadn't completely moved out yet, but had moved their major equipment. Hearing this, I suggested he talk to them to see if they would be amenable to my moving in while they finished moving out. I said I'd sign a lease immediately. The renters agreed.

Now I had a place, but not all the equipment I needed. I went to Federal Equipment Company, which liquidated chemical plants and re-sold the equipment. I was able to buy two mixers with a two-thousand-gallon capacity and with explosion-proof motors and mixing gears.

Within a couple of days, they were delivered, installed, and wired. Additionally, I had purchased a six-thousand-gallon, glass-lined tank originally designed to be used in a brewery. I needed the tank for storing solvents, which were used for manufacturing the concrete sealer.

As for The Golden Dome, when POLY-CARB moved to its new location in Parkman, the rest of the building in Newbury was large enough so that it could be used to warehouse The Golden Dome inventory for the franchisees.

We were all set to move forward with the franchises and also begin production on the Indiana contract, but there were two problems: (1) The Golden Dome was in Newbury, and POLY-CARB was now even farther east of Cleveland in Parkman; and (2) The Indiana contract of 16,500 gallons needed to be delivered in a month. Being in my position, I needed to devote all of my time to POLY-CARB to deliver the product on time.

Dolly and I both felt uncomfortable with her having the merchandise and cash in the shop and working alone. Plus, I really needed her assistance at POLY-CARB. The decision then was to not only shelve the franchise concept but also let go of The Golden Dome completely.

After that, when we made the move to Parkman in 1977, the men from Newbury didn't want to travel so far, and I ended up hiring several local Amish men from Parkman to work in production. We'd grown so much that we ended up building an additional ten-thousand-square-foot concrete pad to store the inventory.

So now, after several years of intense work and development, POLY-CARB was ready for phase two of its journey—right in the middle of Amish country.

Chapter 5

Bets That Paid Off

Looking back over the company's formative years, we'd had our ups and downs. There were plenty of successes, yet I could also see the why and how of our fumbles. Part of it was my own lack of business acumen, and the other part was from having followed the advice of others instead of relying on what I already knew deep within myself. Oneness was always as close as my heartbeat, yet I had allowed myself to be swayed by outside influences. And though the staff and I made a number of mistakes over the years, my inherent instincts did manage to come through. Here's one such instinctual action I took that proved very successful.

Early in POLY-CARB's history, someone suggested that for us to gain greater exposure in the industry on a national level, we should attend the World of Concrete conference. It would be a great place for us to exhibit, get some exposure, and network. So, we reserved a ten-by-twenty-foot booth space.

The show was conducted by the Aberdeen Group, which published the industry magazine *Construction Marketing Today*. They'd put on this show for the first time in 1978. Their second show would be our first.

I went to a local advertising and promotion company to see about redesigning our company's logo. I didn't want a graphical symbol of any kind, just the name POLY-CARB. That way, people wouldn't be trying to decipher who we were by some artistic graphic that might be pretty and interesting to look at, but wouldn't give a clue as to who we were and our business. I wanted them to see a logo that was also the company's name.

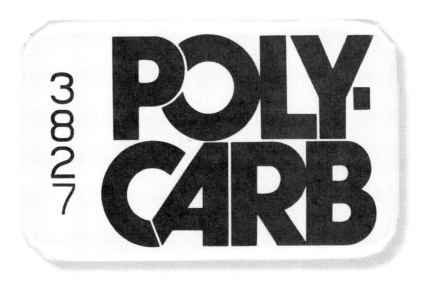

We asked ourselves what the purpose of our attending this show was. Obviously, people would not be giving us orders, as they had never heard of us. So the best thing to do was make everyone aware of the name POLY-CARB.

We came up with the idea of distributing badges with not only our name on it but also a four-digit number. We announced to everyone visiting our booth that there were many pairs of identical numbers on the badges. If two people with matching numbers found each other at the show, then they would receive $100 each.

Vanna White before Hollywood and fame.

To assist us at the booth, we hired two local models to distribute the buttons while we dealt with introducing the company and networking. One of those models was a young Vanna White, long before she joined *Wheel of Fortune*.

You can bet that the $100 incentive motivated people. We knew that by doing this contest, people would see the badge everywhere plus look at it closely while trying to match numbers. As a result, our name would be burned in their minds long after the show.

We distributed over seven thousand badges at the show. It was a tremendous success. The Aberdeen Group was amazed at how POLY-CARB completely dominated the entire show. Our name was everywhere and on people's minds.

Later, when I visited the Departments of Transportation for other states, the people I met remembered POLY-CARB, the buttons, and our marketing strategy. We carried the badge as our hallmark to all the shows we attended. Years later, we included lanyards with POLY-CARB written on them in black and white. Our name was everywhere.

In subsequent years, our booth expanded to twenty by twenty feet, one of the largest booths in the industry. It was classically designed. People often complimented us as having the best booth in the entire show, the best-designed literature, and the best-dressed people. Our POLY-CARB representatives had an amazing energy and enthusiasm.

Because of our congruent presentation, people attending the show would come up to us and say that they didn't care what we were about, they just wanted to join us and establish business relationships. It was quite a compliment.

From that point on, we exhibited every year at the World of Concrete trade show. The venue of this show, which was exponentially expanding each year, alternated between Atlanta, Georgia, and Las Vegas, Nevada.

In 1979, our attendance at the World of Concrete show introduced me to Las Vegas. We followed our tested and successful marketing game of distributing POLY-CARB badges with numbers. Attendees with matching numbers were winners, and each was given $100. It was so successful that we distributed over ten thousand badges. We saw people wearing them at the hotels. One of the waitresses, who must have been given badges by show goers, was wearing them all over her cocktail uniform. People were wearing them in the restaurants, at shows, and in the casinos.

The trade show ran from nine to five for four consecutive days. When I returned to my hotel on the first day, one of my sales managers, a blackjack junky, had me sit next to him at the gaming table. He taught me how to play blackjack.

The next day, when I returned to my hotel, my sales manager was not with me, as he needed to see some customers after the show. As I was passing through the casino to get to my room, I stopped at a blackjack table where no one was playing. I thought I'd see if I could play the game.

As I sat down to play, I was unaware that the minimum bet at the table was ten dollars. It would have been embarrassing to get up and leave, so I ended up placing ten dollars on my first bet ever. I lost. I played another ten dollars. I lost again. The third time, I took out more money and handed it to the dealer without realizing that I'd given him fifty dollars. The dealer thought that was my bet, so he continued. Amazingly, I won. To my chagrin, it was only when the dealer handed me $100 worth of chips that I realized I'd bet fifty dollars.

For the next bet, I returned to playing ten dollars. As you might guess, I lost. I repeated this twice and lost both times. Then, on my next bet, I increased the amount to fifty dollars, and I won. By now, I was beginning to get into the game, and every time I played ten dollars, I lost. Every time I bet fifty dollars, I won. Tempting fate, I doubled the amount to $100—and won. Then I tried ten dollars again and lost. This was really getting interesting!

By now, there were several people gathered around the table, watching me. It was a toss-up as to whether it was my strange betting pattern that attracted them or the fact that I was dressed in a business suit with a turban. I overheard a woman remark, "Look at him; he's throwing money around like water and still winning. I bet he's already loaded and needs money like a hole in the head. But he's still winning."

My largest bet at that table was $500, and you guessed it, I won. It was an amazing feeling. I suddenly lost any sense of money's value. It was like playing with Monopoly money—fake money. In fact, for the first time in my life, I felt as if the entire world were an illusion. It wasn't even me playing. It was as if I were having an out-of-body experience and watching me, the body of Ratanjit, sitting at a blackjack table surrounded by lots of people watching me in astonishment.

Suddenly, my sales manager showed up and woke me from the trance I was in. He was flabbergasted at my winnings, which came to $2,670. I simply could not go on with the game at any level and asked him to cash in my chips.

When I returned home and told Dolly about this strange winning experience, her immediate reaction was, "You simply can't keep this gambling money, as you did not earn it. It is, in fact, dirty money, and we must give it away to a charity." The next day, she gave the money to the nearest church to feed the hungry.

As you can see from these two stories, maintaining one's composure in this frenetic and highly distracting world is a serious challenge. Ingenuity, combined with the innate integrity of oneness, is key. As exciting as the World of Concrete convention was in Atlanta, my focus was still on adding the highest value at all levels of that experience. Dolly had to remind me of that when I returned from the Las Vegas show. The wisdom of oneness—*every thought, word, action, and decision must be completely immersed in oneness*—is the only means of sustaining any measure of success and maintaining clarity of vision and action at all times.

> Creativity and imagination are essential tools that need constant exercising.

In addition to the wisdom of oneness, creativity and imagination are essential tools that need constant exercising. Those of us at POLY-CARB got many a chance to try out our wings, go out on a limb, and push the envelope. It was a very heady period when we sometimes felt we knew where we were headed and other times felt as if we were stranded in the dark without a candle. But, we kept at it every day, some days taking lots of baby steps and other days having breakthroughs and taking a giant step forward.

Not being fortune tellers, we had no idea what the future held for us, but we diligently kept our noses to the grindstone and envisioned a bright future for ourselves. Little did we know ….

Chapter 6

Remembering My Roots

B ack at that heart-stopping moment in 1980 when my accountant and lawyer made their announcement about POLY-CARB being broke, I was in utter shock. How was I to face my family, parents, friends, staff, suppliers, and customers? I felt such shame—I'd failed. I did what anyone would do in such circumstances and started to go into depression.

My ten-year-old daughter, Nisha, witness to the unfolding drama in our lives, felt my pain and jumped in my lap, saying, "Dad, don't worry; everything will be all right." Her words suddenly reminded me of a conversation I'd had with her not long before.

It is often the young- est members of humanity who help us remember

> It is often the youngest members of humanity who help us remember the core of our being.

the core of our being. My daughter, Nisha, was one of those, al- ways questioning, wanting to know the *why* of everything. The following conversation will give you an idea of her keeping me, the adult, on track.

When Nisha was in third grade in a Chagrin Falls school, her teacher called. She started out by saying that children can be cruel and then said that because Nisha was the only non-white person in the entire school, it would be better if she were enrolled in a private school. This was news to us, as Nisha had never complained about the other kids teasing her. Upon questioning Nisha, we learned that school had been very difficult for her for years. So, we put her into a private Catholic school.

Although she was a little more comfortable at the private school, she came home one night and said, "Dad, why are you sending me to this Catholic school? Isn't our religion Sikh?"

> God in any form remains God, and all religions of the world are merely institutions designed by humans as a means to teach spirituality.

I sat her down and explained, "God in any form remains God, and all religions of the world are merely institutions designed by humans as a means to teach spirituality. The wisdom and understanding of the teachings of great saints and avatars comes from their being conduits for God. After all is said and done, when you understand this, it doesn't matter which path you follow as long as you remain spiritual." In her young years, she didn't really understand what the word *spirituality* meant and asked me to explain.

"Spirituality," I said, "is the absence of duality, when you don't

> Spirituality is the absence of duality, when you don't differentiate between people based on the way they look or their gender, age, habits, or color and are able to see the common link of Divine power within each of them. That is spirituality.

differentiate between people based on the way they look or their gender, age, habits, or color and are able to see the common link of Divine power within each of them. That is spirituality."

She then asked, "Then why do Sikhs tie a turban?"

I replied, "There are many reasons why Sikhs tie a turban. The most elementary one is that by Indian custom, when we go to the Sikh temple, or gurdwara, everyone covers his or her head, which is a sign of respect to elders. When young adults are with older people, they cover their head. Therefore, the highest order of respect is given to God. Sikhs believe that God is everywhere and in everyone. In respect to His omnipresence, we cover our heads.

> Sikh, literally translated, means "student." We are always learning and carrying out our mission of serving humanity, and we are continually improving our skills and capabilities, which keeps us down to earth and humble.

"More importantly, our tenth guru, Gobind Singh, wanted to create an ultimate servant for humanity who would be a combination of a saint and a soldier. Once you become a Sikh, you basically let go of your personal identity and personal religion and become an unconditional, loving, and serving entity—serving God, the Divinity present in every living being. That is why in India, in public places, when people see a Sikh, they feel safe, as that Sikh will protect them and provide help without hesitation. In northern India, it was the ultimate honor for a family to dedicate their oldest son or daughter to Sikhism. Now do you understand who you are?"

"I'm a Sikh ... but what does that word mean?"

"*Sikh*, literally translated, means 'student.' We are always learning and carrying out our mission of serving humanity, and we are continually improving our skills and capabilities, which keeps us down to earth and humble. We seek to always add higher value to whomever we come across."

"Why wear a turban to serve others? Can't you serve without wearing it?" Nisha asked.

"As humans, we have the best of intentions, but we continually need reminders to remain steadfast on our path. For instance, as you know, Sikhs do not cut their hair, and it is also part of our religion to be very clean. Therefore, it takes us longer to get ready in the morning, as we not only bathe and tie up our long hair, we then tie our turbans. Going through this demanding exercise of cleanliness and maintaining a turban shows our commitment to the cause of serving unconditionally. When we look in the mirror, our turbans remind us of our mission on an ongoing basis.

"Secondly, if we want to stay on a mission, we have to tell the world this is our mission so that we can be held accountable. By wearing our turbans, we're declaring to the world that this is our mission unconditionally, and we stay on the path of constant learning and serving unconditionally."

"When you were in school, Dad, how many Sikhs were in your class?"

"Because we moved to Rajasthan, we were the only Sikhs at the time, but later on, other Sikhs came. I was always the only Sikh student in my classes."

"Didn't the other students make fun of you?"

"Yes, they did, but I had to work harder than the other students. This was not just so I'd be a better student, but so that I could help other students become better students themselves. This helpfulness eventually became my asset, and instead of making fun of me, they became my friends. If I became a better student and didn't help them, I would have been challenged with even more trouble, as the other students would have been jealous and resentful."

Sikhism was founded by Guru Nanak Dev in the late 1400s. Sikhism is the fifth-largest religion in the world.

Nisha grew more comfortable at the Catholic school. She initially resisted going to church and reciting their prayers, but she slowly became a part of their system, yet remained steadfast to the basic tenets of Sikhism. Fortunately, my wife, Dolly, had also gone to Catholic schools as a child in India and was very familiar with their religious doctrine, and she would often take Nisha to local churches to light candles on special days, etc. We would also visit Sikh temples (gurdwaras), as well as Hindu temples.

The most amazing part of that conversation with Nisha was that it re-connected me to my core. The fundamental roots of my being, oneness, emerged, and I was able to listen to what I was saying and to benefit from it more so than Nisha. It made me ask the questions "Am I being a true Sikh? Are the hurdles I'm experiencing in business because I'm not remembering my true path?"

The answer was that I was on track to getting myself centered again in the oneness concept. What I needed to do now was get POLY-CARB headed in a new direction. Was it possible, and *how* would I do it?

Life, as we all know, can be chaotic and confusing. We do the best we can to weather the challenges, obstacles and demands of life, and most of us manage to lead full lives. Do we know where we're going? Are we truly getting the most out of life in a way that speaks to our hearts and souls?

Generally, we make plans and try to stick to them, yet life has a way of throwing wrenches into our best-laid strategies, formulas, and agendas. What do we have to fall back on when things fall through? What guidelines are available to anchor us, shed light, inspire, and uplift?

> One of my mother's favorite sayings was "When things happen to you and around you that don't make sense, look instead for hidden opportunities to add value and make a difference."

For me, my roots are in Sikhism. I was raised in the Sikh religion, just as my mother and father were. Both tirelessly strove to impart the deeper meanings of its core principles. My mother was not only a student of Sikhism, but an avid student of all sacred scriptures, from the Bible to the Koran, the Upanishads, the Bhagavad Gita, and the Guru Granth Sahib. She taught me that there are four key tenets we Sikhs need to practice and live by. What struck me was the universality of these tenets, which are applicable to all aspects of life.

1. **Remember and serve God at all times.**

   My mother explained this tenet in the following manner: "This can only be done by first seeing and feeling God as the unifying link and omnipresent power present in all of us that enlivens us and unites us all in one. This oneness means we recognize and understand that we are each an integral aspect of the bigger One—the Divine. We are not God, but God's power is present within each of us. Knowing this, we strive to see the Divine in everyone and everything. In other words, we knowingly and in full awareness remain in the presence of that One—God—at all times.

   "Even when we are alone, we see the presence of that humbling yet empowering Divine power right within us. This tenet compels us to unconditionally serve that One in everyone we come across, which includes complete strangers; the rich and the poor; our families, friends, team members, contractors, and customers; and people from all walks of life."

As this thought process was going through my mind, I realized that the reason I was generating 90 percent of my company's sales was that I somehow became one with my customers and put all my efforts into enhancing the operations and profitability of my customers. The business I generated was merely a by-product of that process. Now, if I had brought the essence of this Sikh tenet of serving God in them, I would have further elevated my service to my highest level. In serving God, there is no room for mediocrity or cutting corners.

This understanding unveiled the first Law of Oneness: The Law of Purpose, which states: *"Our sole purpose in life is to add the highest value we can in all our endeavors unconditionally and continuously."*

#1 – The Law of Purpose

"Our sole purpose in life is to add the highest value we can in all our endeavors unconditionally and continuously."

Our focus is always on the bigger One—including for all of humanity, life, and the environment.

The corollary of this law is that anything that isn't in compliance with oneness and consistently seeking to add the highest value—such as people working in silos, teams of people working not for a single purpose but for their own agendas, and company products and services that are not integrated into what is required by society as a whole—will backfire at some time and in some way.

Now I understood why my company had failed. Each sales manager had his own territory and their entire focus was on selling, not looking at what our products were and whether they were appropriate for customers, and the sales reps didn't talk to the other salespeople except in competitive terms. Everyone was working in silos instead of working together, and I was spending a lot of time cleaning up everyone's messes.

Suddenly, another consequence of the absence of the oneness truth hit me. It made me realize that regardless of how intelligent, knowledgeable and experienced we were, we would always remain mediocre when acting on our own. To add the highest value, we needed to share or incorporate other people in our endeavors and bring in their expertise so that our teamwork moved us forward and upward, whether that was on the home front or within our company.

What this told me was that our personal best would always remain mediocre because we were not positioned to add the highest value when operating alone and not as a team. For POLY-CARB, only my team's best would give us an excellent product. The inescapable truth was that we couldn't escape oneness if we wanted to sustain our business, our success, our viability, and, most importantly, our sanity.

> If all of our value systems were a by-product of oneness, we wouldn't have to strive to become honest and respectful or to behave with integrity—those attributes would automatically spring from this universal truth of oneness.

What oneness meant for us was that everything we did impacted the world around us and vice versa. Therefore, were we adding positively to the world or causing pain and sorrow? From this vantage point, if all of our value systems were a by-product of oneness, we wouldn't have to strive to become honest and respectful or to behave with integrity—those attributes would automatically spring from living the universal truth of oneness.

The truth of oneness can be equated with our human bodies. For example, our eyes never lie to us. They provide us with information or data to the best of their ability. The eyes are not separate entities, but a part of the whole, our body, which is analogous to the bigger One we can call society, the universe, or simply the Divine within ourselves and all others.

The reason we at POLY-CARB didn't share the complete truth was that we considered ourselves separate entities. We didn't see the Divine in ourselves and others and didn't understand divine connectedness.

The eyes work in concert with all other parts of the body without conditions or separate agendas, and it was the same with us once we immersed ourselves in oneness. Acting in oneness, we became integral with everyone around us, and the natural outcome was honesty, respect, and integrity.

2. **Practice acceptance.**

   This tenet of the Sikh following, as my mother explained to me, simply states that the first step in moving forward is to accept the situation we are placed in with utter gratefulness. The second step, she said, is to look for the hidden opportunities to make a difference or add value to the bigger One, one person and one project at a time.

   I remembered what my father said to me when I was younger and experiencing a challenge: "This is the best thing that could happen for you. If we did not have challenges in our lives, then we would never grow, never attain wisdom. Challenges force us to stretch and be creative, to not become stuck in what we know and our past accomplishments." He emphasized, "Be grateful for this gift from the universe, and learn to accept life as it comes with grace and gratitude."

Both of these lessons remind me of the first award I ever received, which was around age thirteen. I was jumping up and down with excitement and joy. I felt I'd really accomplished something great. My mother, ever practical and wise, said, "I'm so very happy and proud of you. But, I want for you to continue to achieve bigger successes. Let me give you a thought process that will keep you on the path of success."

What my mother explained to me next was shocking, but it has stuck with me my entire life: "Every success is a failure for the

> Every success is a failure for the simple reason that you can always do better. There is no such thing as a finished product or perfection, only the evolution to something greater.

we can always do better, and we succeed in spite of our hidden weaknesses that are camouflaged by our so-called successes. There is no such thing as a finished product or perfection, only the evolution to something greater."

She further explained that every failure is a success and needs celebration, as it has hidden within it the seed of success—because every failure exposes every shortcoming, weakness, and opportunity to improve and learn and convert our weaknesses into strengths. She then emphasized that the secret to our sustainable, long-term success is to remain totally detached from our successes and failures and focus on what our mission in life is, which is to make a difference, add greater value, and make our best better. All of this has to be done with utter gratefulness, which must be unconditional.

At the time, I couldn't comprehend what my mother was telling me. I thought I'd already made my best better and had been rewarded with an award. I was a success. I also wondered about how a person could possibly celebrate failures. Failures were cause for sorrow and depression. I also couldn't grasp the concept of unconditional gratefulness, as I felt that only occurred when someone gave you a gift and you thanked them. Her words were confusing for me and seemed like a paradoxical puzzle.

It wasn't until many years later, when Dolly came into my life, that I began to understand what my mother had explained to me. Dolly was continuously focused on taking something I thought was great and helping me see that I could do better and further elevate whatever I was doing. She always remained in the mind-set of constant improvement.

Initially, this used to bother me when we planned something. Dolly was improving on the plan up to the last minute. Just when I thought we were finished with something, it changed again. It was quite unsettling for me.

Once I realized the consequences of this thought process, though, I grasped how it actually worked in my favor. The journey, whatever it is, is not an end. It's an ongoing process. This simple truth applies to every facet of our lives: relationships, events, products, vacations, projects, etc. Becoming aware of this process allows us to see things we otherwise would never see.

Here I was lost in the past or worried sick about the future and blaming my well-meaning advisers, my staff, my judgments, my lack of experience, my circumstances, etc., by not gratefully accepting the present situation gifted to me with endless opportunities to achieve my mission of adding the highest value to my fellow human beings, the bigger One.

I suddenly remembered what my father used to say: "Crisis will devastate you if you play the blame and revenge game. Crisis will enhance you if you look for the opportunities to add value."

This is where our true power lies: not in the past and not in the future, but in where we are right at the present moment.

What was becoming clear to me was that things were what they were and I should not waste time and resources on what was, but should move onward by letting go of the past and beginning to operate in the present. This is where our true power lies: not in the past and not in the future, but in where we are right at the present moment. It is in our present where all our opportunities to add value exist.

I remembered how my father always lived his life. He was a man of few words, but in a crisis, he was the family pillar, making decisions and serving the situation by adding the highest value possible, which moved the situation to a higher level. He never questioned why things happened, just accepted things for what they were and moved forward.

I knew that this was not a form of denial or avoidance. Rather, it

Acceptance is taking whatever cards we've been dealt, playing the game with our maximum intensity and attention, and moving forward.

was not crying over spilled milk, holding on to grudges, or pining away for what was. People must take responsibility for their words and actions and, at the same time, move forward with their lives.

I also realized that experience is taking what we've learned and putting it into practical application. Acceptance is taking whatever cards we've been dealt, playing the game with our maximum intensity and attention, and moving forward. The knowledge and experience we've gained give us the ability to play the game.

#2 – The Law of Acceptance
"Accept life as it comes to us with gratefulness and without conditions."

It dawned on me that this thought process could be summed up in the second law of oneness: The Law of Acceptance:

"Accept life as it comes to us with gratefulness and without conditions."

To enable ourselves to stay on the path of adding the highest value, we must first accept life as it comes to us—with utter gratefulness and unconditionally—without prejudice, fear, judgment, or regret. As a consequence, we will operate in the present and will then be in a position to explore the hidden opportunities—in both our failures and successes—to add the highest value.

Accepting life as it comes to us can be very challenging. We want to have things work out a certain way, achieve specific goals, and not be faced with obstacles. Life would be so much easier if everything worked out the way we wanted it to. Realistically, that isn't going to happen as often as we'd like, especially with really important things. Yet, everything happens as it does for a reason—and it's always about our growth, no matter what the situation or event might be. This reminded me of the MADD initiative.

Two women, one whose thirteen-year-old daughter was killed by a drunk driver while she was walking to a carnival, began Mothers Against Drunk Driving. Instead of sinking into permanent despair or seeking revenge, the women accepted what was and then took positive action on an issue that was claiming the lives of tens of thousands yearly.

Their determination sparked a volunteer movement that swept America and has saved hundreds of thousands of lives. They created something that triggered national awareness so that others would not experience the grief and heartache they'd experienced.

The last part of the equation of acceptance involves the concept of unconditional gratefulness, something that eluded me for many years until my daughter, Nisha, who was twelve years old at the time, enlightened me. It happened one day when I was taking her to school.

On some mornings, I would drive Nisha to school, which was about fifteen miles away. One day, I said to her, "Most of the time, you ask me questions. Can I ask you a question?"

"Since we're really early, you have to buy me a McDonald's breakfast."

"Okay, that's a deal," I replied.

While sitting at McDonald's and enjoying our breakfast, I said, "I want you to think about this seriously. It's a simple question that you don't have to answer right away. Here's the situation: What if God appeared and said, 'My child, you've been a good kid, and because of this, I'll grant you one wish—whatever you want.' My question to you is this: What would that wish be?"

"I can ask for *anything*?"

"Sure, God is all-powerful. He can give you anything."

Nisha thought about it and answered, "I can ask for tons of money?"

I replied, "You could ask for unlimited money. He can give it to you."

She thought some more. "If I have all the money in the world, then when I go to the store, I can buy all the things in the store."

"Not only that, but you can buy that store, ten stores—all the stores in the world."

Nisha paused a second in thought, then said, "But then the value would be nothing because if I already own all these things, the excitement of when I buy you something or you get me something new—well, the excitement is gone. The fun of getting things and the warmth of gratefulness I feel in my heart is wonderful, and that is far more important to me. I'd completely miss out on that."

"That's true; maybe that's why God has given us enough. That keeps us excited about getting new things."

Nisha was silent. "I don't think I want all the money in the world."

"Then what would you want? You could ask for a long life."

"If God can give me a long life, I can live forever, right?"

"Yup."

"But, Dad, that would be boring. God is very smart. He must have designed something very beautiful for after we die. I would miss out on what happens after death. And living without knowing how long you have is exciting in itself, and it brings a feeling of gratefulness for every day I live. I don't think I want to live longer than what I'm supposed to. Oh, but wait—God could make me famous. I could become a big star. I could go anywhere, and people would stand in line to see me."

"That could happen, too. Do you want to be famous?"

She thought again and said, "Yeah … but, I wouldn't have a private life because no matter where I went, people would be chasing me. I want to do what I want to do when I want. That would be lost. Plus, whenever I got an award or some recognition, because I'm famous, instead of being grateful, I'd become arrogant and conceited."

"To some degree, that's true," I replied.

Nisha was quiet as she ate her breakfast. She suddenly piped up with "What if I know everything?" Before I could respond, she said, disappointed, "That wouldn't work—life would be completely boring,

"Is there something wrong with me if I don't ask God for anything and am just utterly grateful for what He has already given me?"

as I would already know everything. I wouldn't be surprised by anything or even in awe of anything. I'd already know everything there is to know; nothing would ever be new. I wouldn't feel gratefulness for people sharing their knowledge with me. Instead, I would be a complete know-it-all, intimidate people, and no one would want to be my friend. I would become very sad and lonely."

I didn't say a word, just waited patiently as Nisha thought this through.

"Dad, is there something wrong with me if I don't ask God for anything and am just utterly grateful for what He has already given me?"

I couldn't believe my ears at the words of this little twelve-year-old child who had such profound wisdom and understanding. Maybe this is the reason great scholars have called children the fathers of the human race. There's such purity in them that they are able to clearly see things we grownups can't see. Nisha's wisdom helped me tremendously in finally understanding the meaning of unconditional gratefulness.

Finally, I understood that unconditional acceptance and gratitude are the essential elements to practice in making my best better and adding the highest value in all facets of life.

3. **Make an honest living.**

This third tenet is one my father drummed into me from the time I was a young boy, and it is one we Sikhs must follow.

My father worked for the government PWD (Public Work Department) as an engineer. He reviewed all the contracts that came in. The PWD was known for taking a lot of bribes, but my father never did. He was an anomaly in a corrupt system. Once, he threw a contractor out of our house because the man had brought a bag full of money.

This gave me the answer to a missing puzzle piece and further crystallized in my mind why my company was in its current predicament.

One piece of advice that came from every expert I met with was "To be successful, one has to be an aggressive marketer. Good salesmen are priceless, as they create and capitalize on the opportunities to grow the company." All the success stories I'd heard were of people who had made a killing in some deal and were now retired to the Bahamas.

One of my sales vice presidents concocted such a quick get-rich scheme for POLY-CARB in 1978.

Prior to 1978, our market focus had always been on highway-and construction-related fields, and we sold our products only to professional contractors engaged in commercial or highway construction. We did not do any retail business geared toward the do-it-yourself homeowners market. Our sales vice president came up with a brilliant idea to bring in a lot of quick growth and cash. For a small, struggling company, *growth* and *cash* are the two magic words.

I asked him if the idea was legal and ethical. His answer was a resounding yes. He added that it not only was legal and ethical, but also would create a win-win situation for all parties. He elaborated and said, "We are going to set up local distributors in each major metropolitan area for our new line of products geared toward retail outlets. We do not have to develop any new products, but can simply repackage the existing, proven products in small, user-friendly retail packages. These products will then be placed in local hardware stores on consignment on specially designed racks. Each distributor will purchase inventory of these products and racks from POLY-CARB on a cash basis, guided by the number of hardware locations he or she would like to service. We will select the retail hardware location for each distributor, negotiate with the hardware store to set up a display and a consignment agreement, and simultaneously train the distributor on the uses and benefits of our products."

He continued, "Our sales pitch is that this is the first time that our well-tested, industrial grade products will be available for retailers—an incredible value in long-term performance and reliability."

Our sales VP was excited while making his pitch about his new concept and, without any break, continued, "The best part is that the distributor doesn't need to have any prior sales or marketing experience. The distributor relies on walk-in traffic at the store and simply services the account by refurbishing the inventory and collecting the money on the sales made by the store. The store gets thirty-five percent profit without investing in inventory or worrying about reordering or managing the product rack."

I was not sure if we wanted to get into managing hundreds, possibly thousands, of distributors and answering thousands of questions from retail customers. But instant cash flow and growth were tempting. So I asked, "What would the distributor and POLY-CARB make on this deal?"

He replied, "Distributors will make thirty-five percent, and we will double our money on each transaction. The best part is that we get all our money up front, as the initial investment, as well as all future inventory, will be paid by the distributor on a cash basis. We have no risk. Not only that, but all the sales commissions and support force to set up location and training is already figured in the up-front, one-time franchise fee paid by the distributor. We do not have to put special sales and training people on our payroll, as they are going to be strictly on commission."

It sounded too good to be true. Something inside me was screaming to say that this was not for us. But my brain was supporting it through all kinds of calculations and analysis based on the facts presented by our VP.

I didn't know if it was the quick and easy cash coupled with unlimited fast growth that blinded my vision, but I was unable to foresee all the pitfalls of this venture, and POLY-CARB jumped in with all that we had.

We selected six products that addressed the needs of the do-it-your-self market and designed new packages for retail sales. We also designed a headboard to go over each rack as a marketing and sales tool for the products. In the meantime, the sales VP who'd come up with the idea assembled a team of commission-based sales and training people. I was still not sure if anyone would buy the distributorships and pay us money in advance. So when our VP asked my permission to start selling the distributorships, I said yes.

I was pleasantly shocked when our VP handed over checks worth a total of $50,000 in the second week of this new venture. I was still somehow not sold and expressed my doubt as to whether the same sales could be repeated the following week. However, we did even better the next week, bringing in $55,000. The numbers escalated every week for the next six weeks. By then, we were all convinced we'd found a gold mine. It was a stunning success beyond my wildest expectations. I thought we had hit a jackpot and all of our financial problems were finally going to be over. Little did I know that this get-rich-quick scheme was just the beginning of all our financial challenges.

So what went wrong? We were totally out of our expertise and league. All our previous experience was with bulk packaging. The smallest container we had ever packaged was a one-gallon can. We were now packaging from two-ounce bottles to half-pint containers. Manufacturing was simple, but packaging was turning into a nightmare.

First of all, we simply could not buy just a few thousand bottles or cans because in order to get a good price, we had to purchase close to half a million or more. Not only did we have to tie up lot of capital in the inventory of packaging and special shipping materials, but we also had to hire over fifty people to do manual packaging of our products in the small containers. We even explored custom-packaging houses and found that to use their automated processes, we had to order materials worth several million dollars each time.

Our stunning success was quickly becoming a massive failure. In the meantime, our sales force was busy selling distributorships, and we were falling further behind in delivering the materials. Whatever orders we filled were immediately sold, and new orders started coming in. Our customers were irate, as we simply could not package our products fast enough. And the worst part was that instead of doubling our money, we were actually losing money on each order. We'd not calculated the real packaging costs or the additional labor cost required for packaging.

Some of our distributors were threatening us with lawsuits, as we had not kept our end of the bargain. It quickly became clear that we had a big mess on our hands. Now our problem was how to stop this snowballing of events that was digging us into a deeper hole every day.

Finally, I bit the bullet and asked the sales VP to stop the program immediately. He was rather surprised, as in his view, it was the most successful sales and marketing campaign we had going. Why would we want to stop it? He was simply unable to relate to the fact that the company was losing money. We could not come to any terms, and I was left with no choice but to fire the sales VP and his entire commissioned crew and stop selling new distributorships.

Now how was I to deal with the existing distributors whom we could not support or supply with product? I chose to visit each distributor individually, and leveled with them, explaining what had happened and how I could not sustain this business model. I ended up arranging cash

> The final economic result for me and POLY-CARB was our throwing away half a million dollars of our hard-earned money to get out of this get-rich-quick scheme.

settlements with most of the distributors, and the final economic result for me and POLY-CARB was our throwing away half a million dollars of our hard-earned money to get out of this get-rich-quick scheme.

Now, one can argue that what we did was not really dishonest, and we did not violate the intent of the third Sikh tenet. But the fact is that I was swayed by making quick money, and in the flow of things, I didn't do my due diligence and check out all the facts properly. That, as I understand now, was dishonest.

In the oneness paradigm, which is directed by our first tenet, we really do not own anything. Everything is allocated to us, including our wealth, creativity, knowledge, and even our human bodies. If we selflessly serve the bigger One, our fellow humans, then these resources are enhanced. If we're not serving the bigger One, but serving our greed and/or personal needs, these resources will be depleted and we'll lose everything.

In this paradigm, working hard is not enough. Serving and consistently challenging ourselves to enhance our servicing ability are required.

My mother and father

4. **Share.**

My mother was always reminding me of this fourth tenet. Basically, it implies that what we share enhances and grows, and what we do not share shrinks and diminishes. This tenet calls for unconditionally sharing what we have with others to add value to them, as well as to equip them to add value to others, whether through knowledge, wealth, food, or anything that can make a difference in the lives of others.

I felt that I had failed to create an environment of true sharing at POLY-CARB, and that explained why I was facing bankruptcy.

All the employees at POLY-CARB were in their own zones and silos and did not make any effort to share what they knew or learned that could help other team members to serve our customers or even our team members by enhancing their value-adding capabilities or helping them perform better.

Life, as my mother explained it, and our connection to everyone and everything are similar to our bodies. Our bodies are made up of trillions of cells that form every aspect of our physical features. In essence, we view our bodies as one, not a collection of individual parts. When we eat food—which supplies us with the resources to function optimally—the nutrients, vitamins, and minerals are shared with every part of our bodies without exception.

It is the same with society, but instead of sharing our resources, wealth, knowledge and skills, we exploit the needy, often unreasonably, or hoard resources. Typically, sharing is then interpreted as giving the poor or disadvantaged things like money, food, and clothing. But that kind of sharing is inconsistent and conditional.

#3: The Law of Abundance
"Abundance comes from the realization that resources do not belong to us, but are merely allocated to us to add the highest value."

What this comes down to is the concept of abundance. Most people's understanding of abundance is actually conditional. Generally, the subtext when sharing our abundance is "What's in it for me?" and/or there's the sense that we're superior in some way, no matter whether we're giving to a charity, donating our time, etc. We develop expectations for some kind of return, even if it's just a thank-you or some kind of recognition or award. What we want is some level of ownership.

Why, then, do we work so hard to own anything and everything? The answer hit me square between the eyes: the Law of Abundance, law number three: *"Abundance comes from the realization that resources do not belong to us, but are merely allocated to us to add the highest value."*

In order to operate in an abundance mentality, it is important to understand that it is not possible to own anything, as all resources belong to the bigger One and are merely allocated to us. Their allocation is either enhanced or depleted based on whether we are adding the highest value to the bigger One or not.

With my painful and intense exposure to impending bankruptcy, I understood that true sharing was a much more elevated concept because we share at all levels at all times. If you want to be a good student in class, you share your knowledge with others in the class. By doing this, you increase your own knowledge through giving of what you know and learning from those with whom you're working. I am sure we have all heard the old saying "The best way to learn is to teach." When you share with your fellow workers, what you've shared and learned strengthens your entire team. Even sharing with your competitors strengthens the industry. At the personal level, when you share your home with others, you make and strengthen friendships.

> The process of sharing must generate gratefulness within us, as the credit must go to the bigger One, the originator and true source of everything.

The concept of true sharing is an amazingly revolutionary concept that offers enrichment in every aspect of life. In reality, giving is merely sharing because the truth is that we don't own anything, as everything is gifted to us by the bigger One. Therefore, we can never claim to be the one giving anything. The process of sharing must generate gratefulness within us, as the credit must go to the bigger One, the originator and true source of everything.

In later years, POLY-CARB, in the true spirit of sharing, would hold instructional seminars and invite our customers and even suppliers. When we held these seminars, Dolly would personally prepare several dishes in addition to other dishes we'd order from caterers. The spread of food would outperform five-star hotels in variety and presentation. At the end of the seminar, we'd hand out a comment sheet to see how we rated. Everyone would invariably add another column for food/ presentation and give the highest rating for that. That became a standard for us.

When I visited customers, the first thing they'd remember was the food Dolly prepared. I learned from Dolly that the expression of gratefulness is not just in the words we speak, but in our actions. She chose Diwali—the Indian "festival of lights"—which is in the fall, as one means of adding higher value to people's lives, whether they were working at POLY-CARB or otherwise.

In India, the Diwali festival is epitomized by expressing gratefulness to our fellow human beings and sharing

> Diwali celebrates the victory of goodness over evil. Every home is decorated with clay lamps, which signify banishing the darkness of ignorance and bringing the light of wisdom into our lives.

with our friends and foes good wishes through fruits, nuts, and sweets. Everyone in India, regardless of his or her background and religion, celebrates this festival. The entire home is whitewashed, and wardrobes are refurbished. It's like New Year's and Christmas celebrated as one. It celebrates the victory of goodness over evil. Every home is decorated with clay lamps, which signify banishing the darkness of ignorance and bringing the light of wisdom into our lives.

We would design a beautiful card that stated the core principle of Diwali. Every year, Dolly would prepare over five hundred gift baskets to send to friends and POLY-CARB's key customers and suppliers from around the world. The gift baskets would then be delivered to everyone. Each year would have a different theme.

Dolly would travel to world trade fairs and specialty stores throughout the year to select items from around the world to include in the baskets. People would wait each year with bated breath for their Diwali basket, wondering how Dolly would improve upon and surpass the previous year's basket, their surprise and pleasure were immense as they discovered Dolly's treasures. Somehow, Dolly always outdid herself, arranging the gifts in evermore artful and touching ways that made hearts glow with joy.

The gift baskets allowed us to touch not only the people the gifts were for, but also their families and friends. This yearly event allowed us to establish close ties with so many people, and we never thought twice about whether we would celebrate Diwali in this manner or not. Diwali was one way of expressing unconditional sharing and gratitude.

I now fully realize that the concept of sharing also works well in hard-core business situations and practices. It brings reason and responsiveness to all our business transactions. Greed, which inspires gouging, disappears. Trust sets in, bringing sustainability to the business. Our marketing strategy shifts our focus from simply profitability to customer profitability to adding value, which results in enhanced profit as a by-product.

Adding value does not work on a simple pricing formula based on our costs and profit needs, but, instead, works on the value our products and services bring to our customers. We begin to think differently in terms of the elevation of the value that we offer rather than the product or service we sell. Our products and services are merely tools moving us toward a much loftier objective of adding the highest value by sharing everything we collectively can offer.

Recalling these four tenets actually freed me from the fear of failing or losing anything and empowered me with unending creativity. Somehow, I felt connected to the abundant resources and power around me and within me. I also knew that my team members and I must operate in student mode, as we were continuously learning. It was becoming clear that this was the thought process needed for our sustainability, as we would position our company to continuously make our best better; this thought process would also keep us internally motivated without the crutches of titles, trophies, rewards, and medals.

Importantly, this mind-set would give us the capacity and wisdom to make the right decisions, as our decision making would be in full compliance with the unfailing universal wisdom of oneness. I was beginning to understand that it is only through operating in oneness that we will free ourselves completely from insecurity, fear, greed, and ego. Of course, I needed to truly get myself back on course and stay there in order to avoid being swayed by the world around me. This task would entail a lot of self-discipline, and I had to make sure my mental habits shifted to a continuous mind-set of adding greater value no matter what challenges I faced. It would require approaching everything as an opportunity to learn. By constantly remembering and practicing my Sikh roots, I would eventually get there.

> It is only through operating in oneness that we will free ourselves completely from insecurity, fear, greed, and ego.

The four tenets of Sikhism—remember and serve God at all times, practice acceptance, make an honest living, and share—formed the exact springboard I needed as I began writing down the immutable and intrinsic laws of oneness.

Though it is fundamental to our very being, capturing the spirit of this wisdom was not simple. As with all truth, it is designed to be simple. Humans being what they are, we tend to complicate things, so I wanted to ensure that this wisdom was easily understood and would require little supportive explanation. Thus, my weekend, which had begun with seemingly bad news, turned out to be one of deep contemplation, epiphanies, and insights.

One understanding was paramount, though: The bottom line for me that weekend was acknowledging that I'd become derailed by the external world and its intense push to incorporate more and more people into its myriad and convoluted systems. Those systems are what have brought the world to its present predicament on so many levels. It was time I re-aligned myself with the greater truth of the wisdom I was unveiling. The universal secret of all success was staring me right in the face: the integration into oneness.

#4: The Law of Integrity

"For true, sustainable, and stress-free success and happiness, every thought, word, action, and decision must be completely immersed in and integrated into oneness."

"For true, sustainable, and stress-free success and happiness, every thought, word, action, and decision must be completely immersed in and integrated into oneness."

And that is how we obtain our true integrity—the Law of Integrity, the all-encompassing sphere within which everything else resides. It is also the fountainhead from which all else springs. This fourth Law of Oneness is a simple yet profound truth, and it means that every being and everything around us is part of an integral One. Any decision based on this core human value can never be wrong or unethical and will always stand the test of time.

Not only is oneness always empowering and fulfilling, but it is also the essential foundation of every sustainable relationship, endeavor, happiness, and success in life. It also means that any thought or action by any single person will affect everyone else, as we all are an inseparable part of everyone else. Full comprehension of this truth gives us an understanding of who we truly are.

My mother's explanation of oneness so many years ago was finally coming home to roost. It was like a new dawn for me, one in which I could more clearly see that I was about to embark on a new journey. Actually, though, what was really happening was that I was finally coming full circle. The terrible news that POLY-CARB was heading for bankruptcy was a gift in disguise. The writing I had begun that weekend was proving to be the start of a monumental shift. It was time to head in a new direction.

Chapter 7

Taking a New Direction

Not only did I need to return to my roots and get back to the founding principle of life that could resolve my predicament—oneness—POLY-CARB needed to also. But was it possible to bring my team members onto the same plane of thinking? Was it even possible to retrain the staff? Would they ever understand this new initiative directed by this core principle, especially when they were rigidly parked in the "What's in it for me?" mind-set? Should I bring in new people—people with experience?

The answer was no. People with experience, though they bring important tools and tricks of the trade with them, also bring baggage, and they're not easily retrained. They tend to be closed books, not willing to learn new things. Their baggage, right or wrong, becomes their comfort zone. In this forever-changing world where technology is becoming obsolete every day, where new businesses are being launched and the way business is conducted is changing, experience can often become a liability rather than an asset. Intrinsically, I knew that if you don't embark on learning new methods and technology, you'll become a dinosaur and left in the dust.

The more I thought about it, I realized that each of us needs to remain in the mind-set of a student. At some point, it became crystal clear to me that I must have people who are willing to continuously learn and not stay imprisoned in their prior life and work experiences and/or education. At this juncture, I thought to myself, *What if I start fresh? I'm already broke, and I can't be any worse off than where I am.*

I didn't want experts; I wanted students. To me, an expert is someone with a blocked mind who thinks he or she knows everything

> It's not possible for any human being to know everything. The concept of a person being an expert is highly overstated and grossly misrepresented.

and therefore doesn't need to learn anymore. I also knew that it was not possible for any human being to know everything. The concept of a person being an expert is highly overstated and grossly misrepresented. I needed people who were interested in continuously learning, improving, and progressing with the fast-changing demands of life.

That Sunday morning, I finally got some sleep, and when I awoke, the direction I needed to take was staring me right in the face—oneness. I was really beginning to grasp that we are all one, that nothing separates us, and that everything we do has an impact on the world around us. I was beginning to understand that living oneness as life's primary principle means that our sole purpose in life is to add the highest value at all times in all situations for everyone—unconditionally. In other words, to live to serve that bigger One.

It's a very simple, uncomplicated philosophy, if you will. Yet, it has profound implications in how it shifts a person's thinking and life away from a "What's in it for me?" mind-set to a desire to serve all of mankind.

I was amazed that I hadn't seen the answer before. I told Dolly about the solution I'd arrived at: bring in an entirely new staff. We had customer orders in the pipeline, we'd be able to turn any loss into profitability, and, at the same time, practice what we deeply believed was the right way to conduct business. She was in total agreement.

> Everyone defined me as an engineer, a scientist, a son, husband, father, an immigrant, a salesman. The question still remained, though, "Who am I?"

I was being offered a gift. Now I had a major decision to make, but to do so was going to require some major introspection. In order to implement these timeless and universal tenets, POLY-CARB was going to require a whole new framework within which to operate—a radical and, very possibly, painful shift—beginning with me. That presented a problem. Everyone defined me as an engineer, a scientist, a son, husband, father, an immigrant, a salesman. The question still remained, though, "Who am I?"

I remember in chemistry class a long time ago, my professor posed a question to the students: "Who can tell me what a diamond is?"

Students responded with all the standard answers. He responded by asking, "Do you realize that it is the purest form of carbon?" He held up a pencil for everyone to see and stated that the lead in the pencil was also the purest form of carbon. "What, then, is carbon?"

He went on to explain that if we took the graphite in the pencil and subjected it to very high pressure and temperature, it would transform into a diamond. This is how General Electric manufactures artificial diamonds, which are used in many industrial applications.

"In reality, the lead in the pencil—graphite—and a diamond are merely conditional states of carbon, just like we human beings. We operate under certain circumstances—for example, as a student or teacher—and upon graduation, we take on any number of roles, such as businessperson, parent, judge, homemaker, caretaker, et cetera. These are conditional states of who we are. But do we know who we truly are?

"In science, scientists discovered the truth about carbon by studying its atomic structure and determining what makes carbon carbon. It is only by thoroughly understanding the intrinsic nature of carbon that we have been able to fully use that carbon, which has resulted in the development of all our technology, organic chemistry, polymer chemistry, medicines, et cetera.

"Although this is not a philosophy class but a chemistry class, until you discover who you truly are, you will not achieve your full potential."

It was important for me to find out who I truly was, to utilize my full potential. I needed to understand "Who am I?"

Chapter 8

Who Am I?

This big question was still bugging me. I wanted to move forward, but how would I ever be able to trust other people? They were so full of contradictions, emotionality, hidden agendas, fears and defense and survival mechanisms, and they didn't often speak from their hearts. I then remembered my father's words: "You will never be able to trust others until you become trustworthy yourself, and you can't become trustworthy until you discover who you truly are."

So, again, it all came back to me understanding *"Who am I?"* It's the million-dollar question we all ask ourselves at some point in our lives, usually without obtaining a clear answer. It is, though, something to ponder, as what we discover along the way relates directly to our sense of purpose in life. As the founder and CEO of POLY-CARB, my role was to lead the company forward in a manner that would increase sales and provide sustainable incomes and benefits for all the team members.

Since founding POLY-CARB in 1973, I'd been following the standard business practices of companies and corporations in the US. Most decisions were bottom-line oriented: Were we making or losing money? Actions were taken accordingly. I was now in the hot seat of deciding the fate of the company, as well as the livelihoods of its employees. Was I being an effective leader? Had I ever been?

This thought reminded me of a time when I was about eight or nine years old. A guest had come to visit my family in India. He asked me, "What do you want to be?" I answered that I wanted to be the boss, to become a leader.

> The only way you can lead anyone is to lead yourself first. You can't lead yourself first until you totally comprehend and understand who you truly are. You are fundamentally a part of the bigger One—that's who you are.

My father, upon hearing this, stepped in by saying, "Son, the only way you can lead anyone is to lead yourself first. The irony is that many of us think we are leading ourselves, when instead, it is our egos, insecurities, and greed that end up leading us. The essential prerequisite for leading ourselves is to discover *who in us* should lead *what in us*. In order to lead ourselves first, we must know who we truly are through comprehending the oneness paradigm. You are fundamentally a part of the bigger One—that is who you are." He then gave me the following analogy.

This innate wisdom within us is like the power that runs through and inhabits all of us, similar to the underlying electrical grid of a city. It is a fact that every building in our town is connected to the same power station, which powers every outlet, machine, etc., in all the buildings in our community. A live connection exists between the power station and every building.

When this live connection from the power station is disrupted due to a storm or interruption, all the equipment running on this power simply goes dead. In a manner of speaking, the homes or buildings that have no power are literally dead for all practical purposes. We've all experienced this situation.

We human beings are similarly connected to a power source that is responsible for the life within us, and when this power source is taken away from this human body form, we declare this form dead. This form then has no purpose or use, and we either bury it or cremate it.

You can name that power source in whatever way makes you feel comfortable or that you find compelling. It is the same thing whether you call it Universal Energy, the Divine Force, God, the Supreme Soul, or the Supreme Power. It is what connects all human souls and is fundamentally the same identical power running through us. Most of us, though, completely fail to remember the fact that we're already operating within it at all times and do not have to flip a switch so that we're consciously connected.

Let's take a simple case of switching on a light bulb in your home. By a flick of the switch, you can turn it on. If it doesn't come on, you have three possibilities. The obvious one is that your light bulb is burned out and requires replacing. If you replace the light bulb and it still doesn't come on, then the second possibility is that there is a power failure or the power to your home has been shut off. Perhaps, of course, it could just be that you forgot to pay the electric bill.

When you check and find other appliances working, meaning the power is coming into the house, then the third possibility is that the power coming into your house is not reaching the outlet due to defective materials or some insulating material blocking the flow of the electrical current.

The power source that makes human beings alive is the Universal Energy. If we're still walking and talking, we're alive, which means we're still connected to that Universal Energy.

The power source that makes us human beings alive is the Universal Energy. If we're still walking and talking, we're alive, which means we're still connected to that Universal Energy. Unfortunately, however, we're not aware of it, meaning the "light bulb" within us is not turned on. This could be due to insulation we've accumulated, or blockages, such as insecurities, fear, greed, prejudice, depression, jealousy, anger, etc.—namely, our ego.

It took me years to truly understand my father's words, and here I was again, in 1980, faced with having forgotten my true identity. That's where I had gone wrong. I had been operating in many roles, but not operating as my true self. Suddenly, another amazing secret presented itself, law number five, the Law of Leadership:

"We cannot lead others until we lead ourselves first. In order to lead ourselves first, we must know who we truly are through comprehending the oneness paradigm."

> **#5: The Law of Leadership**
> "We cannot lead others until we lead ourselves first. In order to lead ourselves first, we must know who we truly are through comprehending the oneness paradigm."

I remembered my father telling me who I was, but it didn't sink in until right that minute. I intellectually knew, but it remained only knowledge. I suddenly realized that my personal integrity—my core operating value—could be practiced only by first integrating with my very being and operating in oneness with all the power of the universe present within me and everyone else. It is that power within me that is the true leader.

> Life distracts and derails us from remembering who we truly are and sidetracks us from serving our true purpose.

Looking back, since starting POLY-CARB and during my student career, I realize now that when I operated in unison with this thought process, I unknowingly got amazing results.

But, it never became my standard operating procedure. That's where I had gone wrong. I had been operating in many roles, but not allowing my true self to lead in all of those roles.

Being in a leadership position and not knowing who I was left me vulnerable to the predations of others: their agendas, insecurities, manipulations, and egos. I was being pulled every which way, and therefore, clarity of thought and purpose was lost amid the jumble of others' wants and demands. My personal principles and values became truncated and eventually jettisoned as I was slowly co-opted by outside forces. The outcome was that I became a slave to a system and simply a cog in its moribund machinations. As a leader, any movement or change I hoped to enact would meet tremendous resistance, and it could take a lifetime to bring about real change.

Operating within silos and wearing many hats compartmentalized me and was contrary to the oneness paradigm, which encompasses everyone in a whole, integrated organism. Trying to lead others while I was a non-integrated entity was like trying to put out a forest fire when I and my fellow firefighters had no prior experience in fighting fires. Everyone was running around expending a lot of energy, and the outcome was far from successful. Knowing who we were and working from the vantage point of oneness would automatically put us in a position of clarity of purpose and focus, which would then lead to not only the results we desired, but also levels of success we'd not even imagined. This was the path on which POLY-CARB needed to re-orient itself.

Me, third from the left

There was one specific event in my life that really brought this understanding home. I had heard this message—that we are all one—in a form different from my parents' explanations, but I didn't fully comprehend it at that time. I got a glimpse of it, though, when I attended National Cadet Corps (NCC) training while attending Pilani.

During my bachelor of science studies at Birla Institute of Science and Technology in Pilani, I joined the NCC, which is similar to ROTC in the US and lasts from high school through college. The NCC was an artillery unit. During the year, we were trained in all the military disciplines, except we didn't work with real artillery guns and ammunition. At one point, we had to go to a military base for two weeks of training. This way, we would have actual training with guns and live ammo.

My entire unit took a bus to the military base located on the outskirts of Delhi. Back then, the roads were horribly rutted and bumpy, and we were bounced around for six tortuous hours. Many of the young men on board got serious motion sickness.

By the time we reached our destination, we were exhausted. I was tired but not sick, and I felt great compassion for my fellow travelers. As soon as we were off the bus and standing at attention in several lines, the commanding officer asked for a volunteer to stand sentry duty all night long—a punishing duty even when one is fully rested and in optimum physical condition. An amazing feeling came over me, and I felt one with my fellow cadets. That feeling inspired me to be protective of the rest of the group and their exhausted and sickly state. I immediately volunteered, filled with a sense that the group's welfare was my responsibility.

Having volunteered to save my fellow students from this torture, I was given a heavy gun and positioned at the main gate to the training base for what soon felt like an eternity of sentry duty. There was no one to talk to, remaining fully alert was an absolute must, no food or drink was allowed, and I was periodically checked up on to see that I was at the ready for anything—it should have been one of the longest nights of my life. And when my shift was over, I should have been completely spent. But to the contrary, the thought that my fellow cadets were resting after such a torturous journey somehow made me feel that I was indeed resting. I'd never experienced this oneness feeling before in my life.

Unbeknownst to me, my having immediately volunteered had elevated me in the eyes of the commander, an army brigadier. The outcome was that I was given two extra days to rest while the rest of the unit from Pilani went through practical artillery training. After one day of rest, I was ready to join the rest of the group, so instead of sleeping, I suited up in my fatigues and fell in with the rest of my unit.

Aside from the training, an additional project was announced that involved making signs for all the various areas of the base. Again, a volunteer was sought for someone to take charge of the project. We were asked who among us had artistic talents for sign making. Five of us raised our hands, and they had us each create a sign to determine whose was best. After reviewing everyone's signs, mine was chosen, so I got to make all of the signs for the base.

Back in those days, we didn't have all the marvelous technology we have today for sign making, so I had to hand paint all of the signs. After all the signs were put up, our barracks were reviewed by the brigadier and a guest, a military commander. As it so happened, there were several units from other schools at the camp at the same time. Our unit was selected as number one.

The commanding officers were impressed with the work I'd done on the signs. As a result, all creative projects during that two-week training camp were given to me. One drawback with this, though, was that the projects deprived me of all the hard-core training that the rest of my unit was receiving, such as how to handle real artillery guns that took twenty-five-pound ammo. I did attend a few trainings, but that was not enough for me.

At the end of the two weeks, we were taken to a real firing range. The heavy guns were mounted on their bases, which took several men to maneuver. There were five crews per gun, with five team members per crew, and each team member had a specific responsibility. Position number three had the most critical responsibility, as he was responsible for elevation, angle, and range. He had to record all incoming commands, which were transmitted by another unit that had the exact location of the target. Finally, when the command to fire was given, number three had to pull the trigger.

The scary part was that we were on the outskirts of the densely populated metropolitan city of Delhi, and if the alignment of the gun and calculations were incorrect, we could accidently kill innocent people, as the mortars would land in urban areas of Delhi—the range of the guns being twenty-plus miles. That was how serious this last part of our training was. We were understandably nervous.

One day, everyone was assembled into crews of five to work with the large guns, but I was not assigned to any crew. Then the brigadier asked the trainers who had trained our five crews if they had any doubts about any of their cadets, especially those in position number three. The trainer for crew number two said he wasn't so sure about his number-three guy, as he wasn't as proficient as he'd like. The brigadier said, "Let's not take any chances. Let me give you my most reliable cadet," and he turned and pointed at me. I froze. He asked, "You can do it, yes?"

I found myself in a distressing predicament because if I said no, I'd be directly disobeying him, but on the other hand, I'd not received the full training with the guns. I didn't know what to do, but I had to say, "Yes, of course, sir."

We were handed over to a regular Indian army captain who was also a Sikh. He explained that for the next half hour, he'd answer any questions we had concerning the guns and responsibilities of the cadets in each position or any other concerns we might have. I spoke up and said that our training had been given by Nepalese trainers whose accents had been difficult to understand at times and that it would be appreciated if he would go through the entire process again step by step. That request turned out to be my saving grace, as the captain thought it was a good idea. He announced that we'd be tested afterward. He would give us three test exercises for recording the readings, and whoever entered the maximum number of correct recordings would get the most target-practice shots with live mortars.

> I felt one with the captain, and in that moment, I had a direct hardwire connection with him, as if I were able to transplant all his experience and knowledge into myself.

When the captain was going through each step in precise detail, I felt in unison with him, and every explanation of his seemed to revive and synchronize our previous old, segmented, and patchy training. I felt one with the captain, and in that moment, I had a direct hardwire connection with him, as if I were able to transplant all his experience and knowledge into myself.

He answered all of our questions and then finally asked if we were ready for the test. All sorts of readings needed to be entered and guns aligned. Since I was in position number three, the weight of this responsibility made me anxious. At the end, the captain asked us to step away from the guns and told each trainer to give the reading. This was repeated three times. The readings were recorded and compared. The captain then went to each team and announced the findings for that team. When he got to my team, I realized that none of the other teams had gotten all three recordings correct, not even the best team.

When the captain came and stood in front of me, I was nervous. My heart sank, and I was already lambasting myself for having failed because with the other teams having mixed results, including the best team, I surely must not have done well either. My failure would reflect badly on the captain, who was also a Sikh, and the brigadier who had so confidently recommended me for the number-three position. Yet, when I was taking commands and recording the readings, I had felt that somehow the captain himself was present within me and that he was actually doing the recording. The captain stated that I had all three readings correct. He announced this to all the teams and said that my team had won. Therefore, we would get the most practice shots.

Now, my three correct recordings could have been because I had thrived under the stressful conditions or had paid such acute attention during that last half hour recapping the correct use of the gun. Or my performance could have been because I was so nervous and thus paid greater attention and did not take anything for granted. Or, possibly, my training in the physics lab, with all of its optical equipment, had resulted in my calibrating the gun correctly. Looking back and knowing what I now know about oneness, I actually saw oneness in operation: with the captain, with the commanders, with the artillery machine and recording equipment, and with the entire environment.

Former Prime Ministers Indira Gandhi and Jawaharlal Nehru.
I was chosen to represent BITS Pilani when I was still a student
there. That's me on the right in the light-colored turban.

To top off the two-week training, not only did my correct recordings give my team the chance to have more practice firing the guns, but I was promoted and received the award for the top cadet of the entire camp.

What I'd experienced in that event is similar to what performing artists experience. When they have butterflies in their stomachs, they are in an acute state of awareness that then allows their egos to be put aside, and all that exists is the performance. It is then that the experience is elevated to a whole new level. The same thing had happened to me. I was in the zone.

> People who dig deep within themselves to completely integrate all their energy and concentration in a singular moment end up performing at a much higher level regardless of their prior experience and training.

That military training experience made me extremely humble, as I knew that other cadets were much better trained than I. The point of this anecdote is that in the end, I learned that people who dig deep within themselves to completely integrate all their energy and concentration in a singular moment end up performing at a much higher level regardless of their prior experience and training. This was tapping into the real me—the common, unifying One, the Divine.

I wanted to re-create that feeling of being in the zone not only for myself, but for the entire team at POLY-CARB. Anyone who has experienced being in the zone wants to experience it again and again. It's a marvelous sensation of expansiveness and connectedness—the energy of unlimited possibilities. The trick lies in how to position ourselves 24/7/365 to always be in that flow, the vortex of elemental creativity and beingness. Life gets in the way with its demands and circumstances, though we try our best to stay on an even keel, to stay focused and on track. That was the case with me. I needed to extricate myself from the maze of human confusion and complexity and find the "still point of the turning world," for "there the dance is," as T.S. Eliot put it.

In terms of the core principle of oneness, what I'd done was supplant that principle with someone else's principle—that of typically accepted business philosophies. How could I be a leader if I was simply following the lead of others? What I'd effectively done was borrow the principles, mission, purpose, and values of an established system. But intrinsically, they were not mine, and therefore, they never became one with me. What, then, could I do to get myself back on track? I wasn't operating optimally because I didn't know who I was. Once I understood who I truly was, I was ready to get back to reality and start dissolving my illusions and misperceptions.

Chapter 9

Perception and Reality

I had two contradictory thought processes at work. Whenever I acted alone, I experienced success. Whenever I relied on other people, who had personal agendas, there were conflicts created by the undercurrents of their agendas. They were derailing me. I realized I was working with the common resources of the universe. In my mind, I knew those resources had to be available to me. I just had to find ways to obtain those resources.

It was difficult. Many people had never met or dealt with a Sikh before, and my turban tended to make people apprehensive. This could be called racial discrimination, but through the lens of oneness, I saw it was really just a lack of knowledge, data, and/or experience with me and my customs. An example of one such situation occurred in 2001 when I was in a grocery store.

As a Sikh, I was, as always, wearing my turban. This was shortly after the 9/11 attack on the World Trade Center towers, and people were in shock.

While standing in the checkout line, a woman looked at me and suddenly said, "Why don't you people leave? Get out of our country, and leave us alone!" She was shaking in anger and fear. Other shoppers, overhearing her, began gathering around us. They, too, were experiencing the trauma and pain of the event.

I was taken aback by the intensity of the woman's vehemence. Being a Sikh and immersed in the oneness paradigm, I immediately closed my eyes and was reminded that my purpose in life is to add value. How was I to do that in this situation? Being defensive wouldn't help. That would only worsen the situation. The woman was obviously in pain, as were a lot of people, and she was taking it out on me.

I realized that she was not striking out at me personally, but viewing me as the embodiment of her fear and confusion. What I needed to do was calm her and steer the confrontation away from her fear and hurt and into the larger picture of oneness—that which is found within all of us and connects us all.

I responded by gently saying, "Ma'am, I understand that we're both hurt by this incident. If expressing your pain and anguish at me relieves your anger, then continue; hit me if it helps you. But please understand that we are in this together; we are all one. I am just as hurt as you are. What we need during these difficult circumstances is to express love and kindness."

She looked at me and started crying. She then hugged me.

"Please forgive me," she said through her tears as she continued to embrace me.

> We will be insecure, prejudiced, afraid, stressed, confused, and outright frightened until we remove the illusion of duality within us and begin to see the omnipresent oneness in everyone and everything.

"You haven't done anything. It is the right time for us to come together as one." A number of the shoppers gathered around us applauded, and several hugged me.

Many times, what we see that's different from our everyday experience and knowledge can frighten us or at least make us wary. My turban causes people to pause and wonder who I am and what I'm doing. The woman in the grocery store was afraid and in pain. My turban was not a part of her world, and she equated it with those involved with the 9/11 attack. The old adage "You can't judge a book by its cover" was apt in that instance. Thankfully, my grounding in oneness came to the fore, and the situation ended with all those involved finding greater connection with me and with each other.

Sometimes a simple difference in appearance is cause for curiosity, and people want to investigate. That's exactly what happened when I moved to the US in 1968.

The strange, yet interesting, thing is that the same turban that caused a misunderstanding at the grocery store got me royal treatment in Rome when I first traveled from India for the US. I had told my travel agent I wanted to sightsee a little on my way to America, so he'd arranged two stops: Rome and Paris.

While in Rome, I said to the concierge at my hotel that I wanted to have the best Italian food in town. He made a reservation for me and also arranged for a limousine, though I'd not asked for one. He ordered a limo because I had requested that the hotel staff iron my white silk Nehru jacket so that I could wear it to dinner. The tailor of the jacket was named Maharaja, and his label was in the jacket. The staff, seeing this, spread the word throughout the hotel that I was the maharaja.

That evening, I came downstairs wearing the white Nehru jacket and a maroon turban. The concierge had me ushered to the limousine, which drove me to a fancy and modern restaurant. The entire decor was black and white, so I fit in perfectly, except for my turban.

When I entered the restaurant, the maître d' knew my name and escorted me to my table. The waiter brought a bottle of wine to my table, saying that the Italian couple at a nearby table had sent the bottle over and that they had a question for me. They wanted to know if I was a real prince, or maharaja. I sighed and said that I just couldn't seem to get away. That was enough for the waiter, and shortly after, the wife came over and said she didn't want to disturb me, but had never seen or talked to a real prince. She told me she and her husband would be delighted if I would join them.

I agreed, but I had one condition: I was sure they would want to know all about my background, maharajas and India, but I didn't want any of the questions to be about my identity. They agreed and asked how many wives and children I had in my harem and how many servants, elephants, jewels, etc., I had.

Finishing dinner and preparing to take my leave, I explained that I couldn't give them my real name, but said that if they wanted to meet a real maharaja in India, I could give them the name of a friend of mine, Dr. Karni Singh, the maharaja of Bikaner in the state of Rajasthan. They were extremely pleased and thankful.

When I arrived in Boston a few days later, my cousin, Amrik, a mechanical engineer, decided to impress me by taking me to the Playboy Club. I chose to wear the same Nehru jacket and maroon turban that evening. Ever the jokester, I asked my cousin to introduce me as the prince of Bikaner at the club, which he did.

At one point, we found ourselves at a pool table. Amrik goaded me into playing against the house's best pool player, betting that I would lose. The best player turned out to be a Playboy Bunny. I managed to beat her.

She was intrigued with me, wondering what I, a maharaja, was doing at a Playboy Club. I explained that I was actually in the States to pursue higher education—to attain a PhD at The University of Akron. She was impressed.

I asked what she was doing there. She was an undergraduate student at NYU. Her semester would begin in two weeks. I was impressed that even in that place, the Playboy Club, which sold sex appeal, a Playboy Bunny had a desire for higher education. I told her that she should go for her PhD, as ultimately, an educated woman made a greater impact on society as a whole than an educated man. In fact, the true measure of the civility of any society is directly tied to the level of education of its women and the respect given to its women.

A man can never give birth to a child and is therefore never subjected to the suffering and sacrifices that a woman goes through. A woman can. She can transform not only her life, but, based on her knowledge and understanding about life, also the life of her child—a human in the making—and, thus, eventually society itself.

The Playboy Bunny was surprised to hear such a perspective regarding women from a man and, on top of that, one from India, where she believed women had always been undermined, mistreated, burned alive, sold for money, and, even in this modern day and age, aborted or killed at birth.

I emphasized that every society has its dark side. Although there is some truth to the perceptions she formed by reading news stories, granting the highest respect and dignity to women, especially to mothers, is foundational to Indian history and culture.

Women are central in Hindu mythology. The goddess of wisdom, creativity, and intelligence is Saraswati. The goddess of wealth, prosperity and worldly possessions is Lakshmi, and the goddess of power is Durga. But somehow, in India's male-dominated society, women's education has been grossly neglected, as education has always been a prerequisite for jobs, and men were assigned to be the sole breadwinners in the family. However, that reality is changing rapidly, and today's India is invested in educating its women. We are seeing many women entering the medical profession, teaching, and even entering the corporate and political worlds. It is also interesting to note that the free India gave equal voting rights to its women in 1947.

However, we have to remember that as long as we are focused on short-term gains or temporary glamour, society suffers, and if any woman allows herself to be used as a sex symbol, she is harming not only her gender as a whole, but society as a whole.

I concluded by saying, "The right place for an intelligent and beautiful woman like you is not a Playboy Club, but a university—a temple of learning—so that you are able to empower yourself to make a difference in this world in a way that only a woman can do."

The young lady was greatly touched and astonished, as she had not expected that we'd have this level of conversation in, of all places, the Playboy Club.

Over time, my turban was an icebreaker, a calling card, a means to an end that allowed me many such conversations, and it was a continuous reminder of my mission in life: to serve by adding the highest value at all times no matter where I was or the situation.

Aside from my turban acting like a lightning rod, I faced many hurdles and rejections. I don't know if some of them were because of my turban, but I never let that possibility get in the way of my thinking. I operated in the oneness paradigm and was able to convert many rejections into yeses. An example of this occurred in 1975.

POLY-CARB was taking off, and I had more orders consistently coming in, but I had limited credit with my suppliers. At that time, I had no money, no relatives from whom to borrow money, and no credit.

It was also not always possible to collect money from customers in a timely fashion when orders were filled. How was I to get the money I needed? What did a person in my shoes do?

My attorney suggested a banker, whom I called, and he came to see me at my offices. At the time, I was dressed in coveralls, mixing materials and working. I didn't even have a proper chair to offer the banker to sit in. What I had, though, was a tremendous amount of enthusiasm. I talked about my future and revolutionizing the construction industry by offering long-performing products.

He listened for over an hour. He must have reached his saturation point, because he interrupted me, saying, "I appreciate your enthusiasm, but I have twenty years of experience dealing with businesses and entrepreneurs like you. I have a suggestion: since you have these two master's degrees and almost a PhD, you should do yourself and your family a favor and find a research director's job at a big company. They'll be glad to hire you. Believe me, you are not cut out for business. You're not a businessman."

I smiled and said, "You're absolutely right. But that is where my passion is; that's what excites me and gets me up in the morning. I want to make a difference, make products that haven't been made, and elevate the standards of the industry."

He responded by saying that this was a great pipe dream that would never materialize. He got up, and as he was getting ready to leave, I told him, "I have a little advice for you, too. Business is not for you. My advice is for you to stay with the bank in the secure position you're in and never go into business, as you'll never make it."

He laughed and said I was probably right and repeated that I wasn't either. We parted on good terms.

Then I called the bank where I had my business accounts and asked what a person like me did—someone who had my kind of business and ambition, but didn't have money.

I was told I needed an angel investor—someone who believed in me. I said there had to be another way, and he suggested the Small

Business Administration (SBA). I called them, met with them, and they gave me a packet. I looked at it, and they suggested I contact some of the consultants listed in the packet.

I called all six of them and spent time with them. They looked at my position and business model, and every one of them told me my situation was completely hopeless and no one would give me a loan.

Undeterred, I knew there must be a way. The irony of such situations is that the SBA comes to your aid when you don't have collateral, and the bank is there for you when you do have money.

At that point, there was an unanswered question in my mind because of what the SBA had told me in my first meeting: you have to be turned down by three banks before the SBA will consider you for a loan. Something wasn't making sense to me. I called the SBA and asked to speak to a loan officer, and I set a date to meet with Mr. Cobrer. I asked Mr. Cobrer to give me a half hour of his time, and he ended up giving me over two hours.

He was kind enough and patient enough to sit with me and explain how the entire SBA system works. Obviously, people who come there don't have collateral and aren't bankable. What the SBA is looking for is a well-documented business plan that shows the capacity of the business to repay the loan in a timely manner. They have a direct loan and an SBA-guaranteed loan with the bank. The SBA guarantees 90 percent of the loan, which becomes the collateral for the bank. I learned where their mind-set was: not on collateral and finances, but on a person's proposal showing his or her capacity to pay back the SBA loan.

I returned home and put together a business plan in ten days based on the commitment of the ODOT and customers that clearly showed my ability to pay back the loan. Within two weeks, the SBA approved the loan, and they started using my proposal as a model to show other people seeking a loan.

I found a small bank in Newbury that liked my business plan and especially the SBA's backing to collateralize the loan. They approved a loan for $110,000. I was on my way.

When I'm immersed in the oneness paradigm, I become a conduit for creativity that results in my becoming a magnet for the resources of the universe.

This is what I needed to remember about myself: When I'm immersed in the oneness paradigm, I become a conduit for creativity that results in my becoming a magnet for the resources of the universe. But I needed to initiate that process. What I'd done with POLY-CARB was sidetrack myself by not adhering to this truth. Consequently, as a business, we were in our current position of being broke. I'd not been a true leader.

In order to lead myself, I had to remember who I was, something all religions and spiritual followings state: We are all integral aspects of the bigger One. Therefore, when I deal with people, I see the Divine within them and express the Divine within me. This unconditional respect for self and others is key in all interactions and with my relationships, whether they are personal or work related. Again, though, none of this matters unless I know who I truly am and consistently live and operate in that paradigm.

Something else my mother explained to me involved my quest for knowledge. She said that there are two core concepts that need to be understood. The first is about knowledge: to gain knowledge, you must read a lot and attain an education. After many years of attending schools, we are filled with knowledge, facts, data.

The critical thing we need to understand about knowledge is that it is merely a catalyst generating an ongoing quest for constant and continuous learning. It is essential for enhancing our capabilities to make our best better because knowledge merely gives rise to more questions than answers.

A Nobel laureate who was involved in space research unveiled a key element concerning space. During an interview for the *New York Times*, a reporter remarked, "We must be very close to finding the ultimate answer to how this universe works."

The Nobel laureate answered, "The amazing thing is that every time we unveil a new secret or mystery, it prompts a million more questions." So the quest for knowledge is unending.

The irony in this is that the more knowledge I accrued, the more I realized just how little I actually knew. Knowledge, by definition, is incomplete, as the acquisition of knowledge is unending, and new information, as well as new ignorance continues to be brought to light.

> Knowledge, by definition, is incomplete, as the acquisition of knowledge is unending, and new information, as well as new ignorance continues to be brought to light.

The second concept concerns wisdom, which I, like most people, believed was gained through life experiences. That is only partially correct. True wisdom lies within me, just as it does within everyone. Unveiling that wisdom is like giving birth in that it is usually a laborious and often painful process. It is through facing my life challenges and revealing the core truth within me that I gain wisdom. It is only through that wisdom that the clarity of life is available to me and can be comprehended.

My mother would summarize this line of thought in this manner: "Always remember that knowledge and know-how must always remain subservient to the innate divine wisdom planted right within you, leading you to the path of oneness. In the absence of that innate guiding knowledge, know-how and even real-life worldly experiences will always be guided, controlled and used by your ego, fear, greed, and insecurities, thus putting you in compromising and awkward, challenging situations."

I could feel that I was getting myself back on track, back in alignment with my spiritual roots. This re-alignment was true food for the soul—and I'd never realized until that moment that I'd been starving. I was returning to the true me, reconnecting by choosing to return to the core of my being—oneness. This understanding was the wind that filled the sails of my vessel—me. I'd put myself in the position of leading POLY-CARB, but without a rudder to steer by. That rudder was remembering the complete understanding of who I was. Now, with both of these in place, I could navigate the tumultuous waters of business and life.

> We have everything hidden within us, and our job is to unveil it and nurture it.

Knowing I was fully prepared to sail with confidence into my destiny, I remembered something: My mother had given me a wonderful metaphor many years ago that described what I was currently experiencing. She'd explained that a seed has all the wisdom within its tiny physical being to produce the most minute details of the mightiest tree. That wisdom is intrinsic, gifted to the seed by the bigger One. The seed didn't need to do anything but let that inherent wisdom emerge. I was exactly the same. I had everything hidden within me, and my job was to unveil it and nurture it.

I suddenly had a major aha moment. I was unveiling the inherent wisdom already hidden within me. What was coming through me was not taught in any school anywhere, especially business schools, and not found through life experiences.

My mind lit up as I truly grasped law number one, the Law of Purpose, that the sole purpose of my life is to add the highest value I can in all endeavors—to the bigger One—including for all of humanity, life, and the environment, unconditionally and continuously.

As we've seen many times throughout history and even today, the amount of damage to lives and destruction to property, cultures, and nations is the result of the "I, me, my, and mine" way of thinking. People in general tend to live in microcosms of individual efforts, taking care of their own little universes. This results in conflict when opposing universes collide. Such clashes happen every day in many ways and to varying degrees. Everyone is out for him- or herself. Therefore, what happens to other people is "over there," which translates to "not my problem" and "someone else will handle it."

This attitude was happening at POLY-CARB, and what I was seeing was causing friction among the staff. Our customers were not being addressed at the highest level, our products were not being upgraded, and people were entrenching in their various positions/roles. This meant we weren't growing, improving, or stretching ourselves to better ourselves—essentially, we weren't adding the highest value at all levels.

This realization answered my question as to why I was bringing in 90 percent of POLY-CARB's business in spite of having little business experience compared to those I had hired. Unconsciously, I was focusing on bringing the highest value to my customers by first understanding their business and then going out of my way to find the right solution, whether I sold my product to them or not in the end. This practice produced tremendous confidence within customers toward me and POLY-CARB, and as a consequence, they rewarded us with their business.

As the founder and CEO of POLY-CARB, it was my responsibility to make decisions that would sup-

> As everyone knows, two disparate energies cannot work in collaboration, as friction will occur.

port the company on all levels. But I could now see that with my regrounding in the oneness paradigm, I would be at odds with the rest of the company. As everyone knows, two disparate energies cannot work in collaboration, as friction will occur. After a while, enough friction will cause a combustible situation.

> We're not in the business of manufacturing, supplying, or servicing—we're in the business of adding the highest value.

Therefore, I needed to do something that would help everyone realize we needed to work as a whole to sail the ship of POLY-CARB. "Aha," I said aloud to myself. It dawned on me that as one, the company and I actually had the same purpose in life: We're not in the business of manufacturing, supplying, or servicing—we're in the business of adding the highest value.

What a revelation!

But introducing this idea to the company and having people take to it was going to be quite an undertaking. There would most likely be a lot of resistance. The employees all had their job description and territory they called their own. No one wanted others treading on that territory and authority, and they weren't interested in collaborating with other areas of the company or even learning new things that would expand their capabilities on behalf of the company.

I imagined that staff members were going to respond in fear, afraid of losing whatever they'd accrued in the company by way of position, influence, rewards, and/or paycheck. Combined with their lack of desire to learn more except incrementally, I knew that trying to get everyone to work together under a new paradigm would be about as successful as trying to herd cats.

> Breakthroughs occur only when people are not in their comfort zones and are open to learning.

I needed a new mind-set from everyone, one in which people weren't afraid to take risks and let go of their comfort zones. Breakthroughs occur only when people are not in their comfort zones and are open to learning. I'd come to understand that in life, everything remains in a constant state of motion and change.

I interpreted that to mean that I had to remain in a student mode of learning, which would always position me to continuously make my best better.

My head was spinning, though not from overwhelm. I was in the zone, filled with and thrilled by the strength of having regained my roots. Everything I'd been thinking over this intense weekend of looming bankruptcy was clearing away the cobwebs of illusion and delusions. Then it hit me, like a ton of bricks: part of the problem with the company was that I had structured POLY-CARB just like any other business with a hierarchy of managers, supervisors, vice presidents, and myself as CEO. This immediately put people in the very silos in which I now didn't want them.

> Immersed in oneness, I needed to remember that in this paradigm, there are no bosses or subordinates, only specialized, value-adding entities.

The last piece to this puzzle concerned the nature of the company itself. Immersed in oneness, I needed to remember that in this paradigm, there are no bosses or subordinates, only specialized, value-adding entities.

This was the final component to the entire equation. Now I needed to implement my findings in the company.

Oneness is the seed that has the entire knowledge of how to build a tree, and just as a tree grows and unfolds, this intense thought process was coming through me. Importantly, what I was unveiling within myself was just like the unchangeable laws of the universe, such as gravity and light—universal, unchanging, immutable.

What I had created in my mind I put down on paper. This line of thinking would lead to true and lasting success for any area of life, including business, not just POLY-CARB. This was going to introduce a major shift for POLY-CARB, a completely different business approach. We could no longer be in the business of just making money by filling a market niche. Anyone could do that.

I thought of other businesses, the ones that talk about how they're one big family. That kind of environment is pleasant, but what's the main agenda? What is the company's and the employee's bottom line? Keeping one's job? Getting a promotion? Making it to the top of the leader board in sales? Creating the winning logo? Being named Employee of the Year? Satisfying the stakeholders? Saving enough for retirement?

> POLY-CARB needed to be re-directed, re-aligned, re-vamped, and re-purposed!

For years, I'd followed the advice of those who were savvy in business. They'd told me what they thought was best, based on all their years in business, but my company and I were now in significant trouble. The old business paradigm wasn't working and needed replacing. POLY-CARB needed to be re-directed, re-aligned, re-vamped, and re-purposed!

If POLY-CARB were to be focused on the oneness paradigm, then we needed to approach what we did from a wholistic perspective—100 percent. To do otherwise would be unethical, as we'd be selling mediocrity by virtue of resting on our laurels and being too comfortable. That would eventually allow for someone else to come along and produce something of greater value, and we'd decline.

But the change wasn't simply about keeping ahead of the competition either. The *why* of our existence needed to be about the *big* picture, not just maintaining market share and a competitive edge.

This line of thinking required that I map out the entire company from top to bottom. If our fundamental purpose was oneness, we needed to re-purpose ourselves, which would refocus us. That was when I realized once again that I'd patterned POLY-CARB following the purpose, values, philosophies, and structure generally accepted by business. The truth was, I'd actually launched POLY-CARB without a mission statement, and the primary purpose was to sell the polymer products we'd designed. That wasn't good enough anymore.

Knowing that I had to lead myself first before I could lead anyone else, I understood that I couldn't be the only person in the company approaching everything through the lens of the oneness paradigm. I would be constantly fighting an uphill battle, as the rest of the team would be comfortably ensconced in the old paradigm of business. Everyone had to be on board. Was that possible?

> The concept that we are all one is found in every religious and spiritual text, as well as the writings of every culture.

What I was going to propose to the entire staff was an entirely new way of thinking—a mind-set mostly unfamiliar to everyone there. I was going to share with them ideas that were not part of their upbringing or culture. Most would see the ideas as so-called Eastern thinking. In reality, these are universal laws not owned by or the product of any one religion, spiritual following, or culture. The concept that we are all one is actually found in every religious and spiritual text, as well as the writings of every culture. The reason it's foreign to business is that business, a long time ago, made the decision to leave the heart or soul out of its machinations. Business became cold, unfeeling, heartless, and often inhumane.

With this in mind, I reviewed my staff and their behaviors, job descriptions, agendas, and performances. When it came to garnering clients for the company, I was responsible for 90 percent of the results. Why was the marketing department only bringing in 10 percent? Was something similar happening in other departments, with only a small percentage of the staff producing the majority of the work?

Next, I realized that everyone was dependent on me to continually be the head cheerleader. Yes, I was the CEO, but now I saw that no one was aspiring to that position or even striving to be a leader. Oh, there were managers and supervisors and even seven vice presidents, but the work all still rested on me. I was deemed the company fountainhead.

Revelation: Part of the reason POLY-CARB was in its current straits was because the company was based on an inverted pyramid, with its future resting solely on my shoulders. I had a company of highly skilled and educated people, and no one was taking the lead, striving for constant innovation, or pushing the envelope of his or her creativity. They were all doing what they'd been schooled to do, what they'd learned in their years of business experience. We wouldn't be able to survive.

I now knew what had to happen in order to turn POLY-CARB around: I had to fire everyone.

Chapter 10

A Tabula Rasa

Tabula Rasa, a "blank slate." That's what I needed to create. I had come to the conclusion that though the employees I had worked with for years were highly competent, they were stuck in their past experiences, trapped in silos, unable to see past their own benefit and unable to work as a team, which I now knew was essential for our future success.

I knew that requiring them to fully exercise their creative beings just wasn't going to happen. They'd become rigid, calcified. This reality was no fault of theirs; they just didn't know any better. Wonderful people in their own right, they could remain in their current paradigm and easily make a decent living in other companies. However, if they stayed with POLY-CARB, where I wanted to change their paradigm by asking them to practice oneness, not only would it be a painful change for them, they would always be operating in conflicting paradigms, which would make them utterly unhappy. Firing my staff was a tough decision, but it had to be made.

I had to start with a fresh group of people. This would require that they walk uncharted territory, as they wouldn't understand business or have any experience in marketing. Ironically, I also had no experience in marketing, but there I was, generating 90 percent of the sales. What was the secret? Was I such a great salesman? No, I was just a scientist providing facts to people. Looking back, I realized that three important communication factors—my words, voice tone, and body language—were in complete alignment. I had no inner conflicts in telling people the truth. That was why my customers believed me, and I didn't use jazzy presentations and glitzy marketing.

My marketing team was always grumbling that we didn't have the right marketing and presentation materials and that we had no prior history or long list of product successes with which to convince potential customers. Because of my honesty and congruency of message, I didn't need all those crutches.

> Importantly, feeling myself in the flow of oneness, I knew that this day, this seminal moment in the company's history, required initiating all action based on the fundamental value of honesty.

In the two days since finding out the company was broke, my entire perspective had changed, and I'd refocused the lens of my life. Everything was now in sharp focus.

That Monday morning, I drove to the POLY-CARB offices, my mind clear and at peace. I knew exactly what I had to do: reposition the company. This time, though, it would be totally driven by principles and values. Importantly, feeling myself in the flow of oneness, I knew that this day, this seminal moment in the company's history, required initiating all action based on the fundamental value of honesty.

Therefore, I called my attorney and accountant. They were waiting for me at the offices, though I'd not told them yet of my decision concerning the company. They asked if they could proceed with filing for Chapter 11. They reiterated that I didn't really have a choice.

In response, I suggested we call a meeting of the entire company and share the information about the company being broke. My attorney looked at me, aghast. "You've got to be kidding. Everyone will walk out on you. Who would work for a company that's broke?" I responded that we needed to be honest with everyone no matter what.

So, the entire team was asked to assemble, and I asked the attorney and accountant to please explain the situation to everyone—the entire truth. Unbeknownst to my accountant and attorney, I was fully prepared for everyone quitting. My attorney stood up and awkwardly announced, "The company, for all practical purposes, is broke; there's no money left."

Time suddenly slowed to a crawl as the numbing announcement sank in. The employees sat in complete shock, slack-jawed, barely blinking, their brains struggling to grasp what they'd just heard. The silence lasted for several seconds, then a cacophony of questions filled the air: "What about our raises? Will we get one more check? What about unemployment?" Anger, hurt, and confusion took over, but I remained calm. A glow radiated from me. My serene countenance was unsettling for many, as they expected some kind of dramatic, emotional upset happening within me.

I explained, "I was not made aware of this situation until this past Friday. I didn't want to keep you in the dark, and that's why I brought everyone together. It is entirely up to you to take appropriate actions that are most conducive to your needs. If you walk out, I will completely understand. I will be pleased to help you out in terms of recommendations and reference letters."

It took several minutes to calm the group down, and I stated that they'd heard the truth. I explained that our current financial situation wasn't about raises, but dollars, and there weren't any. Truly, I couldn't pay them. The response I received was that I couldn't possibly expect them to work for nothing. I reiterated that I understood if they wanted to leave. Immediately, 80 percent of the staff got up and left.

Those who stayed wanted to make sure that I couldn't pay their salaries as they mulled over whether they should also leave. I finally had to tell them that I really had no way to pay them and ended up convincing them to leave, clearing out the company completely. The only person who stayed was my closest friend, Dr. Pant. He said, "If you need to further cut back expenses, I can always come and stay with you at your home and help you out of this situation. All I need is a place to stay and food."

> Dolly, Dr. Pant, and I began the process of re-populating POLY-CARB, which now had the appearance of a ghost town.

At that time, I wanted to make sure that Dr. Pant was on the same page as I was, and I shared the intrinsic values-driven strategy for moving the company forward. He absolutely loved it and said that I was finally on the right path and that he was 100 percent with me. So Dolly, Dr. Pant, and I began the process of re-populating POLY-CARB, which now had the appearance of a ghost town.

Dr. Pant and I then began visiting local universities, such as The University of Akron, Case Western Reserve University and Cleveland State, and interviewing students. Dr. Pant was a man of few words, so I described to the students the clear foundational parameters concerning the positions we were hiring for and how we'd operate.

Dr. Pant evaluated them from the technical side, and I evaluated them according to whether they would be able to work within the oneness paradigm. In the final selection of candidates, they met with Dolly, who evaluated them according to her intuitive sense as to whether they were a good fit with us emotionally and ethically.

In the initial interviews, I explained, "POLY-CARB cannot give you a job description. Everything that needs to be done, whether it's cleaning the place, working in production, or making deliveries needs to be handled by any one of us. Secondly, understand that there will be no bosses or subordinates. No title will be assigned to anyone, including me. You will be responsible for the tasks you undertake. Each department will be run by an assigned team rather than a single boss.

"Furthermore, although you may have a master's degree, PhD or MBA, if I find your degrees hanging in your office, it will be immediate cause for termination. We feel that degrees define and limit your potential, when, in fact, your potential is unlimited and can only be realized by staying in student mode. I suggest you frame your degrees and send them to your parents, as they will be very proud of your accomplishments and display your diplomas and degrees with great reverence. But there will be no room for you to display those degrees at POLY-CARB. For the company's purposes, you will be students forever.

"At POLY-CARB, you'll be forever learning and thus enhancing your capacity to serve your team members, customers, and society. Once you join the company, you will simply be a forever-improving team member learning to lead others by leading yourself, which will position and empower you with a true CEO mind-set. Everyone will share responsibility for every aspect of the company's innovation, growth, and sustainability."

During the interviews, we were shocked when 70 percent of the American-born interviewees walked out on the interview after we explained POLY-CARB's working parameters. But conversely, 80 percent of the foreign-born interviewees were fully interested, as they found this new paradigm exciting. We were totally surprised and confused by the response we were getting.

America had been built on ingenuity and a drive to create without restrictions. We were offering just such a scenario, and the American-born students were walking away. Incredible! It almost raised a fear in my gut that if America's future generation could only see themselves working for their self-interests and operating in silos, the day wasn't too far away when this great nation would lose its leadership standing in the world.

Another thing I wanted the prospective POLY-CARB team members to understand is that they would not be considered experts based on their education and could be placed in any department to learn and understand the overall workings of the company. For the next two years from the day of their hiring, they would work in every department, from accounting to marketing to R&D to manufacturing. Only after they'd had intense exposure to each of the disciplines would they be given a choice to determine where they'd like to spend the majority of their time. Even after that, 30 percent of their time would be spent in all of the other disciplines or departments. Only 70 percent of their time would be focused on their department of choice.

Some of the students we interviewed looked at us as if we were crazy. Some absolutely loved the idea. Eventually, we lined up fifteen prospective team members ready to be trained as CEOs working in collaboration. But before we could give them employment letters, we needed to first get our financial house in order.

I was still faced with the reality of bankruptcy. The fact that POLY-CARB was broke was still staring me in the face. Where was I going to find money to make a fresh start? Something my mother used to say, which hadn't made any sense to me at the time, started flashing through my mind: "Your state of perpetual gratefulness to the bigger One facilitates your link with the unlimited wisdom, power, and resources of the universe." Those words produced an aha moment for me!

Once I was in the mode of thinking in the oneness paradigm, I saw no difference between a supplier and myself. We were all one.

Therefore, I had no hesitation in going to meet with Ciba-Geigy, one of my key suppliers. I had orders in the pipeline from contractors pertaining to their contracts with the DOTs from various states, and all I needed was raw materials. From there, all I had to do was manufacture product.

Many of these contractors were willing to pay once I delivered, but I had no funds to buy the raw materials, and I already owed close to a million dollars to my suppliers, including $700,000 to our key supplier Ciba-Geigy, all of which was now more than ninety days overdue. The more I thought about it, the more I realized that I had to have a one-on-one meeting at the highest level with the senior vice president of credit at Ciba-Geigy, which supplied me with epoxies and hardeners.

So, I called Ciba-Geigy and talked to the manager of credit, Frank Marino (who later became senior vice president of credit), saying I wanted to schedule a meeting with their senior vice president of credit, Mr. Duby. Frank asked why I didn't just pay the money that was overdue. He then said that they needed payment before I talked to anyone. I said I wouldn't pay anything to anyone until I spoke with Mr. Duby. Until such time, no money would be forthcoming.

Frank then arranged a meeting with Mr. Duby in New York. When I flew to New York to meet with Mr. Duby, he said, "You owe us all this money, and we're ready to turn this over to our attorneys for collection. There's no other option or grace period I can offer."

I sat there calmly and said, "I'm coming from a meeting with my accountant and attorney. They are ready to file for Chapter 11. As you know, they will ask you to settle for pennies on the dollar. Although this is a common practice in business, it is simply not acceptable to me. Your company was kind enough to trust me and extend credit, selling me the material. I want to pay not only what is due to you, but also interest on the late payment."

Mr. Duby responded that he was glad I was willing to pay and asked why I didn't just write a check—what was the problem?

I answered that I would and that he was going to help me do that. I asked him to please give me the next five minutes, undisturbed, to explain my plan to him. I showed him the purchase orders I had from bona fide state-approved contracts backed by each state.

Mr. Duby interrupted me. "You've always had orders. How is that going to make you profitable? You said you're already broke. How is that going to help me?"

I showed him our financial cash-flow statement from when I'd had fifty-seven employees and the difference with just fifteen staff members. The cash flow also clearly outlined payments to Ciba-Geigy with interest. I pointed out that in the next four months, we'd be brought up to date with payments.

Mr. Duby shook his head. "Wait a minute. What you're asking me to do is insane. You want us to release another half a million dollars' worth of materials on credit when you already owe us close to seven hundred thousand dollars? I can't do that."

I responded, "You're willing to settle for pennies on the dollar under Chapter 11, but you're not willing to have one hundred percent repayment—plus interest—and not only keep a business alive, but also help an honest man keep his dignity?"

There was silence from Mr. Duby as he studied me. Then he said, "Either you are the biggest con artist I've ever seen or you're truly an honest man with the most honorable intentions."

I replied that it took an honest man to recognize another honest man. "You tell me what I am."

By the time I walked out of Mr. Duby's office, he'd told Frank to release an additional half a million dollars in credit. Back at POLY-CARB, I was able to keep my promise; I not only brought POLY-CARB current with Ciba-Geigy in less than three months, but also paid interest on the delinquent credit, as promised.

I became good friends with Frank, who often used POLY-CARB as an example to Ciba-Geigy's many customers. On top of that, everyone at Ciba-Geigy now knew about POLY-CARB and our level of honesty and integrity.

The Ciba-Geigy account was the first component of POLY-CARB's financial equation. The second component still needed addressing. In my formulations, we needed ingredients. Seventy percent were supplied by Ciba-Geigy, but the other 30 percent needed to come from other suppliers. They didn't have such a large stake in POLY-CARB, and they wouldn't provide us any materials until we paid our bills. So, I still had a cash crunch and needed to create a cash flow in order to move forward.

Then, out of the blue, I received a phone call from the Century Fence Company, one of the largest pavement-marking contractors in Wisconsin and one of the largest customers that purchased pavement-marking materials from us at the time. They had just won a bid on a large project that required close to $600,000 worth of materials, and POLY-CARB was specifically named as the company from whom the materials were to be ordered.

We had a strong professional relationship with Century Fence, and they had incredible faith in POLY-CARB's products, quality, and product control. They were also the first company to begin using our breakthrough product, Mark-55, and develop specific equipment to handle our two-part system. The equipment was the first of its kind in the entire industry.

I saw a possibility for creating a win-win situation with Century Fence and set up a meeting with the owner and president, Tony Bryant. Tony was a mentor for me, as he had several successful businesses. He would often give me valuable advice concerning business dealings, which helped me significantly.

I presented all the facts to Tony and mentioned my recent negotiations with Ciba-Geigy and our current situation that required hard cash to purchase additional raw materials that constituted 25 to 35 percent of our formulations. I made him an offer whereby I would save him $55,000 on their current order with us if he would give me an advance of a quarter of a million dollars, allowing me to move forward. We would both win.

Thankfully, Tony agreed to give us the money, but he wanted to make sure that with the new funds, our top priority would be the completion of his order first. I agreed and said that as soon as we had the funds and could purchase the needed materials, we'd work on his job, and once the product was manufactured, we'd store it until they were ready to use it, but they could come and inspect the product first.

Tony showed tremendous faith in me and POLY-CARB. I returned home with the quarter million in cash. Within two weeks, we were able to complete his order. I invited Century Fence to come and not only inspect the finished goods, but also meet the new POLY-CARB team. They were very impressed with the new face of POLY-CARB and its team members. At that point, Tony paid the balance of the order, less $250,000 and the $55,000 we had saved him.

Looking back on this, I had leveraged my technological advantage and impeccable reputation for quality and, with the trust of my customers, was able to refinance POLY-CARB, which otherwise was completely insolvent at the time of that transaction. To this day, I remain highly indebted to Century Fence for the trust and support they showed me throughout my business career.

I'd like to mention how I was introduced to Century Fence, a rather interesting story.

In the fall of 1979, I received a call from Don Lucas, who was the national sales manager of Century Fence Co. and who eventually retired as company president. He said, "You don't know me, but your name has been given to me because I understand you're a brilliant scientist and that you can custom design any product. I have a need for a long-lasting pavement-marking material, and we think a two-part epoxy may be the answer. We'd like you to develop a product that can set up fairly quickly, and we can develop the equipment that can mix the two parts right at the nozzle. Our equipment will saturate the applied epoxy immediately with round glass beads that will impart the retroreflectivity to these striped lines. That will allow the driving public to see the lines more effectively at night."

That call came in September with only a three-week window to test-run the product during the winter to see how it lasted. After getting all the details from Don for the product, I went to work with Dr. Pant for almost three days nonstop. We came up with the formulation and delivered the twenty-five gallons Century Fence had ordered, which we called Mark-55. I flew to Wisconsin with Dr. Pant to oversee the installation. From start to finish, the project was a success, and thus began a long-standing relationship with Century Fence.

We partnered with Century Fence over several years, testing the Mark-55 product in various states. The performance was so uniquely outstanding in terms of its reflective quality and ability to stay intact on the pavement that every test installation resulted in a major project where we were specified by name. Since Century Fence was the only company that had the equipment designed for the Mark-55, they ended up with the projects.

As more and more projects nationwide specifying two-part epoxy marking appeared, Mark-55 drew the attention of giants like RPM, Sherwin-Williams, 3M, and others. Eventually, they also entered the market with their own epoxy formulations. As the market grew, it gave birth to highly-specialized equipment manufacturers that could handle two-part epoxies for pavement-marking installations. Somehow, the focus of most of the new formulations produced by the other companies remained on a quick-setting product rather than on long-term performance. POLY-CARB's Mark-55 stood alone in delivering two to four times longer performance than any other product on the market.

Not only was POLY-CARB's product uniquely designed to last longer, but the flawless application made by the Century Fence team was completely unmatched in the industry. We were a winning team, and we held yearly brainstorming sessions with Century Fence either at our offices or theirs.

In one such meeting, when senior members from Century Fence were visiting POLY-CARB, Tony Bryant noticed the Ping-Pong table next to our conference room. He asked if we had any good players, which we did. He then challenged some of our managers. After several games, I suggested that we take the game up a notch and make a bet: If our team won, then Century Fence would have to pay an extra dollar per gallon for the order we had in hand with them. If POLY-CARB lost, then we'd reduce the price per gallon by one dollar.

Tony, who was very competitive and in good condition, as he regularly played sports, thought he had this one in the bag. Looking over our team, he selected on one of our engineers, Ashok Ganapathy. Ashok was meek, quiet, and polite—not a seemingly dangerous opponent. Tony lost—big time.

Laughing, I said to Tony that this was just a game, not to be taken seriously, and that I had been kidding about the bet. But Tony insisted on honoring the bet, saying that we were a relatively new company and could use the cash. So, POLY-CARB ended up making a nice little profit from our bet to the tune of about $60,000.

Looking back, it still amazes me how I was able to save POLY-CARB from a quick demise. Obviously, it wasn't my cleverness or luck. It was uncompromising faith in my honesty and value system, which Ciba-Geigy and Century Fence were able to relate to, leading them to come forward with unprecedented financial support. Of course, it could have been that winning Ping-Pong game, too.

Now that POLY-CARB had the raw materials we needed for manufacturing, as well as operating cash, Dr. Pant and I began working again but with a new team of fifteen people. We never looked back. We became profitable from day one, as we'd lowered our overhead tremendously and instilled an incredible work ethic and enthusiasm in our new team.

Dolly loved and supported the entire changeover. Many of the students didn't even know how to dress appropriately for work. Dolly would take them shopping and buy them clothes. We wanted our team always to be well dressed, not as a way of

> It was Dolly who'd brought me to understand the difference between elegance and being well dressed as opposed to just being expensively attired.

showing off, but as a sign of respect to the customers we served. It was Dolly who'd brought me to understand the difference between elegance and being well dressed as opposed to just being expensively attired.

After getting married, one of my obsessions was being meticulously well dressed and neat. At the Birla Institute of Technology and Science, we wore mandatory uniforms, and they gave an annual award for the best-dressed student on campus. I'd received the award for three years in a row. In my mind, that recognition somehow made me an expert in being well dressed—until the following incident occurred.

Dolly and I were invited to the high-profile society wedding of one of her family's friends in Bombay. I told Dolly that she would have to wear her best. She showed me the range of her wardrobe, and I rejected all of it as not being good enough. She got irritated with me and my comments. Then, in her innate womanly wisdom, she taught me a lesson. She said, "If you don't like any of these, I'm going to wear a very plain cotton sari with a border, the type normally worn by the house staff. They cost less than five dollars." I objected, but Dolly was steadfast.

When it was time to leave for the wedding, Dolly wouldn't budge from wearing the plain sari. I didn't want to create a scene, so went along with her decision. She had starched the sari, and wore it without the usual heavy amount of jewelry worn by Indian women. The only jewelry she wore was a pearl necklace.

We were driven to the wedding, and once there, I was amazed to see so many glittering jewels being worn. As the evening passed, I was introduced to the who's who of society. I found myself complementing everyone as to how wonderful he or she looked. Then I turned around and saw Dolly nearby, talking with some friends. I was awestruck. I had never seen such an image of purity, elegance, and beauty as Dolly in that plain white sari. I suddenly realized what true beauty, elegance, and dressing well were.

I made a promise to myself that for the rest of my life, I would never criticize Dolly for anything she did. She was my goddess and strength. It was only at that point that I understood the innate wisdom of Indian culture, which assigned a woman to be the goddess of wisdom, music, and the arts (Saraswati); the goddess of wealth (Lakshmi); and the goddess of power (Durga). I had all three goddesses combined in Dolly.

Dolly was full of compassionate care and an amazing tower of strength not just for me but also for the entire team at POLY-CARB. Often, we would work late into the evenings and on weekends, and Dolly would make sure everyone was properly fed and his or her family emotionally supported.

This was how POLY-CARB operated. It took time for employees to acclimate to the mind-set of being values and principles driven, but they eventually grasped the deeper value to them on a personal level, and we accomplished many things on a regular basis that most people would find astonishing.

Chapter 11

Making Our Best Better

Continuously learning and making our best better not only for us, but for the entire industry, meant we needed to operate in the oneness paradigm at all times. Ultimately, it was not about our being better than others in the industry, but about elevating the standards of the entire industry as a whole, of which we were an integral part.

One area in which we found we could be influential in the industry was the Department of Transportation, which was using public funds to build and maintain highways. Their mandate was to have specifications for every product they purchased from vendors. Working with the DOT, we were able to raise the standards of those specifications.

Their process was that they merely accepted a paper certification from manufacturers, stating that they'd complied with the DOT's certification requirements. We thought we could upgrade the standards of the industry by asking the DOT to require that every batch of chemicals manufactured be certified by independent laboratory tests proving compliance to all the properties in the specification.

I presented this idea to our team, and initially, they said we'd be making our own lives difficult. Plus, many independent laboratories didn't have the kind of equipment required to do that level of testing. Even we would have to upgrade our own equipment to verify the tests. So, I challenged our team, explaining to them that based on our value of continuously making our best better, we were not on the path of offering the highest value if we didn't comply with this idea ourselves.

Therefore, we ordered some of the most sophisticated equipment required to upgrade our own small laboratory. But then we discovered we didn't have enough space in our lab for all the new equipment, so we needed to expand.

One Friday in late fall of 1982, we decided that over the weekend, we would build an extension to our lab, effectively tripling the size of the lab.

While constructing the new lab, there was an amazing sense of camaraderie, teamwork, fun and accomplishment, although we worked into the wee hours of the morning. One of the team members on that project was Sanjiv Sidhu, who founded and became CEO of i2 Technologies and is now a billionaire. At the time of the lab construction project, Sanjiv had never lifted a hammer before in his life.

Once we completed the lab, we had positioned the company, as well as the industry, to institute a process whereby every batch was tested and verified in the presence of an engineer from an independent laboratory, who would then issue a certification to the state, verifying that every batch met the requirements of the specifications. The state loved this new process. They found that many times, the original product that had historically inspired them to write the original specification, when opened to the industry, degraded over time even though the Department of Transportation received certifications stating the product met the requirements of the spec. Before the process we'd introduced, they had had no means by which to verify that the certification was true.

With just this one step, we narrowed the list of approved vendors to the DOT to only a handful, as most of the vendors providing paper certification could not supply an independent certification for every manufactured batch. This also gave POLY-CARB the incentive to continuously improve our own products and add an additional means of verification of our products' enhanced performance.

> Following the oneness paradigm, we proved that the best way to compete is to compete against our own best rather than against others.

Following the oneness paradigm, we proved that the best way to compete is to compete against our own best rather than against others. From that day on, in many areas, we almost became the exclusive vendor, as there was a lag in the industry to meet the DOT's requirements.

The upshot of all of this was that it became evident to us that educating the industry, including its suppliers and ourselves, was an essential part of elevating the industry. We talked to the Ohio DOT about providing educational seminars, and we wanted to gather engineers from all twelve Ohio districts to host an all-day training seminar. Then, one day, we received a call from the ODOT, telling us they wanted to take us up on the seminar idea and wanted to schedule the training right away, as they had a small window in their calendar. But to do this, POLY-CARB needed a space where we could conduct educational seminars and classes.

Although we could have conducted the seminar at a hotel, we wanted to conduct a lab tour, thereby demonstrating how we effect and execute quality not only in our manufacturing processes, but in how we did the testing with all the batches we manufactured and with our incoming raw materials.

We had over five thousand square feet of unfinished space in the basement of our office, which was also the ground floor from the back of the building. When I suggested to the team that we create a seminar and presentation room, the task appeared to be too daunting for everyone. They said it was impossible to do, as we only had two days to complete construction. I reminded them that our fundamental initiative was that we never said no. We had to do it. We couldn't say *can't*.

Somehow, I was not able to convince everyone that it could be done. So, I personally undertook the entire project, and they assisted me. We spray applied our product to the walls and shaped it to look like bricks. We created an entire showroom to display our products that could also host 150 people. We installed a large projection screen in the front of the room for presentations. It became an all-in-one media/trade/presentation room.

We worked the entire weekend and into Sunday evening, but I let everyone go home by eight o'clock that night. I continued working and completed the finishing touches on the space and displays, wrapping up at five o'clock that Monday morning—the seminar was to begin at eight. I went home to shower and change. Dolly, meanwhile, had spent the entire weekend preparing food for the officials attending the seminar.

Our new all-in-one media/trade/presentation room

The POLY-CARB team, who had left me to finish up, was amazed at what I'd accomplished and how great the place looked. The remark-able fact that the entire project was accomplished that weekend set a new precedent for the entire team at POLY-CARB: we would never accept *no* or mediocrity. That room became our showroom and elevated the pride of each team member at POLY-CARB.

Very importantly, during the project, I had remembered that leadership was all about leading myself first—I had to truly lead myself before leading the team. If I'd accepted their no, I'd have deprived our team of the amazing mind-set that said, "We can do anything."

Another time, our orders had increased, our plant was working full shift, and there was less attention being paid to keeping the facility clean and organized. On a Thursday afternoon, when I walked into the plant after returning from a trip out of town, I couldn't believe what I was seeing. The place was totally unacceptable by POLY-CARB standards.

I called the entire team together and requested they follow me to inspect the plant. I asked them if the condition of our manufacturing facility was acceptable to them. They all looked at me and said we needed to bring it back to POLY-CARB standards. I agreed with them and said, "We are going to clean our plant, and all production is on hold until it is completely clean and neat. We have two days to complete this task."

I appointed TJ Singh, one of our can-do and quick-thinking team members, as team leader for this project and told him he was in charge. He would need to direct each team member as to what he or she needed to do. I further explained that I was going to be one of his team members and that he could assign me to any task.

TJ enthusiastically took on the challenge. He went to the local Kmart and bought all the necessary tools and coveralls for the team. We all got to work.

TJ scheduled coffee breaks for team members. Somehow, he never told me to take a coffee break. I continued working. After the third coffee break, one of our team members brought this oversight to TJ's attention, letting him know I had been working nonstop. TJ asked me why I'd not taken a break. I replied that I couldn't until he told me to, as he was in charge. He apologized, but I told him there was no need to apologize and asked him to instead think of the situation this way: more work had been done, and we were ahead of schedule.

By the time Monday morning arrived, we had not only cleaned the plant, but also painted the entire place. We probably had the cleanest facility in the entire industry.

This mind-set or attitude is one not prevalent in the business world. Instead, a mode of survival, defensiveness and dominance has taken over, along with a sense of entitlement. POLY-CARB has been an anomaly in that we never subscribed to that type of thinking. We had far more than just a can-do attitude, as the values and principles we instituted throughout the company were taken to heart and integrated into our very beings.

In the absence of oneness, when we try to practice values, we write them down, post them, and form societies and groups around them, yet we only follow them when we're being watched by others. We merely act them, but don't integrate them. That's why when no one is watching us, we don't practice them and we violate their intent. We've seen this time and time again. Our most decorated, revered and respected citizens fall victim to a lack of integrity, as they are not practicing the oneness thought process.

Looking through the lens of oneness, the purpose of our lives becomes clear. Otherwise, all our purposes are driven by our insecurities, egos, greed, selfishness, and fears and end up dividing society. It is through the total immersion in oneness that we understand the Law of Purpose: *"Our sole purpose in life is to add the highest value we can in all our endeavors."* We do this unconditionally and continuously—to the bigger One—including for all of humanity, life, and the environment.

This is the fundamental basis of our success in anything, including business, relationships, politics, government, sports, education, and the arts. In the absence of oneness, all our intelligence, education, experience, and hard work might produce occasional successes, but those successes cannot be sustained in the long run.

The amazing outcome is that oneness forces us to never settle for mediocrity; we must continuously make our best better. We ourselves become our own true competition. We're no longer competing with the rest of the world, which merely provides data and information for us to elevate our standards.

In the absence of this thought process, all we can practice is mediocrity, which, in the indisputable oneness paradigm, is an unethical practice that has continuously inhibited and imprisoned the human race.

This relates to business in that POLY-CARB never created a product and then did not seek to improve it. Otherwise, we would have become stagnant, and our competition would have overtaken us. To rest on our laurels is inherently unethical, as what we are essentially doing is practicing mediocrity. Life is forever changing; nothing remains the same. If we don't change, our brains calcify, so to speak. It's that old adage: "Use it or lose it." That applies in business, in one's personal life, and in all our relationships.

Most businesses conduct themselves by stating that the customer comes first, yet the agenda behind that statement is making as much money as pos-

> Everyone was number one in our book. Our strategy was not based on money, competition, and market share. Rather, it was all about continuously enhancing the quality of life from top to bottom.

sible with as little overhead and outlay as possible. At POLY-CARB, looking through the window of the oneness paradigm, we sought to consistently and constantly add the highest quality in all our interactions, whether with our team members, customers, contractors, suppliers, or society and environment—everyone was number one in our book. Our strategy was not based on money, competition, and market share. Rather, it was all about continuously enhancing the quality of life from top to bottom.

As a consequence of this thinking, we transformed our business model from one of selling for profit to one of "pay for performance," meaning that we would be paid after our product had delivered performance-wise in the field and not just by installing the product and meeting specifications based on lab testing. We realized that there's a vast difference between the results found in the controlled environment of a lab and the performance obtained via the unpredictable, uncontrollable elements out in the field.

In the final analysis, the DOT was looking for actual performance in the field and *hoping* that the lab results would assure acceptable field performance. They even tried asking for performance guarantees from the manufacturers, which didn't pan out, as the manufacturers argued that they had no control over the installation, which was done by separate contractors. There was always a blame game going on between the DOT who had written the spec, the manufacturers, and the contractor who actually did the product installation. When the product failed, everyone blamed the other guy. Conversely, we were taking entire responsibility for the performance of the product, and if our product failed, we didn't get paid. We, in fact, leased the product on a yearly performance and got paid after the performance was delivered each year.

The situation was this: our products were constantly outperforming our competitors in their specific categories. And yet, when we went nationwide, many DOTs, with their lack of differentiation between highly-sophisticated polymer formulations, grouped them all in the same category. Many times, they would consider low-grade, mediocre products as equal to ours. When contractors bid on a contract, their only criteria for selection was often just the price. They weren't interested in whether the product would outlive by three to four times the lower-cost products. They weren't being paid for higher performance; they were being paid for job completion.

This reality subsequently led us to an important understanding of just who we were and how we comported ourselves in the marketplace. We remembered *our sole purpose in life was to add the highest value at all times.* We were not in the business of manufacturing, supplying, or servicing; we were in the business of adding the highest value—period.

One day, I received a call from one of our marketing reps who'd just returned from a major trip. He appeared to be upset and wanted to meet with me and the marketing team for a brainstorming session. He explained that we'd lost four road-striping-material contracts in a row because our competitors were selling similar products at a much lower price than we were.

One of our team members said that the other products didn't perform anywhere close to ours. The sales rep responded by saying that it didn't matter, as the DOT was equating our product as equal to others. Since we couldn't bid directly to the DOT, we were only an approved product supplier; contractors bid the projects and bought products from vendors who offered the lowest price.

The rep's solution was that we needed to lower our prices and become more competitive. The team discussed the issue. I asked, "What bothers us most? Is it that we lost the business or that by allowing an inferior product to be placed on the road for striping with one-third the life span of our product, we're endangering the life of the public? The driving public is going to be exposed to the application trucks three times during the same period if inferior products are used."

Based on our value system, we had to add the highest value. The only way we could do that was to have our product used by the DOT. The marketing manager jumped in and said that was why we had to lower our prices. It was generally agreed that that model would not provide sustainability in the marketplace for us and that, sooner or later, we'd not be able to continue adding the highest value. We needed to think of a different model.

We continued brainstorming. By the end of the day, we came up with the pay-for-performance concept, something unheard of in our industry.

Traditionally, DOTs were known for buying products based on already written specifications. The majority of vendors focused their efforts on meeting those specifications and then manufacturing their product at a lower cost so that the DOT would award them the contract. This process often diminished the product's quality.

> By its design, business in general focuses intently on lowering costs, which generally results in lower product quality.

DOTs developed their specifications based on a product's success. Unfortunately, as time passed, the quality of the product continued to decline. By the time the specification changed again, an incredible amount of time and money had been wasted, as the DOT, having awarded the contract to the lowest bidder, needed to have the work redone or corrected. By its design, business in general focuses intently on lowering costs, which generally results in lower product quality.

How does one practice adding the highest value in a market such as this? Intrinsically, I knew that producing a product with a lower price and quality would be not only a waste of our time and resources, but simply unsustainable. Plus, based on the oneness thought process, when we asked ourselves who our true customer was, the resounding answer was that it was the driving public, not the DOT, even if they were the ones writing the specifications and awarding contracts.

The contractors weren't our customer either, though they ended up buying the material from us. I always felt the DOT, contractors, and POLY-CARB were the three entities collectively providing value to our real customer: the driving public.

The driving public, who appeared to have no say in the matter concerning product quality and contracts, had a clear need for a product that would last longer for driver safety, and they didn't want to be subjected to unsafe driving interruptions because of striping trucks on the highway. Drivers were moving at speeds of sixty-five miles per hour and greater, whereas the stripers were driving at less than ten miles an hour and blocking one lane.

Another great concern was that we couldn't apply a product composed of almost 50 percent volatile, toxic solvents that polluted the environment. Most importantly, the highway lines faded when drivers needed them the most: in wintertime. The lines' visibility at night, the lack of which was responsible for 50 percent of fatal accidents, was highly questionable or not there at all.

Here's how our approach worked with DOTs many years ago, when we were still drumming up business.

The product POLY-CARB produced lasted longer by seven to ten years, but was more expensive up front. Typically, the fast-drying paint used in striping only lasted four to six months, which meant that highway lines required repainting several times a year. Additionally, the products sold under the category of long-life markings only lasted two to three years maximum on asphalt roads and less than six months on concrete pavement.

Painting costs varied per foot. With millions of miles of roadway to paint, the annual painting costs added up. As a result, many roadways remained with unserviceable lines due to restrictions and limited budgets.

POLY-CARB's price was three to five times more expensive per foot than other products, including labor and material. A contractor's immediate thought when seeing our project bid was that we were too expensive, even though the product would last up to ten years. Since the lowest bidder got the contract, contractors were obviously not interested in our product, as it was classified in the same category as other products that were less durable.

Even other epoxy products that used two-part epoxy kinds of paint didn't last as long as our product, as our product was a hybridized epoxy, a molecular marriage between molecules to give higher value.

Departments of Transportation recognized POLY-CARB's long-lasting product value, but state laws made competitive project bidding mandatory. Their suggestion to us was to become more competitive. Instead, POLY-CARB approached DOTs with an idea: Since performance was what they were looking for, instead of the DOT providing the specs, why not approach companies with their problems and ask for them to come up with solutions and submit a proposal?

Here's why this suggestion worked: DOTs don't have qualified polymer scientists who understand their own requirements. At best, they have civil engineers who are not equipped to understand the various products in terms of strength and longevity.

In addition to our suggestion, we asked DOTs to require companies to furnish a proposal that included price, how many times the lines would require re-painting, the paint's visibility, durability, and so on. Once this was done, POLY-CARB produced a proposal that almost none could match based on safety, durability, reflectivity, and affordability.

> There is nothing more precious than the gift of life. We therefore have an obligation to save lives by making a commitment to prevent accidents with better roadway visibility.

We began our proposals with "There is nothing more precious than the gift of life. We therefore have an obligation to save lives by making a commitment to prevent accidents with better roadway visibility."

In keeping with this opening statement, we proposed to broaden the stripe from the standard four inches to five inches and to contrast it with an eight-inch black line so that daytime visibility was not reduced because of wear and tear. Night visibility of the lines was not an issue, as the retention of the glass beads we imbedded in our product was much higher than in any other product on the market due to the unique binding strength of the polymer used in our product.

We did not charge a one-time price, as other vendors did. We leased the lines for four to six years, receiving payment on a yearly basis, which was tied to performance. In other words, we set a mutually agreed upon requirement as to how our lines would be evaluated. They would be assessed by independent laboratories, and if we met the criteria, we would get a certain amount of payment at the end of the year.

This put POLY-CARB within their yearly budget for their lowest-cost material—fast-drying traffic paint—as typically, they had to buy and install traffic paint two to three times a year. Our cost was within that budget. Yet, they were getting the highest-performing product, which would have otherwise cost them four to five times the amount if they had paid up front to other vendors using lower-quality products.

POLY-CARB was taking the entire risk because if our products stopped performing, the state would stop paying us. No one in the industry could match that offer, as to begin with, they had to have a product that would last at least six years and have full faith in it to wait for four to six years to receive their entire payment.

We knew the entire industry's paradigm wasn't to add the highest value. By staying on the course of adding the highest value, we became the exclusive vendor for many DOTs and eliminated the competition completely. It was a highly profitable model, though that wasn't the original incentive that brought us to this outcome. We then applied this business model to other products and markets.

> Our thought process was always challenged to not just do extraordinary things, but doing ordinary things in an extraordinary manner.

Building long-term relationships and staying at the top of our industry was merely a consequence of staying on the path of adding the highest value at all times in all of our transactions. Our thought process was always challenged to not just do extraordinary things, but doing ordinary things in an extraordinary manner. From a big-picture perspective, our primary objective was to never do just our best, but to continuously improve on our best. It was a different approach to doing business.

POLY-CARB now had an unbeatable strategy. *Strategy*, though, isn't the right term because anything derived through the oneness paradigm is not a strategy, but a mind-set, a way of being. We were now primed to make a difference in the world via POLY-CARB and the individual and collaborative efforts of our new team members. We were a whole new entity!

Chapter 12

Shattering Limitations

I knew that in order for POLY-CARB to earn its very existence and sustain its growth, it had to continue to provide the highest-quality products in the marketplace; we needed to continue to be innovative. This could only happen if team members were willing to push their personal envelopes and not stay safely ensconced in their comfort zones.

Yes, that was it—a mind-set of being in student mode and break-throughs! Being the eternal student allows freedom from attachments to what was—we wouldn't get stuck in a mental and emotional rut. Instead, we'd remain in a fluid state of inquisitiveness and exploration. We'd then be available to take in new information and see where it took us.

Prior to letting everyone go, stagnancy was what I was afraid of in my team members, and its signs were clearly visible throughout the company. People wanted to stay where they were, sort of like robots programmed to do a set of prescribed tasks and nothing more. If they tried to do something outside what they could handle, they could end up frying their circuits. They wanted to stay safe in their little cubicles, the proverbial box.

> The universe—Nature—is in constant motion on levels we haven't even discovered yet. That includes us, no matter how hard we try to maintain our sense of reality. Every moment of our existence is in a state of flux.

I knew, though, that the universe—nature—is in constant motion on levels we haven't even discovered yet. That includes us humans, no matter how hard we try to maintain, organize, and control our sense of reality. Every moment of our existence is in a state of flux. It's our choice to either flow with it or resist—and "resistance is futile," to quote a famous *Star Trek* declaration. In addition to the fear that makes people avoid change, people feel safe when they can say they own something, whether that's a physical object or intellectual property.

POLY-CARB required a motivational force, a catalyst to facilitate endless inspiration through a self-generating and organic process, a process that wasn't about self but about oneness and our actions radiating out into the world.

I know that most humans have within them the desire to be known by others. For many reasons, we derive our security from what others think of us, and we assess others' feelings through their compliments, awards, or recognitions—even from our accumulated possessions. That's the ego at work, ensuring that we don't live in anonymity and aren't forgotten by the world. Hence, the ego works to make sure the world knows us by our possessions, progeny, titles, wealth, fame, accomplishments, and legacies.

What is interesting about the constant drive to be known and remembered is that it can all be taken away. Nature can destroy our possessions in a flash. We can lose our ability to utilize our skills and talents through a simple accident. We can be fired. Banks can repossess our property. People re-write history to suit their agendas. It's all ephemeral.

Why, then, do we work so hard to own anything and everything? The answer hit me square between the eyes: the Law of Abundance. In order to operate in an abundance mentality, it was important to understand that it's not possible to own anything, as all resources belong to the bigger One and are merely allocated to me. Their allocation is either enhanced or depleted based on whether I am adding the highest value to the bigger One or not.

> People hamstring themselves by relying solely on the attributes of their physical body and mind and the limitations of their ownership mentality. As a result, they begin to operate within limitation and lack rather than abundance.

I've observed that people hamstring themselves by relying solely on the attributes of their physical body and mind and the limitations of their ownership mentality. As a result, they begin to operate within limitation and lack rather than abundance.

The former staff at POLY-CARB had been no different. Because of this, though, they'd become slaves to the pleasures and distractions of their five senses and egos. This produced an inconsistency in their work, their behavior, their productivity, and POLY-CARB's products.

One extremely accomplished gentleman with a most impressive and imposing résumé worked at POLY-CARB. In spite of his many achievements, he constantly got in his own way via his oversized ego, which prevented him from adding the highest value in his work and relationships.

In order to get this message across to him, I once taped a conversation we had—with his complete knowledge—and when I played the tape back, we discovered that 90 percent of our entire conversation of an hour and a half had been dominated by him. Out of that time period, 60 percent was spent degrading and finding fault with others and various situations, and 30 percent was spent describing how great he was and his amazing achievements, which I'd already heard many times prior to this conversation. Only 10 percent was spent on new ideas that were remotely meaningful to POLY-CARB.

In addition to this, he felt that he should be given ever more power and control in the company, which he felt he deserved due to his past achievements in other companies. What he was completely unaware of was that since joining POLY-CARB, he'd managed to degrade our products and processes simply to cut costs, demoralize team members, and alienate himself from everyone.

The amazing thing was that this person was so much about himself that he didn't even have a meaningful relationship with his spouse and children, let alone have any close friends.

In spite of my efforts to make a difference in his life, he never caught on to what I was conveying to him. By his own admission, he found comfort in our relationship and not only considered us close friends, but also felt that I was his mentor—though he never listened to anything I said to him. I finally realized that I couldn't help him overcome his inherent insecurities, which made him consistently condemn others and talk only about his achievements. We eventually parted company.

In this man's mind, his comfort level and security came only from putting his name on and trying to take ownership of everything. Any idea from a team member was slightly changed by him, and he would then call it his. I noticed that when the company secured a contract or invented anything, he had no hesitation in claiming it as his own. He never understood the fundamental concept concerning ownership.

Owning promotes insecurity, greed and manipulation, whereas the Law of Abundance recognizes that everything is allocated to us, which gives rise to gratefulness, frugality, responsibility, and creativity. This resource allocation by the bigger One can either increase or decrease based on whether we're adding the highest value or not. Therefore, there is no room for mediocrity in our thinking and operations in life, whether in private or in business.

Owning promotes insecurity, greed and manipulation, whereas the Law of Abundance recognizes that everything is allocated to us, which gives rise to gratefulness, frugality, responsibility, and creativity.

This law applied to me in my situation at that time because by letting go of an ownership mentality and operating within a mind-set of being the manager of the resources of the common One, I'd shatter limitations and reach out for all the resources of the universe toward the common goal of adding the highest value. Within this new paradigm of abundance, I could now begin seeking help from within and without the company. I was focused on finding the highest value-adding solution and innovation, whether it was a product or service, and continuously leading the company in making our best better.

Our true competition is with our own best rather than with someone else when we consistently stay on a path of making our best better.

This gave rise to a clear understanding that POLY-CARB's true competition was with our own best rather than with someone else when we consistently stayed on a path of making our best better. But we couldn't make our best better until we fully accepted the situation at hand and operated in the present rather than complaining about what was wrong with the current situation and playing the blame game or wishing and hoping that things would go away or improve.

Conceptually, we had to first honor the Law of Acceptance: "*Accept life as it comes to us with gratefulness and without conditions.*"

To enable ourselves to stay on the path of adding the highest value, we had to first accept life as it came to us—with utter gratefulness and unconditionally and without prejudice, fear, judgment, or regret. As a consequence, we would then be operating in the present and in a position to explore the hidden opportunities in both our failures and successes to add the highest value.

A lot of POLY-CARB's time and mental energy was wasted on "woulda, coulda, shoulda" and "the grass is always greener" thinking and/or not taking action because of preconceptions, preconditioning, and the projecting of our fears and judgments onto someone or some situation. Any time we were in this mind-set, we became our own obstacles to and saboteurs of success, joy, peace, and fulfillment.

I needed to convey to the new team at POLY-CARB that all of life's great inventions, architecture, artworks, compositions, novels, movies, technology, and innovations began with making current conditions better. Instead of complaining, bickering or blaming anyone for the way things were, we had to take the current situation as the starting point and move forward by using our imagination, creativity, and intuition.

> Opportunity lies within everything that comes our way, not in the crass manner of being opportunistic, but in seeing the silver lining or hidden gold within what life offers us, no matter with what we're faced. Through this lens, we are able to see the possibilities of creatively adding greater value.

I wanted to get across to the team members that life does not move forward by maintaining the status quo or running away. Imagine what the world would be like today if this were the case. We'd still be living in caves, afraid to come out for fear of something terrible happening. We've progressed as civilizations and cultures because of one thing: challenge—*Per Angusta ad*

Augusta, which, from the Latin, translates to "Through difficulties to greatness."

Essentially, opportunity lies within everything that comes our way, not in the crass manner of being opportunistic, but in seeing the silver lining or hidden gold within what life offers us, no matter with what we're faced. Through this lens, we are able to see the possibilities of creatively adding greater value. Conversely, seeing life through any other lens causes things to spiral downward, and the next thing we know, we are stressed, unhappy, and paralyzed.

Prior to bringing on the new team, I experienced plenty of resistance, friction, reinvention of the wheel, positioning and power plays, staking out of territories, finger pointing—the whole enchilada of corporate dysfunction. All of this happened because people were stuck in their erroneous expectations and unwilling to accept challenges and work in the present.

How often have we heard that challenges are really opportunities in disguise? Looking through the lens of oneness, I realized that the prerequisite for converting challenges into opportunities was by first accepting life as it comes to us—unconditionally. When we introduce the element of unconditional gratitude in our acceptance, we catalyze our creativity in finding solutions and unveiling opportunities in any challenge.

Once POLY-CARB was ensconced in this mind-set, we'd no longer be slaves to anything and would therefore be free to be creative, inventive, and visionary as we sought to add greater value. We'd no longer be held back by the constraints of others' thinking, dictates, and conventions.

But we had to accept that no matter how difficult an unexpected situation was, the only way to get out of it

> No matter how difficult an unexpected situation is, the only way to get out of it is to first accept it as it is and then utilize all of our creativity and resources to find a long-term solution.

149

was to first accept it as it was and then utilize all of our creativity and resources to find a long-term solution. I was always amazed at how Dolly used these principles when dealing with many unexpected and challenging situations.

Each of our key customers had a special relationship with Dolly, and when they wanted material shipped on a certain date and time, they would bypass everyone and call her directly. Dolly would then work her magic, and—voilà!—the customers' needs were met.

Dolly had an uncanny ability to engage people to do things. An example of this occurred when my mother passed away in 1988. That June, while our house was having a major overhaul and additions built, I flew to India. I realized my father, who had never spent a day away from my mother, ought to accompany me to the US to avoid being lonely and depressed. At the same time, his presence would help me fill the void brought about by my mother's passing. My flight to the US was to leave from Mumbai (formerly known as Bombay), so my father had to come with me and get his visa from the American consulate in Mumbai.

Dolly's family lived in Mumbai, so we stayed with them. While we were there, Dolly's father had a heart attack. The doctors recommended bypass surgery. I wanted him to have surgery in the US, so I called Dolly and told her I was bringing her father and mother, as well as my own father. This development meant that Dolly faced a superhuman effort to create a bedroom, add a deck in front of the kitchen so that people could enjoy the outdoors, and add an additional room to the kitchen to sit and eat in only ten days. She said, "Don't worry. I'll get it done."

Dolly had the four contractors working day and night in order to meet this unexpected ten-day deadline. She made food for all of them and smothered them with kindness. They couldn't say no to anything she asked for. When I returned with our parents, I was flabbergasted and wondered how one person could get all of the house additions completed in just ten days.

We waste a lot of time and energy trying to resolve and/or mitigate current circumstances. If we get caught up in a current event, we're likely to miss the beauty, lessons, and opportunities of the present. Dolly didn't fret about suddenly having to complete the house makeover in just ten days; she just figured out ways to get it done and collaborated with others to do so. The more time we spend caught up with circumstances and minutia, the less time and energy we can devote to creative problem solving.

> The more time we spend caught up with circumstances and minutia, the less time and energy we can devote to creative problem solving.

Have you ever watched any of the *Star Trek* television series? Each episode involves some type of challenge, and then we get to watch the crew members quickly come up with ideas and solutions. They try different avenues and angles, and sometimes they're immediately successful, while other times, they miss the mark and have to put their creative thinking caps on once again. Thankfully, most of our decisions and challenges are not of such high, stress-inducing levels. The point is that the *Star Trek* crew members don't hang about worrying about challenges; they immediately get into a creative mind-set and see what happens.

> A way is always found by simply asking, "What if …?"

All of humankind's inventions, developments, and creations are based on stepping out into the unknown and not being held back. A way is always found by simply asking, "What if …?" Unfortunately, many of us look only at the downside of possibilities, primarily out of fear: failure, humiliation, loss, abandonment, rejection. The secret to life is boldly stepping outside of your comfort zone and seeing what transpires, who shows up on your doorstep, and where your journey takes you. Most assuredly, mistakes will be made, but they are simply stepping stones in disguise that lead to further enlightenment and discovery. And that was what I wanted for POLY-CARB and the team. It was going to be quite a shift!

How could I create an environment that nurtured innovation?

Could the discipline needed to stay on course co-exist with the free thinking needed to nurture innovation? Those two concepts appeared to be diametrically opposed. Discipline reflects a rigid adherence to rules or order, whereas freedom is synonymous with the absence of rules, and a fluid state of being.

I didn't have a clear idea of what the answer was, but I did know that the word *freedom* was integral to everything.

Chapter 13

Discovering True Freedom

My dilemma was going to take some further thought because I needed to understand what true freedom was.

In our so-called civilized world, we have laws of the land, and we are not free to break them. If we do and are caught, then we are put through a process that balances the scales of justice. In fact, we create all our societal freedoms by following these laws.

However, in our current system, our laws can be modified or vastly changed with the consent of the majority of the voting public and Congress.

But beyond the laws of man are the totally unchangeable laws of the universe that no power can modify or change. It is by unveiling, understanding, and applying these laws of nature that science and technology are born. To teach and fully understand these laws, we have divided our formal learning into various academic disciplines, such as chemistry, physics, mathematics, biology, etc. The applied side of these disciplines is taught under engineering principles.

My understanding of freedom is that it comes about when we first know and follow the rigid laws of the universe as seen through the window of science and technology. For example, only by knowing and fully understanding the implications of gravitational force and realizing that it would always be present and could not be changed that were we able to create aviation technology. In other words, the freedom to fly came about when we first understood and then applied the rigid law of gravitation.

Other laws of nature (e.g., relativity, electromagnetics and thermodynamics, as well as quantum, radiation, and motion) have opened extraordinary portals of technological development that affect every aspect of our lives. Think about what an understanding of these laws has provided us in terms of everyday living, and then try to imagine what life would be like without any of them. What would our experience of freedom be like then?

Aside from the freedoms derived from laws instituted by mankind and created by understanding the unbending laws of nature, there is another freedom: personal freedom. I can eat what I want. I can sleep when I want. I can read what I want, say what I want, think what I want, live where I want, and so on. However, I must also realize that with every choice I make, there are associated consequences for myself, my relationships, and the world at large. For instance, if I eat pizza every day as part of my freedom of choice, then I might pay with the consequence of poor health. If I choose to drop out of school, then I lose the freedom to earn a higher salary. Similarly, if I choose to speak with disrespect to a person, I will lose the freedom to talk with him or her. So where is the freedom if I consider the consequences that eventually hinder my true freedom?

It therefore appears that the only freedom I have is the freedom to choose my disciplines, which eventually creates my true freedom. Thus, if I have the discipline to talk respectfully with you, it is only then that I gain the freedom to talk or communicate with you.

Now the real question is this: How do I gain the wisdom to choose my disciplines, which will give me my true freedom?

As I was thinking about this, I had another epiphany, realizing what true freedom is:

"We create real freedom through the discipline of oneness, which guides us in choosing and living our values unconditionally."

It is only the wisdom of oneness that gives us our

#6: The Law of Freedom

"We create real freedom through the discipline of oneness, which guides us in choosing and living our values unconditionally."

---

core value system, and we are then able to practice those values even when no one is watching. It is through living these values that we create our true freedom. This is law number six, the Law of Freedom.

Over the years, I'd had conversations with successful CEOs and business leaders. Their well-seasoned advice was that in order to grow my company, I needed a well-trained and experienced management structure in place that was guided and controlled by a well-documented rule book for the entire company. My banker, attorneys, and accountant always told me that I needed to create a rule book for everyone in the company to follow and to which to adhere.

After understanding the core wisdom of oneness and its implications, it became clear to me that I needed to breed leaders and not managers. To me, a manger is someone who follows rules and procedures set by someone else. Eventually, managers become stumbling blocks to real innovation and progress, especially in a time when technology, products, and services are rapidly becoming obsolete and are constantly being reinvented. This unprecedented rapid and constantly changing environment has even left the largest giants of commerce and industry and well-established companies vulnerable.

In my mind, a leader is a person who makes the rules and often re-defines or breaks the previous rules set by others. History has two extreme examples of such leaders who were known to break all the rules and impose their own: Adolph Hitler and Mahatma Gandhi.

Hitler was guided by his extraordinarily power-hungry, selfish agenda fueled by his insecurities, fear, greed, and forever-inflating ego. On the other hand, Mahatma Gandhi was guided by an organically empowered value system that was completely immersed in oneness, which directed him to add maximum value to all mankind.

I've had the privilege and honor of sitting on the advisory committees of some well-recognized universities. I have often been asked by deans and presidents how they should position their university so that its students stand out and so that they are considered to be offering higher value than other universities.

Based on my experience with my own company, my statement has always been to stop producing managers and start producing leaders. Unfortunately, this advice has always fallen on deaf ears, as our school system is entrenched in curriculums based on teaching that engenders thinking and placement in silos, defining a student for life as a chemist, a civil engineer, an attorney, etc. What is really needed is education that is holistic, value-guided learning that will inspire innovations and purpose in life.

Rigid rules never inspire me, as I value freedom most. Rules actually do more harm than good, as they eventually become so complex and we become so reliant upon them that we end up being strangled by them.

Essentially, any rules and operating strategies should be the outcome of a strong value system.

Essentially, any rules and operating strategies should be the outcome of a strong value system. If I am not imbedded in a clearly defined and integrated value system, then all the rules in the world will not help me. Instead, I will continuously employ technicalities and rationalizations to supplant and distort my espoused values. That's what I see all around us today. For example, look at our legal system. Could there be a more rigid system? Yet, when a gross crime is committed and we ask an astute attorney what the chances are of convicting the perpetrator, the response is a fifty-fifty chance. What happened to our values?

Society has paid an incredible price by exchanging our values for rules. It comes down to this: The height of a civilization is determined by the number of laws or rules it has—the more laws needed, the less civilized the society. The more laws we have, the less true freedom we have.

I thought about the world's conflicts, from one-on-one to disputes between entire nations. All of them were due to not having the discipline to live our values. We are always managing to get in our own way and sabotage the very efforts we think will bring us our heart's desires. The world of politics, government, and society's well-being is a prime example of hijacked values and a lack of discipline, which has resulted in a Byzantine jungle. Ironically, an amazing amount of discipline is exerted toward endeavors for personal gain, whether for an individual or a group.

Interestingly, we seem unable to see just how much further we'd go and the greater sustainable, long-term success we'd enjoy if we disciplined ourselves to maintain our values. Instead, values seem to have become a commodity as part of a means to an end.

Values are espoused and supported by volumes of rhetoric, yet are easily re-fashioned to fit situations, replaced with more convenient and expedient values, or retracted altogether so as to be non-existent. Once we begin weaving these tangled webs, we become slaves to our intricate entanglements. We've lost our freedom, and re-establishing the discipline required to aright ourselves will turn into a monumental task.

Until POLY-CARB's values were tied into oneness—our true purpose in life—we wouldn't have the inspiration or discipline to follow those values of freedom.

Chapter 14

Forging a New Company

With the new POLY-CARB team members, we had, for the most part, individuals with little to no business experience. One thing about unformatted minds is that they are not bound by the strictures of prior business systems; they're not hemmed in by the proverbial box that we're so often told to think outside of.

> **If you believe you're in a box, then you're going to expend a lot of energy trying to get out of it. Instead, remember that the so-called box is just a convention, a fabrication—there really is no box.**

To begin with, if you believe you're in a box, then you're going to expend a lot of energy trying to get out of it. Instead, remember that the so-called box is just a convention, a fabrication—there really is no box. Therefore, the entire universe is your playground; its unlimited resources at the standby for you. Now you're ready for unrestrained and uninhibited innovation. To channel and properly utilize these resources at

POLY-CARB, we brought our operating principles and values into full action to guide us.

The driving power of POLY-CARB was not its markets, technology, customers or products, but our well-thought-out values and operating principles. Imbedding this new paradigm mind-set into POLY-CARB's team members and the people with whom we did business was the primary objective. It would enable the company's long-term sustainability in the environment of forever-changing technology and marketplace, which continuously demands innovation and breakthroughs.

As I stated earlier in the book, breakthroughs occur only when people are not in their comfort zones. The previous staff members had become akin to couch potatoes, content to stay where they were, to not rock the boat, not strive to change anything, not dare to take a stand, or break through barriers. They were unwilling to say, "What we've created is great; how can we improve it?"

Fresh minds tend to think freely, unencumbered by past experiences or co-opted by the dos and don'ts of existing structures. Breakthroughs happen more easily and on a more constant basis. Coupled with the mind-set of oneness, fresh minds become an unstoppable force—not in the sense of steamrolling over others and disregarding their input, but of adding the highest value in collaborative efforts so that everyone benefits and wins.

When Dr. Pant and I had made the rounds of the universities to recruit new hires, we'd described to applicants our new-hire operating guidelines, sharing with them that everything remains in a constant state of motion and change. Therefore, we told them they must remain in a student mode of learning, which would position them to continuously make their best better.

We had six guidelines to go by in implementing the core of our recruiting and training strategy. As I pondered these guidelines, another law began formulating in my mind, number seven, the Law of Change:

#7: The Law of Change

"Living in the reality of constant motion and change, we must remain in a student mode of learning and making our best better."

"Living in the reality of constant motion and change, we must remain in a student mode of learning and making our best better."

Remaining in student mode is something most people don't want to do. They've already been through years of school, so the thought of continuing their education isn't a happy one. But life is one unending series of lessons designed to help us grow. We're constantly learning new things; we just don't realize it. Often, what we have to learn is attached to something we need. Most of the time, we just deal with learning something new. Other times, though, we resist having to learn yet another thing and forget about getting the thing we desire—even if it's something that will make us happy, alleviate problems and pain, and possibly improve the quality of our lives and relationships.

The fact is that the more we know, the more we realize how little we actually do know.

Unfortunately, our universities unknowingly do us a great injustice by giving us degrees, such as master's and doctorates; the reality is that they are merely putting us on a life-long journey of learning. The fact is that the more we know, the more we realize how little we actually do know.

Intrinsically, we have an unending desire to learn new things, and we get bored when we deal with the same old things over and over again. Ironically, our educational system has instilled a fear of failure in us, which deters us from trying to learn new things. We like to explore new, untapped territories and look for new places to stimulate us, yet when something comes packaged in formal learning, we freeze, stress out, rebel, or do our best to avoid it. We often see highly-educated people resist further education even within their own arena, for fear of failure, rejection, humiliation, loss of their safety net, etc. Many college grads throw their textbooks away because they believe they're finished with their education.

In our constantly changing environment, only change is constant. Learning new things is absolutely vital to our existence. However, we need to create an environment and initiatives for constant learning without fear of failure. We achieved this at POLY-CARB by implementing the following six guidelines.

1. *No one will have a job title. There will be no hierarchy of managers and supervisors. We are all responsible for everything within the company, not just our particular jobs.*

   There are no bosses or subordinates, only specialized, value-adding entities.

   There are no bosses or subordinates, only specialized, value-adding entities. Job titles pigeonhole people and often set up a class system with what can many times be considered unequal and, thus, unfair pay scales. Those at the bottom of the scale might feel disenfranchised and think their ideas and opinions don't matter as much. This can lead to a lassitude in one's job, which leads to mediocre performance, productivity, and products and low morale and resentment.

   With no job titles, everyone will be on a level playing field; everyone will have equal say and input. No one will ever be put in the position of being discounted or underestimated.

   An extension of having job titles, a hierarchy in a company automatically encourages the following four things:

   • Job titles establish division and exclusivity. If there is one thing that feeds the lust for power and prestige, it's the sense of being superior to others and being able to order them around. People become protective and defensive about what little power they have within a company, and they'll do all manner of things to hold on to their fiefdom.

- Job titles leave responsibility to the next tier above, finally ending with the CEO. This means that no staff member needs to take full responsibility for his or her decisions and actions. This is where the term "pass the buck" rears its irresponsible head. In tandem with this, job titles allow people to hide behind others in order to avoid blame or taking the heat.

- Job titles box people into specific roles and responsibilities and close them off from other areas, which leads to what is referred to as specialization. If you only know your specific job in a company, then you cannot be effective in other areas if called upon to help out.

- Job titles lead to a sense of entitlement, one of the big ego traps not just in business, but also in other aspects of life. Our unions are now ensconced in the concept of entitlement—whether earned or not—and they've fought battles over entitlement, thus shrugging responsibility to their peers, their industry, their society, and even their families.

We must continually work to better our best and not rely on rewards and certificates bestowed on us to speak for us.

2. *No one is allowed to hang their diploma in their office. If they do, it will be grounds for immediate dismissal.* Diplomas are a statement about what we've accomplished in our education, but they say nothing about who we are and how we are in business. Just as the adage in show business states that we're only as good as our

last performance or production, we must continually work to better our best and not rely on rewards and certificates bestowed on us to speak for us. People who rely on these visual aids, also known as crutches, are letting you know that they are not fully comfortable in their skins and aren't living fully in the present.

3. *Everyone will learn everyone else's job so that any one of us can run the company and produce anything needed by our customers. No one is allowed to say, "I can't." Instead, be creative and inquisitive.*
The driving idea behind this guideline is for each person to essentially nurture the mind-set of a CEO. The only way to truly be in that role is to understand the company inside and out. To facilitate this requirement, each new hire was rotated in every department and cross-trained in all areas of our business. This process was carried out for at least two years. At the end of their cross-training, they were subjected to the rule of 70/30: 70 percent of their time was spent in an area where they found their passion lay, regardless of their formal education, specialization, or the job for which they were originally hired. The other 30 percent of their time was to be spent working in other departments and, thus, staying connected to all aspects of the company's operations. This system nurtured true team spirit in its core structure, as well as in actual operations. We had well-trained and completely vested "CEOs" working in total collaboration.

4. *We are in the business of adding the highest value in everything we do. Anything less than that is unethical, mediocre, and grounds for dismissal.*
One of the major and endemic challenges facing business is a lack of inspiration and morale. Many people just want to be in a position that doesn't stress them, doesn't ask too

much, and allows them to create a familiar and comfortable rut within which to work every day. They don't want to have to strain their brains, don't want demands put on them that can't be easily met, and don't want changes coming into their workspace that will upset their routine.

A work environment of this sort breeds a mentality of numbness. Literally, the light goes off inside, and people are there more or less like automatons day in and day out. Creativity and imagination are stifled, replaced by the monotony of patterns. As this attitude spreads throughout a company, the focus is no longer on creating products that serve, but on maintaining what is. The spark of ingenuity is forgotten, and mediocrity sets in, showing up in the products, productivity, and customer interface. The job becomes just a job that provides the means to collect a check and merely sustain oneself.

This kind of attitude breeds contempt and a lack of empathy toward others, both within and without the company. Eventually, thoughts begin forming of getting away with things we think no one will catch or miss. And this can lead to much larger issues, such as employees stealing from the company, cheating customers, and even making mediocre products that can harm or kill people and/or destroy the environment.

> In our quest for continuous learning and training, we found the best way to learn is to teach.

To avoid this calcification, we continuously presented the challenge of constant learning to our team members. In our quest for continuous learning and training, we found the best way to learn is to teach. Therefore, every Thursday from eleven until two o'clock, we had a continuing education session to challenge and expand the learning of team members, which would also sustain the company. A staff member's name was pulled from a hat that had everyone's name in it. Then, the name of one of the departments was pulled from another hat or a subject was selected, covering anything about the company and our industry.

The lucky staff member was to then give a presentation one month later on the fundamentals and principle processes of that department or the subject he or she had randomly picked. In this way, each staff member became quite familiar with each department and could easily work in it. Accountants learned to operate the research lab, polymer scientists learned marketing, and marketers learned to manufacture our products. This process occurred throughout the company in all departments. Team members were then rotated in these roles over and over again. Thus, together, we nurtured the CEO inherent in everyone.

Everyone also became knowledgeable about aspects of our industry. This meant that a customer could receive top-quality assistance from any staff member and not be shunted around until the right person became available.

We also assigned people a technical subject that was beyond their background. They'd research the subject and give a presentation to the entire company. This elevated their understanding of the subject, and sharing the information with everyone elevated the team's knowledge base. This facilitated the entire company learning together.

5. *Collaboration is the primary operating procedure, so egos are to be left at the door. We're all in this together as one.*

A person's ego can be the biggest stumbling block in any process or group effort. Egos want to own things as a way of attaining acknowledgment, notoriety, prestige, and potential rewards. Egos are based on insecurity and focused on one thing: survival. Therefore, egos are collections of erroneously compiled information—baggage—that impede true forward movement and innovation. When ego is present, all processes and decisions are filtered through private agendas and conditions, which means that the decisions we make and actions we take are not based in the reality of adding value, but in the illusion of insecurity.

With the oneness principle, our sole purpose in life is to add the highest value at all times in whatever we are doing—unconditionally. That means we're operating without agendas, without ego-based needs, and without our insecurities running the show. Our decisions are without hesitation, reservations, expectations, or conditions.

All our team members were encouraged and often required to form small complementary teams to solve problems or address specific projects. This elevated performance and brought about collaborations without nurturing individual egos. We even encouraged inclusions of team members outside POLY-CARB to further elevate our final outcome. Many times, some of the outside team members were our suppliers and even our customers. In addition to helping with the project at hand, this practice nurtured close relationships and camaraderie.

Our greatest learning and growth occurs when our egos are left behind and we become the student again. Ego blocks, while a mind-set of unconditionality embraces without judgment and seeks the best

> Ego blocks, while a mind-set of unconditionality embraces without judgment and seeks the best and highest in all situations.

and highest in all situations. Collaboration becomes a way of life to serve humanity by adding the highest value at all times.

6. *In the CEO mind-set, you have full responsibility to make decisions. Do not be afraid to make mistakes. The only requirement is that when a mistake is made, we share it with the team and make it a learning experience so that it's not repeated. No one will be penalized for making a mistake.* We live in a litigious society, one based on punitive conditioning, which starts at a young age. Therefore, making mistakes and taking responsibility for them is not high on our list. We're so afraid that we'll be castigated, humiliated, rejected, kicked out, fired, criminalized, financially penalized, and maybe even incarcerated. We could lose everything, including our freedom. Consequently, our only option seems to be to pass the buck, watch some other poor schmuck take the blame, and hope no one finds out the truth.

Not only have we become a slave to our fear, but we're also walking around with a perpetual black cloud hanging over us. That is not living.

In any company—no matter how large or small—each team member should be endowed with the role of being a CEO. Decisions are based on doing our due diligence in researching pros and cons and then moving forward.

Since we're all working in collaboration, we've no qualms about inviting others to give input, question, or expand on our vision or plan. Then, when we're satisfied that we're on track, we're ready to take action.

> We do the best we can to avoid costly mistakes and actions that might harm others, but we are also not afraid to step out on a limb.

If, after a decision is made, the outcome doesn't turn out as planned, we can celebrate, as we've just been provided the opportunity to learn something. We do the best we can to avoid costly mistakes and actions that might harm others, but we are also not afraid to step out on a limb. Instead, we share what we've learned, as we have the support of our team members no matter what the outcome.

Essentially, life is a series of discoveries about what works and what doesn't. The only way we know which is which is by taking action. We can observe the actions of others, which provides clues, and then we can extrapolate new ideas and actions from what we've learned. That's how we learn and grow, how we evolve to be greater versions of ourselves.

> As CEOs, we learn to listen and listen to learn, as well as guide, encourage, envision, and set in motion.

As CEOs, we learn to listen and listen to learn, as well as guide, encourage, envision, and set in motion. If we're all CEOs working in collaboration, then the sky's the limit, as we seek to add ever-greater value to all our endeavors and relationships, to the people around us and the world at large.

The stage was set, and new hires were introduced to an operational approach very different from what they'd heard, read, or learned about. They were about to become value-adding entities.

Chapter 15

Empowering the Real Boss

The vibrancy of oneness resonated throughout our company, keeping the creative juices—the lifeblood of the company—flowing and instilling an infectious spirit of bettering our personal best. Oneness became a beacon of self-evolution and empowerment.

We immersed all of our team members in working every Saturday for a number of years to bring about our vision.

> **OUR VISION**
>
> We must realize that we are all an inseparable part of the bigger ONE, and that it is only through serving this bigger ONE continuously and unconditionally that we could ever truly serve ourselves.
>
> Therefore, we must understand that to serve this bigger ONE, we could never even conceive of mediocrity, personal egos, and self-agendas. We must always think and create WIN-WIN situations through every thought, decision, and action.

Once our vision was clear and bought into by every team member, we were ready to give our team and company a well-defined mission and a path to follow our mission. The depth and breadth of POLY-CARB's mission and path is remarkable. It is a call to action and service that asks each individual to be fully responsible and accountable at all times. It moves each person out of the realm of personal interest and ego satisfaction and into the broader expanse of humanity and its welfare.

> The depth and breadth of POLY-CARB's mission and path is remarkable. It is a call to action and service that asks each individual to be fully responsible and accountable at all times.

Here are the mission and path that the POLY-CARB team composed over a period of time, based on aligning ourselves as a team with the oneness principle.

> Both the mission and path encourage each person to be an integral component of all collaborative efforts and to always support others' efforts, ideas, input, and creativity.

Both the mission and path encourage each person to be an integral component of all collaborative efforts and to always support others' efforts, ideas, input, and creativity. In essence, it's a self-illuminating path to realizing one's true self and purpose in life.

OUR MISSION

To provide unparalleled Value, Performance and Service to our team members, customers, business associates, society, and our environment.

OUR PATH

Creating and sustaining an environment based on and driven by Truth & Truthful Living that is conducive to total honesty, human dignity, and unconditional love ...

Thus, encouraging personal growth, courage and team spirit and simultaneously cultivating, nurturing, and elevating boundless creativity and self-driven ethical leadership in each team member ...

Thereby continuously inducing and enhancing extraordinary Quality in every thought, action, product, and endeavor, resulting in the innermost fulfillment for each team member, thus positioning us to achieve our MISSION.

There are very important words involved with this path: *creating, sustaining, truth, truthful living, honesty, dignity, unconditional love, personal growth, courage, team spirit, cultivating, nurturing, elevating, ethical, quality,* and *fulfillment.* They are not just words, but the intrinsic truth of who we are. And it all ties in with the sole purpose of our lives, which is to add the highest value at all times in all ways for everyone.

Truth is higher than everything; higher still is truthful living.

To achieve our mission and vision and follow the path we'd created for ourselves through the fundamental truth of oneness, we unveiled a core operating value: *truth is higher than everything; higher still is truthful living.* Under this value, we created fifteen operating principles by which to live. Every decision complied with these fifteen principles and thus helped us eventually achieve our mission.

These fifteen operating principles were developed over a period of years at monthly Saturday meetings where we would discuss, debate, and understand the implications and applications of these values, continuously polishing the verbiage.

The Fundamental Truth:
Oneness

Core Value:
Truth is higher than everything.
Higher still is truthful living.

Operating Principles

I. Honesty
    I will practice and encourage total honesty.
    Continuously search for truth and distinguish between apparent and real truth. Always evaluate and verify the truth.

II. Human Dignity
    I will have and express unconditional and genuine respect for all.
    First understand others and practice win–win situations at all times. Induce and retain high self-love, be humble, be kind, be respectful, be fair, be clean.

III. Value
    I will improve and add value to everything I undertake. Without compromising my fundamental principles, I will practice only excellence, and not tolerate or encourage mediocrity. Always market value, buy value, and reward and preserve value.

IV. Commitment and Loyalty
    I will keep my promises and commitments to all.
    My loyalty is to my inner core value and my operating principles. My loyalty is extended to my family, team, customer, supplier, and our society simply through following my value system.

V.   Disciplines

I will carefully choose and live my disciplines.

Manners, punctuality, dress code, proper eating, and exercise. Evaluate my actions by introspection and develop 7 habits, as per Stephen Covey.

VI.   Leadership

I will develop a clear vision and a mission.

I will lead myself and serve others through pursuing my mission. Lead by example and compassion, not by rules, commands. Be proactive and take full responsibility. I realize that the only competition that I have is myself and my biggest obstacle is me.

VII.   Team Spirit

I will keep the team's priorities ahead of my own.

Always take the blame and give credit. Take responsibility as "I" and accept accomplishments and successes as "We."

VIII.   Focus

I will maintain clear focus without losing diversity and creativity.

Keep my eyes on my principles, mission, and goals at all times.

IX.   Time Management

I will plan intensely, carefully & thoroughly.

I will not procrastinate, and I will do it now. Let my priorities and time utilization be dictated by my principles, my mission, and my goals. I will always think and operate in the present rather than be imprisoned by the past or day dream about the glory of the future.

X.   Knowledge

I will be an excellent student.

Listen attentively, read voraciously, question intelligently, always take notes, and share my knowledge with others.

XI.   Innovation

I will always work to improve my best.

I will never say impossible. Think, innovate, search, ask questions, take chances. Try, try, and try again.

XII.   Positive Thinking

I will live and work with enthusiasm.

Smile while talking; talk, walk, and act with vigor. Always be grateful for what is gifted to me and not take anything for granted. Everything in life is a gift and I own nothing.

XIII.   Control

I will know my resources, limits, and values.

Think and plan all my actions thoroughly and continuously. The only thing that I truly control is my thought process and nothing else. All my success and freedoms are created through how I think and implement my thoughts.

XIV.   Responsibility to Family and Society

I will make my family and society (my family at large) one of my top priorities.

I will spend quality time with my family and contribute time, talents, and resources toward social causes.

XV.   Non-Judgmental and Forgiving

I will not judge people, just actions and/or decisions.

I will develop a sense of humor and learn to joke about myself but never, never about others. I will learn to forgive and forget.

We held monthly Saturday meetings where we focused solely on the understanding and application of the company's vision, mission, core values, and operating principles in day-to-day business practices. A team member would give practical examples of how he or she was able to put any of the operating principles to use and describe where he or she had difficulties practicing any particular principle. We'd then discuss the principle to gain greater clarification and understanding.

Additionally, we held company retreats in the late autumn. We'd rent a place within a two-hour driving distance, and the Friday before the retreat, everyone would arrive at the offices with bags packed for the weekend. We'd leave around four o'clock in the afternoon to arrive at six. After checking in at the retreat center, we'd have a dinner meeting in a private room, where we'd set the agenda for the weekend.

Everyone understood that as a team connected by our common values and mission, the purpose of our retreat was to completely dismantle POLY-CARB and reassemble it, moving forward under the rigid umbrella of our core values. Therefore, everything, including the company's products, customers, marketing strategy, name, etc., was on the table for discussion. The only things that were inviolate were the company's fundamental truth of oneness, core values, and operating principles.

THE FUNDAMENTAL TRUTH:
Oneness

CORE VALUE:
Truth is higher than everything.
Higher still is truthful living.

OPERATING PRINCIPLES:

I. **HONESTY**
I WILL PRACTICE AND ENCOURAGE TOTAL HONESTY
Continuously search for truth and distinguish between apparent and real truth. Always evaluate and verify the truth.

II. **HUMAN DIGNITY**
I WILL HAVE AND EXPRESS UNCONDITIONAL AND GENUINE RESPECT FOR ALL
First understand others and practice win-win situations at all times. Induce and retain high self love, be humble, be kind, be respectful, be fair, be clean.

III. **VALUE**
I WILL IMPROVE AND ADD VALUE TO EVERYTHING I UNDERTAKE
Without compromising my fundamental principles. I will practice only excellence, and not tolerate or encourage mediocrity. Always market value, buy value and reward and preserve value.

IV. **COMMITMENT AND LOYALTY**
I WILL KEEP MY PROMISES AND COMMITMENTS TO ALL
Be loyal to myself, my team, customer, supplier, and our society.

V. **DISCIPLINES**
I WILL CAREFULLY CHOOSE AND LIVE MY DISCIPLINES
Manners, punctuality, dress code, proper eating, and exercise. Evaluate my actions by introspection and develop 7 habits, as per Stephen Covey.

VI. **LEADERSHIP**
I WILL DEVELOP A CLEAR VISION AND A MISSION
Pursue my mission. Lead by example and compassion, not by rules, commands. Be proactive and take full responsibility. I realize that the only competition that I have is myself and my biggest obstacle is me.

VII. **TEAM SPIRIT**
I WILL KEEP THE TEAM'S PRIORITIES AHEAD OF MY OWN
Always take the blame and give credit. Take responsibility as **"I"** and accept accomplishments and successes as **"We."**

VIII. **FOCUS**
I WILL MAINTAIN CLEAR FOCUS WITHOUT LOSING DIVERSITY AND CREATIVITY
Keep my eyes on my principles, mission, and goals at all times.

IX. **TIME MANAGEMENT**
I WILL PLAN INTENSELY, CAREFULLY & THOROUGHLY
I will not procrastinate, and I will do it **now**. Let my priorities and time utilization be dictated by my principles, my mission and my goals.

X. **KNOWLEDGE**
I WILL BE AN EXCELLENT STUDENT
Listen attentively, read voraciously, question intelligently, & always take notes.

XI. **INNOVATION**
I WILL ALWAYS WORK TO IMPROVE MY BEST
I will **never say impossible**. Think, innovate, search, ask questions, take chances. Try, try, and try again.

XII. **POSITIVE THINKING**
I WILL LIVE AND WORK WITH ENTHUSIASM
Smile while talking; talk, walk and act with vigor.

XIII. **CONTROL**
I WILL KNOW MY RESOURCES, LIMITS AND VALUES
Think and plan all my actions thoroughly and continuously.

XIV. **RESPONSIBILITY TO FAMILY AND SOCIETY**
I WILL MAKE MY FAMILY AND SOCIETY (MY FAMILY AT LARGE) ONE OF MY TOP PRIORITIES
I will spend quality time with my family and contribute time, talents, and resources toward social causes.

XV. **NON-JUDGMENTAL AND FORGIVING**
I WILL NOT JUDGE PEOPLE, JUST ACTIONS AND/OR DECISIONS
I will develop a sense of humor and learn to joke about myself but never, never about others.
I will learn to forgive and forget.

POLY-CARB

Signature: _____

In later years, team members were given Franklin Planners with which to schedule their weeks and months. They were also given printouts of the operational principles, which they would sign, signifying that they were pledging to uphold and live these principles. The principles were then laminated and created as an insert to the Franklin Planners. Team members would always have a reminder of their pledge so that when challenges arose, they were feeling down or bored, or they were feeling overwhelmed, they had the insert to help realign them to a higher vision and purpose.

Each new hire would go through a week of intense soul searching, a systematic approach that included listening to tapes on the principles, followed by in-depth discussions and probing questions with team members. These values and principles had to become their own—they had to have a vested interest—and the principles were always touched upon in all of our daily morning meetings so that we were all focused as a team. It was absolutely essential that all of our values and principles were completely imbedded in the core thinking of each team member.

POLY-CARB was now poised for success far beyond what I'd originally envisioned when starting the company. Now it was a matter of putting the team's vision, mission, path, operating guidelines, and operating principles into practice. This brought to light the understanding of law number eight, the Law of Values:

#8: The Law of Values

"We can only live our inherent, true values, true integrity, when we are completely integrated with and immersed in the one Divine Power—oneness."

"We can only live our inherent, true values, true integrity, when we are completely integrated with and immersed in the one Divine Power—oneness."

Operating void of the oneness paradigm, we're subject to all manner of distractions that get us enmeshed in ever-complicated scenarios, heartbreak, stress, and derailment from our true purpose in life: adding the highest value in all our endeavors. Integrity doesn't stand a chance in this environment. POLY-CARB had been waylaid by egos, personal agendas, and the attractions tied to our five senses. That was now going to be a thing of the past.

> Oneness will result in the removal of our illusionary egos, and we will become truth and trustworthiness—essentially, integrity itself.

We knew that true values could not be practiced unconditionally until they became completely integrated within our very being. That could only happen through the oneness paradigm, but we couldn't switch from where we were to the oneness paradigm in one fell swoop. Initially, before practicing the oneness paradigm, we had to tie principles to results. Otherwise, practicing the principles wouldn't be reinforced under our current operating mind-set.

We made it mandatory for all team members to summarize their activities at the end of the day by writing in their Franklin Planners. They were to evaluate each decision they made that day to determine whether each decision was in compliance with the operating principles or not. They then documented each decision appropriately so that they could see the outcome of that particular decision brought about by practicing our value system.

At the end of the week, the entire team would meet and discuss each team member's decisions. They'd be asked how they had arrived at each decision and whether they had been able to use the core understanding of our principles in their decision-making process. They also determined whether they'd done so in full compliance, partially, or not at all.

One example of this process involved a bridge-decking project in Chillicothe, Ohio, in the early 1980s. POLY-CARB's product was specifically asked for by name by the Ohio Department of Transportation (ODOT). The contractor, who was the lowest bidder, purchased the

product from POLY-CARB. In spite of our detailed application in-
structions, the contractor somehow failed to follow the correct procedures for applying our product. The project was completed toward
the end of October, and due to early snowfall that year, we could not
properly inspect the bridge until the spring of the upcoming year.

When I inspected the bridge work that March and saw the horrible
job that had been done, I felt sick to my stomach. Our product had been
badly applied. I wasn't sure why it looked as it did. When I returned to
the office, I gathered the team and asked them what we should do. We
discussed the situation at length and realized, based on typical business
practices, that we had been paid, and it wasn't our fault that the contractor hadn't done a good job; therefore, that was the end of the story—we
wouldn't need to do anything for the moment. We decided we should
recommend more stringent requirements and restrictions in the state's
specifications for the future so that this scenario wouldn't happen again.

But, as we did with all our major discussions and debates, we
brought in the big boss: POLY-CARB's core principles and values.
We reviewed them to see if our decision complied with them, along
with our mission and vision statements. We realized that we didn't have
any other choice but to re-do the bridge job ourselves, as we knew we
would not be able to convince the contractor or the state to bear the
cost of re-doing the project.

After doing a quick calculation, we realized it would cost us about
$250,000 to remove and re-apply the product. When we looked at our
internal value system, we had to follow it. I had to make the decision to
re-do the work not just because we had to comply with those values, but
because if I didn't comply with them, I destroyed them in the eyes of each
team member. They would only be paper tigers. It was critical for us to do
this. I went to the ODOT and asked their permission to redo the bridge job.

The state engineer in charge of this project was rather puzzled because the state had not issued any such orders to us or to the contractor. Furthermore, per their records, the state had fully paid the contractor and also confirmed from us that the contractor had paid us in full. In fact, it was suggested that we should not waste our money, as it would not make a difference to ODOT since this had been an experimental project to begin with.

We insisted that it was not a matter of cost or money or even compliance with state regulations. It was strictly a matter of our company values and our operating principles. We maintained that we would be greatly indebted to the state for their permission to let us to redo the project. That way, the state would help us uphold our value system. They thought we were crazy but gave us permission to redo the decking with our material.

Back at POLY-CARB, we had a company meeting to decide how we should handle this situation. Our initial decision, based on our discussion, was that we should find another contractor to do the job and negotiate the price, etc. We then brought out The Boss—our fundamental truth, core values, and operating principles. It became apparent that the correct thing to do, which would be an important lesson for our team, was to redo the project with our own hands. This would expose our team to the problems and shortcomings of our products and system and written application procedures. It would also help us to discover and institute a full-proof method for future applications.

We completed the job ourselves. The state was amazed to see the finished product and more amazed that the entire project was done at our own cost. In the history of the state, nothing like this had happened before—someone re-doing work at their own expense just to meet their own internal standards of quality. This news spread like wildfire and ended up being discussed at the national American Association of State Highway Transportation Officials (AASHTO) Conference. A most unintended consequence was the amount of free publicity generated by our actions, a possibility that had never entered our minds.

But even the intended consequence of mastering the application procedures gave us an amazing window to the future application of this product. Our product was manufactured in our plant in two parts that needed to be mixed not only in correct proportions, but also within a specific range of temperatures. Even after correct apportionments, proper mixing was critical to the product's performance. Moreover, the mixed batch needed to be placed on the deck surface immediately or it would start losing its optimal adhesion and long-term performance.

Now, given the uncertainty of the skills and training of unpredictable contractors coming through the doors of the low-bid process, this product would always face unpredictable performance. Plus, there were uncontrolled field conditions and weather.

If we were going to be able to add the highest value to everyone involved—state DOTs, contractors, the driving public, and the environment—then we had to have a method independent of weather, skills of the workforce, and contractors that would give us totally reliable results.

We needed to develop application equipment that could be leased to a contractor with a trained crew. This equipment had to have a separate large storage container for both parts of the product and be equipped with temperature controls. It further had to be equipped with a meter mixing device capable of mixing and dispensing the properly mixed material on the bridge deck.

It took us two years of working with three different industries to develop equipment capable of producing and dispensing enough material to cover twenty thousand square feet per hour. We continuously upgraded this equipment over several years and pioneered and led the industry in prolonging and protecting our highway bridges.

The most important thing we learned was that if we had defined our core business to be solely the manufacturing of high-performance infrastructure restoration and preservation products, like any typical competitor, we would have never embarked on the development of such a unique application technology. Fortunately, we were directed by our mission: to provide unparalleled value, performance and service to our team members, customers, business associates, society, and the environment. This equipment not only provided unparalleled value and performance, but prevented the workers from exposure to the chemicals and eliminated the need for shipping containers that ended up going to landfills.

It was amazing that when our decisions complied with the operating principles and their intent, the results were overwhelmingly game changing. This exercise was extremely effective, as it didn't come across as preaching the principles, but merely reflected the consequences of following or not following them. As the adage states, "the proof is in the pudding." This process slowly and steadily moved us closer and closer to the oneness paradigm, and the value system began to blossom from the seed of oneness effortlessly and organically.

Chapter 16

Help from Uncle Sam

In all the seminars and business meetings organized by state and federal agencies to help small businesses, we were told that the federal government was by far the largest buyer of every kind of goods and services through the General Services Administration, commonly known as the GSA.

The GSA was established by President Truman in 1949. Its focus is to streamline the administrative work of the federal government, and it's the centralized procurement arm for services for the government. In turn, it provides small businesses the chance to sell billions of dollars' worth of products and services to the government. The GSA's "set-aside" program offers female-owned, HUBZone, veteran- and service-disabled-veteran-owned, and 8(a) small disadvantaged businesses the opportunity to attain government prime-contract and subcontract awards.

In our eyes, POLY-CARB qualified as an 8(a) small business, as we were minority owned. The Small Business Administration (SBA) created the 8(a) Small Business Development Program to help small businesses compete in the marketplace, as well as gain access to federal and private procurement markets. They offer mentoring, procurement assistance, business counseling, training, financial assistance, surety bonding, and management and technical assistance.

The Asian-Indian immigrant community discovered in the early 1980s that we were not being afforded the same economic equality and consideration in procuring government contracts as American-born people were. So I became a founding member of a national group gathering data to spearhead a petition to the SBA to help them understand that we were grossly discriminated against despite the fact that we were fully capable, qualified, and equal to the SBA's qualifications. Even in the job market, Asian-Indians were typically paid lower salaries for the same jobs, though we had the same or better qualifications than non-immigrants. Through our efforts, we were included as a qualified minority under the auspices of the SBA.

POLY-CARB then endeavored to become an 8(a)-certified company. It took a lot of paperwork being filled out, and we hired a consultant from Washington, DC, to guide us in the process. Once we were certified, we then had to locate a contract in the federal government where they'd buy our products or services. We started examining bids put out by the GSA.

What we discovered is that the GSA bought high-performance epoxy and urethane coatings used for military equipment and on naval ships. The bids came out in late fall, and the product was to be supplied during the winter months. That was perfect for us, as our construction projects slowed down after the fall months and came to a screeching halt in the winter months. We could use our facilities during the winter to manufacture the products for the government. Perfect!

The only problem with this scenario and our thinking was that even though we were approaching this endeavor through the lens of oneness, we forgot that anyone not versed in the oneness paradigm was going to be playing by his own rules. Those rules could morph or turn to concrete, depending on the mood and agenda of whomever we were dealing with. The following experience with the GSA really brought that truism home to us, and we learned that it really didn't matter whether others were practicing oneness as long as we were. Then the outcome would always be elevating, growthful, and rewarding.

We approached the GSA and asked how we could qualify as a vendor for these epoxy and urethane coatings. We never heard from them, even though we called them a number of times. Eventually, they did respond, stating that we didn't meet their criteria—we were too small for them. I asked what size had to do with anything, as we had everything they needed to comply with their quality and production requirements. The GSA wouldn't budge.

We contacted our congressman, Ed Feighan, and explained that the GSA had rejected us without even evaluating us and had not given us an opportunity to prove that we could meet their criteria. The GSA was focused on strict quality control, which was on a par with that required for the nuclear industry. As a result, we had to fill out a huge and very complicated document. We were told we'd never survive the process.

Congressman Feighan contacted the GSA and asked why they hadn't evaluated the POLY-CARB company in Ohio. If they inspected us and determined that we didn't meet their criteria, then they could reject us, he said. But he advised them to at least give POLY-CARB a chance to prove that they could comply with GSA's requirements.

So, one early morning and without notice, an agent from the GSA came to visit us, a Mr. Longfoot. Asking to see me, he explained that he was from the GSA, that he didn't have much time, and that he was there to advise us on GSA's requirements. He flatly stated that if we didn't have the time to complete the required document, we'd be rejected.

Unfazed by Mr. Longfoot, I invited our core team to come listen to his explanation of the requirements. He assured me that this was all a waste of time. When I offered him coffee or tea, he said he was not to be bribed. Wow!

Upon concluding his explanation to me and the POLY-CARB team, he said that we had only one week's time to put the four-hundred-page quality-control manual together and that it had to be fully integrated and in place, functioning with every aspect of our operation. He would give us the one week starting as of that moment and would then be back. If the document wasn't completed to GSA's strict standards, we'd be rejected. He reminded us several times that not only he was truly the toughest guy in the industry, but that no one had ever gotten qualified on a first attempt under his watch.

A week later, he returned, again having only a short time to review our completed document. What he didn't know was that during that entire week, we'd worked twenty-four hours a day to put the document together and re-align our entire mind-set and our entire operation, including the lab, to meet the GSA's requirements.

After two hours of going through every detail in the quality-control and operation manual we had put together, Mr. Longfoot couldn't believe what we'd accomplished. In the same breath, he reiterated that he wasn't done yet and assured us that no one had ever passed muster with him on the first attempt. He was doggedly looking for faults. At the end of the day, he said that he was sorry he couldn't find any reason to reject us and that he'd never seen anything like this situation before. Since he was only a field agent, he would have to return to the GSA with our documentation to have them also review our work before they issued an approval order, and then someone from the GSA would contact us to explain the next steps.

A month later, after hearing nothing, we called the GSA and were told that our report was too detailed and that they didn't have the manpower to go over it diligently. Hence, no qualifying letter would be issued to us.

We called Congressman Feighan again, and he called the GSA. GSA's response was that, yes, we met their quality-control requirements, but they now needed to send in a technician to witness all the tests performed on the products that were to be submitted for approval. There were thirty-six different formulations and colors, some requiring over six months of testing in the presence of a GSA field engineer.

To their surprise, we not only developed all the formulations and passed all the tests with the GSA field engineer present, but also met all their criteria and obtained an approval certification. In our conversation with the GSA office, we were told that this was the first time any company had achieved the privilege of certification in its first attempt—and with all thirty-six formulations. When we conveyed this message to Congressman Feighan, he was excited for us. The GSA then had to set aside a $2 million contract for us, and we were ready to go.

We thought we'd won a big battle, and with the help of the 8(a) umbrella and GSA, we now could build a strong growth base that would propel us into new horizons. Little did we know that we were being set up and trapped for a quick demise.

The GSA set-aside contract approval was made in the early fall. We thought we were well positioned to begin manufacturing during the winter months. Looking at the bid documents from the past five years, we knew that most of the material GSA would be purchasing would be in five-gallon containers, which we were well equipped to package. We kept on waiting for the details on the order and made several calls to the GSA, inquiring as to when the order would be released. No response was forthcoming for the entire winter period.

After waiting five months, we finally received a contract at the end of March. To our huge surprise, the order was mostly for quart and one-gallon containers instead of their usual five-gallon requirement. It was as if, knowing our manufacturing capacity and schedule, they purposely were punishing us, knowing full well that this order would have to be manufactured during our peak season, when our primary contracts would be coming in. Packing the product in these small containers would tie up our entire facility.

Furthermore, the GSA order required that products be packed in a special manner and shipped to numerous destinations and with different bar codes, etc. We could manufacture the product, but the packaging became the stumbling block. We were paralyzed and struggled to fulfill the order—simply because of the small packaging requirements and highly complicated shipping specifications.

The entire company was consumed with fulfilling the GSA order. In the process, we couldn't resume some of our regular business that had much higher profitability. Although we fulfilled the GSA's contract, we had to forego some of our major business. As a result, we basically broke even on the GSA order, but lost other business and ended up having a major financial loss that year.

We learned a lot from this contract with the GSA, and instead of falling into the trap with the set-aside program and subjecting ourselves to the whims and unpredictable terms and conditions, we decided to go head-on with the open market, where GSA's terms and conditions were specified in advance in their public advertisements. We carefully studied an advertised contract and sent in our bid on a $10 million project. In the bidding document, we clearly spelled out our conditions and schedule and limited our supplies to five-gallon containers, as this particular bid stipulated. Our earlier $2 million contract had thoroughly trained us to manufacture these products in the most efficient manner.

When the bids were opened, we were the lowest bidder, but the GSA declined awarding us the contract, stating that we weren't financially able to handle it. As per GSA rules, being a small company, we were allowed to challenge the GSA's decision, and automatically, the local SBA office was called in to evaluate the situation and determine whether the contract should be awarded to POLY-CARB or not.

We were scrupulously investigated by the local SBA office of Cleveland. They found us fully capable of fulfilling the order and made a strong recommendation that the $10 million contract be awarded to us.

Per official procedures, the GSA had the right to accept or reject the SBA's recommendation. They rejected it. Automatically, the second tier of the SBA, located in Chicago, was given the task to re-evaluate POLY-CARB. We again were comprehensively investigated by the Chicago SBA office. We passed their inspection with flying colors, but despite Chicago's overwhelming recommendation, the GSA chose to reject us.

We were then given the choice of accepting the GSA's rejection or being inspected by the SBA office in Washington, DC. We requested they proceed with the inspection. Unfortunately, the Washington office of the SBA blindly endorsed the GSA rejection without even inspecting us.

We had thirty days to register an appeal with the federal court. The upshot was that the federal court was only going to decide whether the GSA had had the right to reject us. The ruling was that the GSA had. Strangely, though, in that appeal, there was no challenge to the Washington SBA office as to what grounds they rejected us on.

In the end, the contract went to the second-lowest bidder, whose bid was much higher than our bid. Our bid would have saved the GSA about $1 million. Historically, the other bidder was always receiving the contracts, regardless of whether they were the first, second, or third bidder. The GSA had been rejecting everyone else except this one bidder.

If we had wanted to take further action, the next round of litigation to challenge the GSA would have been expensive. We were advised it could cost us several hundred thousand dollars to litigate. We weren't in a financial position to do that, so we had to live with the ruling in favor of the GSA.

In this process, we lost the chance to recover our loss that the set-aside $2 million contract had left us with. We were in a position to not only recover, but, if given the chance, to take a giant step forward, which we had earned through being a legitimate low bidder, to fulfill the $10 million contract with the GSA. This fiasco left us extremely cash poor and vulnerable, and it became difficult to even fulfill the orders we had in hand.

This was the second time in POLY-CARB's history that our well-meaning legal advisers brought up filing for protection under Chapter 11 bankruptcy laws, even after knowing that I would never consider that as an option. Banks were not willing to extend our credit line until we brought fresh cash into the company, despite our flawless, highly profitable history and product acceptance and demand.

Fortunately for us, Century Fence Co. landed several large contracts with three different state DOTs with our product specified. I approached Tony Bryant, the owner of Century Fence Co., and related my predicament. Tony, after giving me his judgment that I was a poor businessman for getting entangled with the GSA and not staying with what I knew—dealing with state DOT business—agreed to advance some money against the orders they had in hand. I came home with a check for $500,000. Thanks to Century Fence Co. and Tony Bryant, we survived Uncle Sam's "favorable" treatment.

Following our experience with the GSA, we realized that there were vast amounts of steel used on bridge structures that needed protection. By elevating the GSA-prompted technology and coming up with even more unique products, we were able to capitalize on the highway steel-bridge market.

We took all of these experiences to heart as windows into a greater understanding of how the wisdom of oneness truly works. In order for us to move forward, it was important for us to understand the following: "*Fundamentally, success evolves from a continuous quest to search for and find goodness and usefulness in everything, every situation, and every human being."* No matter what the situation and how many obstacles we face, oneness trumps all.

What was paramount for us at POLY-CARB—looking at the GSA experience as an opportunity in disguise—was remembering that the Laws of Purpose, Acceptance, Abundance, Integrity, Leadership, Freedom, Change, and Values were the ultimate matrix from which to approach our work lives, as well as our personal lives.

Even though the entire experience with the GSA seemed tilted against us, we comported ourselves most admirably despite all the obstacles. We outdid ourselves in a number of ways, raising the bar even higher. This stood us in good stead as we moved forward as individuals, team members, and POLY-CARB as a whole.

We were definitely positioning ourselves to proceed in a manner that helped us remain steadfast in our values and galvanize our mission to make our best better. Keeping in mind that life is "less about winning and more about not accepting failures," we would be able to sustain ourselves on a path to a bright future.

Chapter 17

Principles in Action

POLY-CARB was in stage two of its development and liveli-
hood. It now had a core structure in place that was well defined, well documented, and, most importantly, thoroughly tested.
We always got overwhelmingly favorable results, often even beyond
our expectations, when we assiduously practiced our core values
and operating principles.

However, in spite of our amazing results through these principles
and our constant reinforcement to practice them, some team members
ended up taking shortcuts or an easier path and bypassing our values and
operating principles. It happened more with new hires. We handled this
challenge in a completely unorthodox way. Instead of punishing the offenders, we made it a practice to appoint the offenders as the watchdogs
of our values and operating principles.

We did have to part company with some chronic offenders who
simply could not see the value in our way of life. This happened more
with team members who came in with experience and entrenched in

the typical corporate practice of attaining results at any cost. Values, if any, were only window decorations or a marketing ploy for them.

We were growing quickly and needed new team members all the time. Once, we placed an ad in the paper that stated our mission and path and said that if any applicants wanted to be a part of helping us achieve this mission, they could apply for the position. We had an amazing response.

One person applied who was used to working in Fortune 500 companies. He'd been a senior executive who had taken early retirement with a golden parachute from a mega-international conglomerate that was downsizing and cutting costs. He showed unusual interest in our advertised position and kept calling us. I invited him for an interview.

He had been working in international marketing and found our approach refreshing and unique. One of the reasons he was taking early retirement, though he was in his early forties, was that the stress of the job was getting to him. He explained that he'd had to put away his conscience to work for his previous company, as the company only cared about results at any cost. He had felt that if he didn't leave, he'd burn out. He couldn't give us details, for fear of a lawsuit, which was a common occurrence with some of his company's past employees. The gentleman had been earning a six-figure salary with a hefty bonus, something we simply could not match. We concluded the interview and wished him happiness and prosperity in his new life.

He called me again the next day and wanted to meet for lunch, which we did. He had additional questions about the inner workings of our company, such as the absence of titles and the use of our values and operating principles as our only guidance. The more he questioned, the more interested he became.

We met three more times, as he wanted to make sure we were for real and that our message was not a sales pitch. In the end, he wanted to join POLY-CARB at any salary, as he'd never seen or heard anything like us before in a real corporate environment. He agreed to come on board at less than half the salary he'd been making at his earlier company and further agreed to become a student and work at different assignments to learn our business at its core.

As time progressed, he found our environment and culture not only extremely challenging, but also helpful in re-defining and breaking through the comfort zone that earlier life experiences had planted in him. In his previous job, his title had always shielded him from being answerable to subordinates and co-executives for his decisions, whereas at POLY-CARB, every decision made by every team member was weighed against our values and operating principles. He was used to making decisions based on profit and loss. Although our values and operating principles looked appealing and powerful on paper, he could never totally immerse himself in them and was therefore not able to follow them.

Over time, the very values and operating principles that had attracted him to us became his biggest hurdle. He openly started opposing them, arguing that if they worked, big corporations, which were successful without them, would have adopted them. He thought we had a silly experiment that had no practical application in the real corporate world. He discounted all of our unparalleled and unconventional business successes, calling them flukes and maintaining that they had nothing to do with practicing our values and principles. Unfortunately, we ended up parting company after only six month into the game.

His leaving was painful for me. After all the adjustments this gentleman had made and all the enthusiasm he'd shown, I had been sure he'd be able to align himself with and see the truth of our mind-set. His leaving made me wonder if our mind-set could only be implemented in fresh minds out of college; I feared it wasn't applicable for experienced people with set habits and unloadable baggage that they'd accumulated from earlier jobs.

I was deeply concerned, as I had always thought that every person had an internal and natural inclination to gravitate toward and practice this thought process. It's the same with any piece of iron. In order for it to become a magnet, all that's required is the re-aligning of its north and south poles under the influence of electromagnetic force.

I also began to notice occasional diversion from our path even among our seasoned team players. I didn't know if it had always been there or if I had become supersensitive after the departure of this gentleman. POLY-CARB's team members made sincere efforts to enhance their understanding and practice of our values and operating principles with a clear focus on our mission and vision. Yet …

Over the years, I somehow could never get this gentleman out my mind. Almost two years after his departure, I ran into him in the presidential lounge at O'Hare International Airport in Chicago. He came up to me and extended a warm greeting.

After the usual exchange of "How is everything?" and other pleasantries, he sat down, looked me straight in my eye, and said, "Ratanjit, I want you to know that there isn't a day that goes by that I don't think of you and POLY-CARB. The funny thing is that the values and principles I resisted while I was there are the very ones that have saved me in so many situations. I have successfully put them into practice even in the typical corporate environment. They have helped me stay stress free and most productive. I can never thank you enough for bringing about this incredible change in me."

Somehow, I wasn't surprised. I would have been surprised if it had been the other way around and he had not been touched by exposure to POLY-CARB. After a brief silence, he continued, "You know, Ratanjit, people at POLY-CARB would never realize the true power of these oneness laws out in the world. I think you should teach these to corporate leaders. They're starving for them." He got excited and said, "I think you're underutilizing your true potential by just running POLY-CARB. You are badly needed in the real world of big businesses. You can make a difference to so many people and companies!"

Just because the team at POLY-CARB had endeavored over the years to create and align ourselves with our values, mission, path, and core operating principles didn't mean it was a breeze. We struggled both individually and as a group to maintain and sustain ourselves in this environment. Coupled with dealing with customers, suppliers, contractors, and various agencies, it seemed we were on a never-ending quest to truly live these principles. But we did endure, and we strove tirelessly to immerse ourselves ever more deeply in this mind-set.

Everything POLY-CARB was evolving toward encapsulated the entirety of our focus and standard of operation from individual to company; we were completely integrated with our vision, mission, path, guiding principles, and operating principles, and they became our prime mandates.

This kind of thinking, lifestyle, and behavior was the complete opposite of what we saw exhibited by POLY-CARB's team members at the time of the bankruptcy. They were caught in their egos and agendas of survival, ownership, and the need for acknowledgment and recognition. We had to realize that ownership of everything, from possessions to intellectual property, had led to innumerable conflicts, whether among family members, neighbors, communities, or entire nations.

As was shown in chapter 6, the answer to this dilemma is found in recognizing the Law of Abundance: *"Abundance comes from the realization that resources do not belong to us, but are merely allocated to us to add the highest value."*

In order to operate in an abundance mentality, it is important to understand that it is not possible to own anything, as all resources belong to the bigger One and are merely allocated to us. Their allocation is either enhanced or depleted based on whether we are adding the highest value to the bigger One or not.

At POLY-CARB, we wrestled with this line of thought and how it affected our working relationships outside of the company. On a larger scale, this line of thinking is something many people find challenging. We've become so inured to claiming ownership of everything and anything that we have thousands of laws to safeguard what we call "mine." Have you ever watched lions and wolves when they're feeding? Get too close to the area where one animal is eating and it becomes highly possessive, baring its teeth, giving warning growls, and readying its claws. Humans are not too far removed from animals.

> The universe is a vast, unlimited, ever-evolving repository of resources, everything from physical resources to creative inspiration. All those resources are available to us.

In the oneness paradigm, it is understood that we cannot actually ever own anything. The universe is a vast, unlimited, ever-evolving repository of resources, from physical resources to creative inspiration. All those resources are available to us.

In dealing with this law of oneness, there is a paradox involved, however. When we are focused on adding the highest value, we become a magnet for the resources of the universe. When we choose to undertake endeavors that only feed our egos and satisfy the pleasures of our five senses, those resources dwindle and gravitate to whoever else is adding the highest value. This means that we human beings are merely vehicles for adding the highest value at all times.

In our discussions at POLY-CARB, we recognized that there were plenty of examples of people who have amassed fortunes and vast physical holdings and power in the world without the mind-set of adding the highest value. What they did was take action on ideas that served humanity in some respect, and what they provided was the best that could be offered, or no one else had something similar to offer. At that point in time, and as an unintended consequence, they were adding the highest value. Hence, the resources of the universe gravitated to the individual or group offering the best at that moment.

At some point, though, someone will come along—humans being as competitive and acquisitive as they are—offering something of greater value, and the resources will shift. This presents a paradox and actually has nothing to do with good or bad, moral or immoral. Essentially, resources will gravitate toward whoever is offering something that does a better job of fulfilling a need. The best business example of this is General Motors.

At one point, GM was the largest corporation in the world. It was said that "What is good for GM is good for America." They reached that plateau by giving consumers a well-designed, highly affordable means of transportation. GM had so much money that ordinary people couldn't even comprehend the number. As a result, GM could afford the best advertising company and campaign, beyond what any other company could imagine.

Then, suddenly, along came new car companies, such as Toyota and Honda and others. Initially, GM considered their cars to be nothing more than toys—not real competitive threats. At the time, the mind-set of these competing companies was focused on continuously improving the cars they were manufacturing. On the journey of making their best better, there came a day when the cars produced by these car companies added higher value to the driving public than those produced by GM. Based on immutable secret number five, the resources of the universe started moving from GM toward the other companies.

GM, used to unmatchable glory and power, thought they could destroy the competition through their marketing muscle and advertising campaign. But the path of continuous improvement followed by the other companies caused them to continue to gain market share—resources kept on moving toward them.

Finally, the day arrived when the biggest, most powerful corporation in the world had to declare bankruptcy. Experts might argue that the unions and economic circumstances caused GM to file for bankruptcy, but after the dust settled and the complex data was sifted through, the truth was that it had everything to do with GM not being able to add the highest value.

At POLY-CARB, we brought the highest value to customers based on earning our keep rather than whatever the market or situation dictated or what we could get away with. In the business world, most pricing is decided by what the market will bear and by competition. POLY-CARB's prices were based on fairness, not the bottom line and getting rich. Our profit was something we earned.

The other car companies—and all businesses in general—of the world have to watch out that they don't fall into the same trap that GM did.

POLY-CARB faced escalating visibility in our industry, and now we had to deal with the repercussions of not only that prominence and the attention it derived, but maintaining our sense of equanimity within the parameters of our operating principles. Our egos were going to be on the line as we were highlighted, scrutinized, dissected, and criticized. In short, under society's microscope, we were either going to truly be an example of our values and principles in practice or just another nice theory.

POLY-CARB began receiving calls from magazines and newspapers that wanted to interview us, to know our magic formula for success.

Aberdeen's
CONSTRUCTION MARKETING *today*

The Aberdeen Group   April 1994   Volume 5, Number 4 $6

A strange formula for success
Poly-Carb and its philosophical founder are doing things their way

By Terrance Noland

Dissatisfied with how the company was operating, Sondhe cleaned house in 1980 and revamped his approach.

Back in 1980, when Poly-Carb Inc. was still a fledgling, 7-year-old construction chemicals firm, owner Ratanjit Sondhe was feeling distressed. It wasn't that his company wasn't making money. It was. What concerned Sondhe ran much deeper. His managers were bickering, his employees were badmouthing their bosses, and his sales reps were misleading customers about their products' capabilities. And though Poly-Carb had a network of dealers, Sondhe still was making 90% of the sales himself.

This is not what Sondhe had in mind when he started the suburban Cleveland company just five years after coming to the United States from India. He wished he could somehow start over.

... So he did. First, he fired all 45 of his employees. Then he cut his 100 dealers loose. Just like that. Talk about cleaning house.

"The company was really suffering," says Sondhe (pronounced *sahn-dee*), now 54. "Everybody just wanted to make money, and they didn't care what they did. It was not a place where you wanted to come. Nobody was happy. It was like self-imprisonment. I thought, 'Gosh, what are we doing?'"

Sondhe tried to zero in on why he started the company in the first place. It was not about making
Continued on page 4

Case breaks its first-ever parts ads
By Jennifer Kolodziejczyk

RACINE, WIS.—In a bid to make over the image of its parts business and overcome a high-priced reputation, J I Case launched its first-ever ad campaign concentrating on parts and service.

The first ad of the campaign, a two-page spread that debuted in February's *Equipment World*, focuses on Case's recent decision to lower prices on certain parts. "If

High Parts Prices Kept You Away, Here's Something to Bring You Back," says the headline.

Three other ads will follow over the next 18 to 24 months. One will tout Case's service and product support. Another will give reasons for choosing OEM parts over will-fit parts. Case hasn't yet decided what the fourth ad will deal with.
Continued on page 8

Con/Agg psychs up for '96 megashow
By Diana Granitto

LAS VEGAS—It was a banner show ... and possibly the end of an era.

The International Concrete and Aggregates Show (Con/Agg), held here in February, boasted a record 373 exhibitors occupying 262,000 square feet. At about

20,000, registration was 2,000 shy of its 1990 peak.

But sharing the limelight with the show's success was the anticipation of Con/Agg's 1996 merger with ConExpo, now officially dubbed "ConExpo-Con/Agg '96." If
Continued on page 28

spotlight

■ **Gerald Randacker is stepping in as president of Hitachi America Inc.** Randacker, formerly Eastern regional manager for Deere & Co.'s industrial division, replaces Nicholas Stahl, who has headed Hitachi since 1991. Stahl moved to Deere, where he will be manager of commercial accounts, a new group catering to large accounts.

■ **It looks like J I Case will be getting a new CEO soon.** Dana Mead is leaving that post to replace Michael Walsh, who is battling cancer, as CEO of parent Tenneco Inc. (see story, p. 9). At press time, no successor for Mead had been named.

■ **U.S. construction equipment exports were down 5% in 1993,** while imports increased 31%. The result was a dramatic drop in the industry's trade surplus from $2.2 million in 1992 to $1.5 million, the smallest favorable balance since 1988. Canada remains the top export market, and China entered the top 10 for the first time.

■ **Don't miss the April 22 early-bird deadline for Construction Marketing '94!** Conference details and registration forms can be found in the insert in this issue.

inside

7 Hitachi stages knockout promo at Con/Agg

12 Desktop publishing is beckoning ... Can you handle it? First in a series

---

For example, let me share a story written about POLY-CARB that appeared in the April 1994 edition of the magazine *Construction Marketing Today*, published by The Aberdeen Group. The article, titled "A Strange Formula for Success: POLY-CARB and its philosophical founder are doing things their way," was written by Terrance Noland.

Sondhe tells the story of one flooring job at a Cleveland food-processing plant [in 1988]. POLY-CARB was contracted not only to supply the product but also to apply it, a job it hired out to a local contractor. At 4:30 pm the day before the job was to begin, the contractor lumbered into POLY-CARB's office.

"I was standing in the lobby, and this gentleman came in with muddy boots and a big cigar in his mouth," Sondhe recalls. "He said, 'I'm here to pick up that gook.' I said, 'Sir, we do not sell gook. We sell only highly respected products. If you don't respect our product, I can't sell it to you.'" The contractor looked Sondhe over and said, "Do you want me to do the job or not?" Sondhe said, "No."

Sondhe called up the plant owner and broke the news that his job wouldn't be complete on time. The owner was livid. The next weekend, Sondhe and his managers went to the plant and laid the floor themselves.

POLY-CARB then picked up the full $50,000 tab. "[The plant owner] was absolutely flabbergasted," Sondhe says. "But, I told him this was not any great gesture. This was simply a lesson we as a company must learn." And what was that lesson? "One of our principles is that what we promise, we must deliver."

Here is what one client had to say about POLY-CARB:

They always conduct themselves in a gentlemanly fashion, and that isn't all that common in our business. It's always a pleasure doing business with them because they're first-class. I think they really try to live by their guidelines.
—Bill Hoye, former president of Century Fence Co.
Waukesha, Wisconsin

The POLY-CARB team members truly did strive to incorporate these guidelines into their everyday lives. Each day always brought some type of challenge, and some of the guidelines were easier to integrate and utilize than others, which required time and acclimation. Such is the process of learning and evolution.

Over the years, POLY-CARB created a clearly stated vision, mission and path, which again neatly dovetails with the universal Law of Change: everything remains in a constant state of motion and change. Therefore, we had to remain in a student mode of learning, which positioned us to continuously make our best better.

> The entire universe is one vast exercise in non-stop motion, which includes us human beings. The only way to stay alive and vibrant is to see change as a gift, an opportunity to grow, to become more than we ever envisioned.

As understood by the POLY-CARB team members, the entire universe is one vast exercise in non-stop motion, which includes us human beings. As soon as we decide to stop moving, we begin taking root emotionally, mentally, and energetically. The last thing we then want to do is move. We become comfortable, then sluggish, and eventually dormant. During that process, we become fearful, afraid that whatever change is introduced will turn our world upside down and that we'll be confused, unanchored, lost, unable to cope, dispossessed, and forgotten. The only way to stay alive and vibrant is to see change as a gift, an opportunity to grow, to become more than we ever envisioned.

This kind of thinking is somewhat elucidated in the missions and vision statements of companies around the world, but the most important key is missing—oneness. Without oneness as the fully galvanized heart and soul of an organization, everything else amounts to just words on paper—nice to look at and consider, but not the compelling force enlivening and inspiring an organization from within and without.

By POLY-CARB learning to consistently remain in student mode—taking full responsibility for our decisions and actions, learning every aspect of the company, living the company's values, always seeking to add the highest value in everything we did, and leaving our egos out of the equation of our endeavors—we approached each day with enthusiasm and the mind-set of becoming a value-adding entity.

This reminds me of an employee at POLY-CARB, Jeremy (not his real name), who was originally hired based on his degree in mechanical engineering. Within the first month of his working with chemicals, we realized that he was highly allergic to some of the chemicals; he broke out in rashes, etc. We couldn't have him working there. It so happened that we had an audit coming up and needed some additional help with the accounting. Jeremy volunteered, discovering he had a natural aptitude with numbers, and asked if he could work in the accounting department. He went on to master the work.

His knowledge of engineering gave him a better understanding of our business, which brought a new dimension to the accounting department, and his interaction with the other team members was much higher. In fact, he elevated the operations of the department. Today, Jeremy is in a senior management position in the accounting department.

When oneness is not lived and embraced wholeheartedly, we then have life as we know it today. We live in a world of competing forces striving to outmaneuver, outcompete, gobble up, diminish, and even destroy the so-called opposition. We're even willing to destroy each other and our planet in the race to see who will be the richest, own the most, control the most, and become king of the mountain. Meanwhile, people suffer, live in abject poverty, starve, and die from others' predaceous, egocentric needs.

POLY-CARB was not that way. Over time, the company became like an incubator, a college of sorts, so that people—unencumbered by boundaries—were able to see who they truly were in this universe. They saw new mountain peaks to discover and explore.

POLY-CARB blessed them, many times helping them achieve their dreams. As you may recall, Sanjiv Sidhu, whom I mentioned earlier, started i2 Technologies, a supply chain management software and services company. He is now a billionaire. Sudarshan Sathe, founder and CEO of New Concepts, a metal-trading company, is now a millionaire. For both of these people, POLY-CARB was their first job straight out of college. Kawshal Shah now has his own successful and fast-growing business in India, supplying the needs of consulting firms in the US. Many POLY-CARB employees have gone on to become

CEOs, CFOs, COOs, and other key positions in business both domestic and international.

Lessons I learnt working with Ratanjit helped me a lot as I started and ran my own company. The innovativeness he deployed in boot-strapping POLY-CARB with no outside capital helped me bootstrap i2 Technologies to be one of the few technology companies to go all the way to a NASDAQ IPO without any venture capital. I learned how to motivate people to excel and rise to levels that they thought were not possible. Ratanjit is dedicated to quality in everything. In business, in thinking about life and spirituality, in the way he interacts.

—Sanjiv Sidhu, from *Mending Souls*
by Khushwant Singh

Adding the highest value is complicated. Until a company has sustainability, it isn't adding the highest value. POLY-CARB was challenged many times on its journey to add the highest value when we brought in sustainability measures.

Regaining people's trust is a long, uphill struggle. There will always be that one little section of people's hearts not fully trusting, always treading cautiously around us. And we'll be wondering how long we'll be able to maintain a constant vigil of integrity within ourselves.

Integrity is not something achieved or obtained external to our being. We can observe others acting with integrity, but until we decide to be integrity itself within our own being, it will remain ephemeral, always just out of reach.

Integrity is not something achieved or obtained external to our being. We can observe others acting with integrity, but until we decide to be integrity itself within our own being, it will remain ephemeral, always just out of reach. It is not something we can grasp, not something we take on like a role in a play, not something to be bartered when expedient. We either have integrity or don't. POLY-CARB learned a lesson in integrity from another contract, one involving parking structures.

One of our waterproofing systems was designed as a waterproofing membrane for high-rise parking structures, where water seeps into decks and begins corroding the rebars. This especially occurs in areas where roads and highways are salted to melt ice and snow.

Some of the salt migrates to the parking decks via car tires. Only a small amount of chloride ions need to be present—less than five hundred parts per million—to activate corrosive cells that corrode the rebars, which impart tensile strength to the structures. The corroded rebars can expand up to seven times their original volume and impart tremendous stress to the concrete surrounding them. When that happens, cracking and de-lamination take place.

It is also known in the industry that when a deck is kept dry, the salt present in the deck remains inactive in its dry state. It is only in the presence of moisture that it releases chloride ions, which are responsible for all the damage.

Based on the unparalleled performance of POLY-CARB's waterproofing membrane system, the nation's leading consulting engineering firms specializing in parking structures started specifying POLY-CARB's products for some of the major projects around the country. The waterproofing system was purchased by contractors who then installed it. During the bidding process, POLY-CARB quoted prices to various contractors who were actively bidding on these large projects.

On one such major project, POLY-CARB quoted prices to one of the nation's leading contractors who specialized in building parking decks and applying the waterproofing membrane system. We had two grades of waterproofing membrane. The lower grade was designed for five to ten years' performance only, and the higher grade was designed for up to twenty years' performance. Most of these types of projects specified only a five-year performance guarantee. This particular project, though, called for a greater-than-ten-year performance guarantee.

We quoted both prices to the owner of this contracting firm, who then made a choice based on the performance guarantee of ten years, which was required for this specific project. The project specification was for a higher-performing waterproofing membrane, which was our more expensive system. When we sent the contractor the invoice, he disputed it, saying that he'd been quoted for the lower-performance product and that that was the only quote he was going to honor and pay.

Contractors are known in the industry to bargain prices down to maximize their profits. In our case, this contractor was expecting me to give him the higher-performing system at the price of the lower-performing system. This was just the way he operated; he was a bargainer.

Taking the owner quite seriously, I checked all of our documentation and correspondence with the team members in charge of the project. In all of our correspondence and documented quotes, it was obvious that we had quoted the prices for the high-performing system, based on the contractor's choice.

A meeting was arranged with the owner of the contracting firm. He, POLY-CARB's marketing manager, and I met for lunch. The contractor brought his attorney and his CFO. I explained, "We have checked all of our paperwork, which corresponds to what we've invoiced you. If I accept the price you're offering, which is for the lower-priced system, I'm also determining that we were not truthful in our agreement with you. That is not acceptable to us. At the same time, we feel that you're an honorable contractor and you will do what is correct."

At that point in my explanation, I said I would give him two choices: (1) he could pay us, but we would only accept the full payment of what we'd invoiced him, or (2) if he felt that he was right, then he should not pay us anything. We were still friends, and I would not have POLY-CARB, a lawyer, or a collection agency calling him to collect any money whatsoever. The case would be completely closed. "Since we're here together now as friends, let's enjoy our lunch," I concluded.

There was a long silence, and then he said, "What do you mean not pay anything?"

"You heard me correctly, because if I accept a smaller amount than we invoiced, I am diminishing POLY-CARB's values and saying that we lied, which is not true."

He replied that he had brought a check for the lower amount. "It's for $200,000. You're willing to forfeit the entire amount?"

I replied that money comes and goes, but once we lose our integrity, we have nothing. So, it was a question of our integrity, not money, I explained. "You are the sole decision maker in this. No one is going to sue you; I won't tell another person. This is strictly between you and me."

From that point on, I refused to talk about the subject. We continued with our lunch. He was still uneasy when we parted. "Look, if you want me to send you the money, I'll send it immediately." I responded that the case was closed and that he should keep the money.

He returned to work and called the head of the consulting engineering firm who had originally specified our waterproofing system on this project. He shared the incident of our luncheon with him and asked him if this guy Ratanjit was for real. He explained that I had refused to take the $200,000 and that I was ready to walk out if I wasn't given the entire amount.

The consulting engineer told the contractor that he'd finally met his match. "Knowing Ratanjit for many years, all I can say is that I have complete trust in him. He's an honorable man. Here is a chance. Why don't you keep the money? I can assure you that Ratanjit is a man of his word, and he won't come after you. The question is not about money at this point, but about whether you can live with yourself because the truth will always haunt you."

In three months, we received full payment. The owner of the firm and I became good friends, and he also became our best reference in that industry.

Looking back, whenever POLY-CARB followed its core values and principles, this entire system and process created a working environment of unlimited creativity and empowerment. Nothing held us back, and if we made mistakes, we learned from them, even if it meant we had to redo work for our customers at our own expense. But our challenge always remained to live our core values and truly bring our vision, mission, path, and operating principles to life. This mind-set became applicable not just to team members' lives at POLY-CARB, but to personal lives and professional work elsewhere.

> Our challenge always remained to live our core values and truly bring our vision, mission, path, and operating principles to life.

I had a dear friend, Dr. Kapur (not her real name), who was the head of the pathology department at a local major medical institution with over four hundred doctors. There was a vacancy on the board. The procedure for joining the board required each prospective board member be nominated and voted on by the four hundred doctors. Usually, the prospective board member would send out his or her CV to the doctors, who then voted accordingly.

Dr. Kapur was a timid and humble woman. Hardly anyone knew her. So, she came to me and explained that she really wanted to be on the board because she knew she could make a difference. The problem was that none of the four hundred doctors really knew her.

She showed me her CV, and I asked just how much she wanted to be on the board. She truly wanted to join it. After reviewing her CV,

I could see that it needed work, and I asked if she would be amenable to working with me to re-shape it. She was all for it.

Over several days, it took me a good deal of digging to find out what her true purpose, mission in life, and operating values that she wasn't willing to contravene were. We also worked on what she in her heart wanted to accomplish personally, professionally, and spiritually. We ended up with a four-page CV. The first page was a statement of her mission and role in life, which was to add the highest value in everything she undertook. On page two, we listed her primary governing values and operating principles. The third page listed her objectives: personal, social, spiritual, and professional. And the last page was a roster of her accomplishments: educational, professional, and personal.

What this process did was bring out who she really was as a person. When she sent her CV out to the four hundred doctors, the response was overwhelmingly positive, and she received the greatest number of yes votes in the institution's history. Additionally, working on her CV gave her the personal direction for her life that she'd been seeking. Since then, she has become well recognized in her field, and the CV has continued to give her direction not only in board meetings, but professionally and in her personal life.

What was interesting about helping Dr. Kapur with her CV was that the four-page document turned out to be a CV for her life, not just for work purposes. The process of re-shaping her CV re-invigorated her sense of self and her life in general—it put her back on track. In essence, she was given a second chance at life, one that didn't entail some big, dramatic event, which is what it sometimes takes to get people to wake up. Dr. Kapur had a second awakening, a chance to re-invent herself—a chance I was soon to have myself.

Chapter 18

A Second Awakening

In late fall of 1986, I got a call from Charlie Snyder, senior vice president of Ciba-Geigy, who was chairing the annual conference for the Epoxy Formulators Association, operated under the Society of the Plastics Industry: The Plastics Industry Trade Association.

Over the years of doing business with Ciba-Geigy, Charlie had been exposed to POLY-CARB's way of thinking and running its business. As a good client of Ciba-Geigy, we'd also had the chance to meet throughout the years for business meetings. His call, though, was for a different reason. He reminded me of the upcoming conference in the latter part of the summer in 1987.

He explained that that year's conference was to be focused on quality and productivity. The reason he was calling me was to ask if I would be amenable to presenting the opening paper for the conference under the title of "The Philosophy of Quality."

I smiled to myself and said to Charlie, "I don't think people are ready for the philosophy of quality yet. I'm sure after I make this presentation, they'll just laugh at me. If they know you've invited me, you'll be in trouble, too."

He laughed and replied, "That's the precise reason for my asking you to do this. I know how you think, and I think it's time for the world to realize from what true quality stems. Your opening paper will set the tone for the conference, and you know it's attended by the who's who in the industry. It'll send a resonating message, which they need to ponder."

I accepted the challenge and asked if I could make the presentation with all the lights off and the overhead slides from my presentation displayed on a giant white screen, with only my voice heard and me not seen. He again laughed and said that if that would cause me to deliver a stronger message, then he'd arrange it.

The conference was held at the Buena Vista Hotel in Orlando, Florida, part of Disney World. Starting at 8:30 am sharp, Charlie announced the first presenter—me, founder and CEO of POLY-CARB, though at POLY-CARB, no one in the company had a title. He explained that everyone in the company was completely guided by the company's vision, mission, path, and operating principles. Charlie announced that the title of my presentation was "The Philosophy of Quality." Because this was a technically oriented conference, there was a lot of murmuring coming from the audience members, who wondered why they were going to be subjected to philosophy and what it had to do with quality. Quality is considered measurable, deliverable, and quantifiable. Philosophy, they thought, was for scholars, not for scientists and technologists.

With about three hundred people in the audience, the lights dimmed until they were completely off, and I then stepped out of the wings up to the lectern. My slide presentation began—the only thing the audience could see. A half hour later, I ended my presentation, and the lights came on in the auditorium. An eerie, dead silence enveloped the hall. Then a few sporadic claps were heard. No questions came from the audience. My prediction that the presentation would not be well received had come true.

The next presentation was by a senior manager from DuPont. His opening remark was "Enough with the philosophy. Let's get into the nitty-gritty of real quality and productivity."

I saw Charlie and told him, "See? I told you it would be beyond everyone's comprehension."

He answered by saying, "Wait and see as the day goes on. Your thought process is going to haunt them."

As the day passed, a lot of people stopped me with a variety of comments and observations. Some said that the thought process wasn't practical. Others said that it was a well-thought-out presentation, but that they'd still had difficulty comprehending it. Still others were in complete agreement and said that it was about time this thought process was brought into the mainstream.

By that evening, as I was having dinner with a friend at the hotel, people were coming up to me in droves, sharing their thoughts and compliments. Some were completely agitated, as if I'd shaken them to their core. It was almost like being a celebrity.

The next morning, around ten o'clock, as I was checking out of the hotel to leave for the airport, a gentleman came running up to me and said, "Congratulations! Your paper won best paper of the conference!" I was in shock. I knew I'd produced quite a reaction from people, but it had never occurred to me that the expert conference committee would even consider my presentation for this distinction. If I'd gone to the main conference room, as suggested by this gentleman who'd come to fetch me, I would have missed my flight, so I had to unfortunately forego their award ceremony.

As time passed, I received many invitations from companies and associations to present the same paper. The most notable was an invitation from The DOW Chemical Company at their Freeport facility in Texas. They'd invited three hundred senior managers from around the world to listen to my presentation. I also gave the same presentation to the American Association of State Highway Transportation Officials (AASHTO).

Every time I presented "The Philosophy of Quality," I could sense an amazing hunger in people for this thought process. Many people thanked me deeply for changing their lives.

Mirroring the shift that was occurring for people when I gave this presentation, I had a different sort of wake-up call, one that helped me see more clearly the trajectory of my life.

In 1991, I had heart bypass surgery, as my main artery was blocked. Before this condition was actually verified, I had an inner vision that my arteries were blocked.

I was hesitant to tell Dolly, because there weren't any symptoms, but to remove any doubt, I went ahead and took out a personal $5 million life insurance policy. This necessitated my going through a battery of medical tests. I was actually surprised when the doctors found nothing. But, I knew there was something going on. To prove this, I'd do crazy physical tests (e.g., I carried a sixty-five-pound bucket up the steps for three stories during our product installation on a parking-deck project in order to see what would happen with my heart, but I had no reaction).

I had such a clear vision of my clogged artery that I finally had to tell Dolly, and she immediately called our doctor. A good friend of ours, Dr. Beg, a well-known heart surgeon who operated on doctors, had me come to the hospital for tests. They put me through a battery of routine tests, such as a stress test, an EKG, etc. After all their monitoring, they couldn't find anything. As I was getting dressed the next day, I told Dolly that all these doctors didn't know what they were talking about. I knew there was something wrong.

When Dolly shared my frustration with the doctors, they immediately scheduled an angiogram. They discovered that my main artery was 90 percent blocked. The doctor explained that even though I had a 90 percent blockage, I had larger-than-normal arteries. Even though I had only 10 percent of the artery open, it was adequate enough for good blood flow, and that's why the blockage hadn't been detected by normal tests. I could still function normally. The fact was, though, this was still a dangerous condition. So, they did heart bypass surgery.

Believe it or not, after the surgery, I didn't feel any different from how I'd felt before the operation. However, the experience did give me a new, realistic outlook on life. If I continued focusing on business success, then life would soon pass me by. I needed to become more involved with making a difference than making products.

Because of my inner knowing and vision of the issue with my heart, I knew that my life had been prolonged for a reason: to continue serving the purpose of spreading the paradigm of oneness and adding the highest value to all of life unconditionally.

This event helped me begin to see life with a fresh perspective. I now saw everything as an illusion and realized that much of the world was focused on simply achieving a means to an end and satisfying egocentric agendas. My personal journey was about the journey of oneness and knowing who I truly was. Before this health issue, I had been caught up in the all-consuming box of business, being a CEO, and running a company. But I wasn't free of them, and therefore, I was enslaved and trapped.

The heart bypass surgery helped me break through all these restraints, connections, and roles and set me free. It became obvious to me that my real purpose in life was much broader than just being tied down to POLY-CARB. The experience also gave me a sense of urgency because life had now shrunk to a limited time frame. It made me ask myself, *If I only have so much time left, what should I be doing?* Running the company was not as critical as spreading the message of oneness. But, the situation wasn't that simple, as I still needed to run the company, which required an incredible amount of my time and energy.

Two weeks after the surgery, I was back in the office. The seed for the quest to do more had been planted and was quickly growing within me. But, I wasn't quite sure how to make the transition and transformation. Fortunately, the POLY-CARB team was well trained and completely ready to take charge of all its activities.

I began to telescope my role down in the company to that of an adviser and coach. And because I was now coming into full compliance with who I truly was and my purpose in life, the transition was happening rather effortlessly.

My mission was reaffirmed when, in 1993, I was at the World of Concrete Conference in Las Vegas and a young man came to our booth and asked to speak with me. He said, "Ratanjit, I don't know if you remember me or not, but I was at the Orlando conference when you presented your paper on 'The Philosophy of Quality,' which was rightly awarded best paper of the conference. I want you to know that there has been nothing that has made such an impact on my life as your paper has. I came here not to compliment or praise you or tell you how much it meant to me, but I feel I need to tell you that this is your real mission and purpose in life—to share this with the world. You can make a difference to millions of people. This is your calling, not manufacturing products or running a business."

"You can make a difference to millions of people. This is your calling, not manufacturing products or running a business."

I thanked the young man. He reaffirmed my inner quest to make a difference since my awakening following the heart surgery. I was definitely in transition and had to think of delegating more and more of my responsibilities in the company to others. The surgery confirmed why I was having the heart issue in the first place. It was clear that I needed to re-order my life and fully take on this mission of spreading the message of oneness. I began taking on more speaking engagements, presenting to business associations, community leaders, and students.

Ray Somich and I, 2000

Then, in 1995, the Cleveland Sikh community approached me and asked if I would be willing to sponsor a weekly radio program that would broadcast Sikh prayers for our community. I said I would, but that we needed to find out if a radio station had time and what their charges would be. They researched stations and found a small AM station on the east side of Cleveland, 1313 AM, WELW, privately owned by Ray C. Somich. He described the radio station as family-oriented and said that he himself was a religious person.

He had no objection to broadcasting our religious prayers, but he wanted to know more about the Sikh religion before airing a show. He was told that I could answer any of his questions. Therefore, a luncheon was set up for us to meet. In the first fifteen minutes, we realized that his radio station's frequency wouldn't reach all the areas where our community members lived. With that idea off the table, we decided that since we were already there, we would have lunch and get to know each other.

This was the first time Ray had ever met and talked with a turbaned Sikh. He was very curious. As a professional radio interviewer who had interviewed hundreds of authors, leaders and well-known people, he was not shy about asking questions. The more we talked, the more he became engrossed. Before we knew it, we'd been there for two and a half hours. He said, "I can listen to you for hours. I have an idea: let's do a talk show."

Not realizing he was serious, I took his remark as a compliment and replied, "Sure." We thanked each other and parted company.

A month later, I received a call from Ray. "We're scheduled to be on the air July eighth at nine a.m."

I said, "Hadn't we decided that your station didn't have enough reach?"

"No, no. It's about our talk show, which you and I agreed to do."

I was in shock, as I had no prior experience with doing radio shows. I didn't want to be subjected to crazed, live telephone callers. He explained that it wasn't like that at all; it was a family station, and we'd talk just as we'd done at lunch, with no one else involved. We just needed to be ourselves and try it, he said. If we didn't feel comfortable after a few recordings, we'd stop.

I said I'd do it, but with one provision: any day I felt I needed to stop, we'd stop without any hard feelings. He agreed.

We started with just a half-hour show and soon realized we needed to expand it to a full hour in order to really cover our topics. For four months, we aired the show live on Saturday mornings. One day, it occurred to me that I was going on the air and answering questions, but was not really qualified, as I didn't have a PhD in psychology. Most of Ray's questions were not technically oriented around polymers or about business, but were focused on life. I never did any preparation and usually had no idea what we were going to talk about; I just jumped in cold. Whatever Ray brought up was what we'd discuss.

Though I was thoroughly enjoying these broadcasts with Ray, I decided that this had been a nice little experience and that I should quit while I was ahead.

One Saturday, I was of a clear mind to tell Ray that this would be our last program. As life would have it, it so happened that Ray didn't show up until two minutes before we were to go on the air. We went straight into the broadcast, live, so, I had no chance to tell him of my decision. At the end of the program, as I was getting ready to tell Ray, the phone rang. It was a lady who wanted to talk to me. Ray gave me the phone, and the lady, after introducing herself, explained that her doctors had given her only four more months left to live, maximum. She was dying.

I was stunned and said, "Is there anything I can do?"

She replied, "I want to know if you'll grant this dying lady her last wish."

I was further perplexed and said, "It is only you and your God who can fulfill this wish, but I'd be very glad to help. What is it I can do for you?"

"Promise me that you'll not take this radio program off the air."

I was stunned and couldn't utter a word. She continued, "Let me explain why I'm requesting this of you. I was diagnosed six months ago, out of the blue, with this nasty condition, and the doctor only gave me six months to live. I'm only fifty years of age. I've been a very good human being. I've prayed, I've helped poor people, I've volunteered.

"When the doctor gave me this news, I became very bitter, doubting if there was a God or any justice. I knew several people who were obnoxious and lived indulgent lives and yet were healthy and enjoying life. At any rate, one Saturday morning, my son was coming to visit, and he happened to switch on your show that morning. As he arrived here, he instead turned around and went to your radio station to see about getting a tape of that day's recording. He brought the tape home to me and played it. I not only listened to that program over and over, but now I don't ever miss your program. I look forward to it every Saturday.

"Let me tell you what it's done to me. Not only am I ready to die, but I'm utterly grateful for life. I'm living life to its fullest every moment that I have. This is all because of your radio program. Do I have your promise that you'll not take this program off the air?"

I was speechless when I left the studio that day. I went straight home to my study, where I kept copies of every program that we'd aired. For the first time ever, I listened to a number of them. As I listened to them, I was shocked. That wasn't really me I was hearing. The voice was mine, but the words were not coming from me. I learned just as much from those shows as the lady who had called. I suddenly recalled the gentleman who'd visited me at the World of Concrete show and told me my real mission in life was to share this wisdom with the world. It dawned on me that I was somehow a conduit for this divine wisdom that had chosen to come through me. I was in awe of what was happening in my life.

To this day, our radio program is still airing with Ray as my co-host. The show was initially titled *Visions* and is now called *Stress-Free Living.* The amazing thing is that the show has given us a remarkable window from which to look at life from many perspectives and different avenues of entry, ranging from leadership to business, relationships, stress, anger, religion and spirituality, and many other aspects of life and living.

> Even in my business meetings with POLY-CARB customers, I found that customers were more interested in talking about real-life situations and philosophy than products and performance.

Life for me at that time took a completely different route. Even in my business meetings with POLY-CARB customers, I found that customers were more interested in talking about real-life situations and philosophy than products and performance.

Quality

Service

Knowledge

Leadership

is

an earned privilege.
never assigned.
an ego for most.
a mission for few.
a title for too many.
not a technique.
driven by knowledge.
practiced by example.
nurtured by compassion.
pioneered by vision.
founded on trust.
empowered by respect.
governed by character.
unpretentious.
uncompromising.
inner strength.
Leadership is a way of life.

In the late 1990s, I became less involved in POLY-CARB's day-to-day business and more focused on expressing thoughts integrated with this universal wisdom. Even our company's definitions of service, quality, leadership, and knowledge were re-defined through this philosophy, so we created posters under the umbrella of a newly created entity called HELP (Highest Entrepreneurial Leadership Program).

At the time, I realized that the thought process that had brought POLY-CARB from bankruptcy to success was one that needed to be taught and coached to others, both students and businesspeople. But I couldn't run this new company in addition to POLY-CARB, so I decided to hire someone to lead HELP. This decision provides a touching example of what can happen to someone who is already inculcated in the old business paradigm when he or she is introduced to this new paradigm.

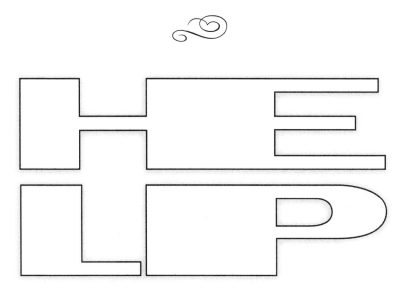

Highest Entrepreneurial Leadership Program

I decided to hire a CEO for HELP, and I found someone during the interview process who was highly qualified and impressive. She was an electrical engineering graduate from MIT, had a PhD in psychology from Princeton, and an MBA from Harvard. Self-assured and confident, she was the epitome of a professional and well-educated American.

Seeking to make sure she understood the oneness paradigm upon which my entire training was based, she asked a number of penetrating questions. Our conversation was exceptionally deep, reflecting her quick comprehension and far-reaching intelligence. The interview went well beyond an hour.

Then, there was complete silence, and she suddenly burst into tears. I thought I'd said something that had offended or hurt her, and I apologized.

After composing herself, she said, "You have no idea what you've done."

I apologized again, deeply concerned that I'd somehow caused this reaction.

She explained, "It's not something you've done; it's what you've made me see so clearly about the oneness paradigm you've described and its all-encompassing wisdom and consequences. It leaves no doubt in my mind that you're absolutely right. But what that's done is destroy every pillar upon which I've built my entire life."

I was amazed that anyone could comprehend this concept so quickly. "What made you realize this?"

"Absolutely everything you've said is true," she answered, "but now I don't know what to do and where to go from here. You've stripped me of everything I've worked for and all my accomplishments."

I responded by saying, "Actually, you have gained the real wealth. You just don't know how to evaluate that new wealth using your old measurements. If you truly understand the wisdom of this oneness paradigm, then the power of this new wisdom will position you to utilize your ultimate potential, which otherwise is not possible.

"I must caution you, though, that old habits die hard. In spite of your realization concerning oneness, you may very easily return to your old crutches because the world around you still validates those. Your glory is still attached to them, and your five senses and ego are still in control of you."

She thought for a moment and then replied, "What you have given me is a sense of my true purpose in life. I'll no longer need these worldly pillars anymore to support me. This is going to make a tremendous difference in my life no matter where I go and what I do. It doesn't really matter if I get this job or not, because I'm walking out of here with newfound clarity, which is going to help me rebuild my life so that it has much greater meaning and depth. And I'm very grateful to you for this. But I feel that this thought process is going to take some time to take root in me and become integrated. So I must tell you that at this moment, I may not be the person you're looking for to lead this incentive."

With that, we concluded the interview, and she left with a wonderful look of conviction and peace on her face.

This interview made me realize that the bigger One was entrusting me with running HELP because it couldn't be run as effectively by anyone else. I also saw that POLY-CARB could be run by a professional manager. The fact was, though, that I had obligations to POLY-CARB and its team members, as I was in the thick of running it and simply couldn't walk away from it. Yet, at the same time, I realized that if this information was presented correctly, it would be incredibly powerful and life-changing for people. I needed to find the right vehicle for presenting this paradigm, and it was going to take some thinking to figure it out.

> Whenever I had to make such decisions, meditation was tremendously helpful.

Whenever I had to make such decisions, meditation was tremendously helpful. Early in the morning, I would sometimes meditate for hours, which often gave me clarity and direction. On one such morning, as I finished my meditation, a thought process started coming through me, and I wanted to make sure I captured it. I immediately went to my study and began writing. I soon saw that the message coming through me like a quick flip-chart sequence of thoughts was very powerful. It started with a question: "What will make us successful?"

SECRET
OF
SUCCESS

Within a week, I had written an entire book, which I titled *Secret of Success*. I printed two thousand copies and was able to put about six hundred of them on display at a local bookstore in Cleveland. They started selling!

I also personalized copies and sent them to my key customers and suppliers. I received an overwhelming response, as the thought process presented was simple, yet powerful. Many have kept the book right on their desk so that visitors can read the book and embrace the thought process. They often read the book when they're having a difficult day, as it not only calms them down, but gives them direction.

I got a copy of *Crain's Cleveland Business*, a weekly publication that lists the names and addresses of the top one hundred CEOs in the region. I sent a personalized copy of my book to each of the CEOs. I was amazed to receive only two acknowledgments, which I took to mean that either the books never reached them or the thought process was too much of a threat to their egos. All the more reason for me to continue on this path, as the oneness paradigm was not available to or making a positive impression with our top leaders, where it is most required. Any leadership not imbedded in oneness is not only unsustainable, but can easily become a dangerous threat to society, as it is only driven by "What's in it for me?" thinking.

In 1999 and 2000, I put professional management in place at POLY-CARB, which gave me more time to devote my energies and time to HELP and public speaking.

Over the next couple of years, I continued to give presentations and corporate training sessions on leadership. Then, in 2002, the president of EXIM Club was in the US doing business. He was looking for someone as a conference keynote speaker. He was told about me, and I met  with him. He was quite touched and insisted I come to India at some point to deliver the message of true leadership, the purpose of life, and the oneness paradigm to Indian audiences comprised of CEOs and business owners.

In 2003, I traveled to Vadodara in the Indian state of Gujarat to be the keynote speaker for a business conference. Business–wise, Gujarat is the most progressive state in India. The conference was held under the aegis of EXIM Club, the Association of Exporters and Importers. This association was formed to promote the exporting business by Indian companies. The Club has over two thousand members.

I was also scheduled on that trip to present at various chambers of commerce in Bombay, Delhi, and Chandigarh under the umbrella of the World Trade Center of Cleveland. This highly scheduled, two-week trip included not only chambers of commerce, but universities, investment banks, and venues for the general public.

A local businessman and good friend of mine, Prakash Keswani, intrigued by the content of my presentation, approached me about an emerging television station he'd heard about, Aastha TV. *Aastha* means "faith." Most of the programs were philosophical, religious, or spiritual. Prakash arranged a recording session with Aastha on the day I was to leave India for the States. When I got to Aastha's studios, located in Andheri at that time, a suburb of Mumbai, I was taken into the makeup room, and for the first time in my life, I was made to wear makeup. They put me in front of the camera and said, "Go."

I recorded a half-hour program. The wanted me to record some more programs and suggested I change my suit, but I hadn't brought a change of clothes to the station. They sent someone to fetch a change of clothes for me at my brother-in-law's home, where I was staying. I ended up recording three shows that day.

That night, my flight was to leave at 2:00 a.m. At 10:00 p.m., I received a call from Mrs. Mehta, the wife of the owner and chairman of Aastha TV. She said she'd just finished listening to the programs I'd recorded and that she needed to come see me, as she'd not heard programs of that caliber before.

Both Mr. and Mrs. Mehta came to see me that evening. She couldn't say enough about the programs and how they'd touched her and brought tears to her eyes. She wanted to know if I could possibly record programs in the US and send copies to Aastha TV. I replied that I'd look into it, amazed at the direction my life was going.

When I returned to Cleveland, I called Ray Somich's son, Ray Jr., whom I had brought in to work for HELP, now known as Discoverhelp, Inc. I told him we were going to record television programs. He knew nothing about television, and I told him to go research it and get cameras and the other necessary equipment. I asked my daughter, Nisha, a professional photographer in New York City, to help us with determining what we'd need. Before we knew it, we were recording television programs in the offices at POLY-CARB.

Each of the programs I recorded was like a discourse where I'd have a particular subject I'd cover. The shows were unprepared, unscripted, and unrehearsed. I'd record several programs at a time on weekends. I would then send these programs via tapes to Prakash in Bombay, who would then deliver the tapes to Aastha TV. At that time, Aastha hadn't gone international and was only broadcasting in India.

I wasn't sure of the feedback I'd receive and always wondered if these programs were making a difference in people's lives. I didn't find out until 2005.

We started the television program in 2003, and I visited India in 2005, when Prakash wanted me to see a newly developed shopping center. As a civil engineer himself, he was proud of the mall. We stopped by to take a stroll through it. The first shop we entered was a high-fashion ladies' clothing store. As I looked around, a well-dressed, sophisticated Indian woman in her mid-forties came up to me, bent over, and touched my feet with her hands. In the Indian culture, this is a high gesture of respect. She said, "Sir, I watch your program on Aastha TV without fail. I'm a big fan of yours. For the first time, you have made me understand the difference between spirituality and religion, and also the real purpose of life."

She then invited her teenage daughter to also touch my feet. I was totally unprepared for this. Embarrassed by her unwanted and unsolicited attention, I made a quick exit, asking Prakash to get me out of there. Talking with Prakash later, I voiced that people were going to make a guru of me, and that was the last thing I wanted. I decided to stop the program immediately, as the program was about the message, not me.

Prakash replied, "Then focus on the message, not yourself. This has nothing to do with you. Let the people deal with your program in whatever way they choose. It is, after all, respect for the wisdom coming through you, not you yourself."

I realized that he was right and that I must go on without getting myself in the way of the wisdom that was coming through me. It wasn't mine. We often get trapped between the ego feeding off of public attention and the truly inspiring truth coming through us or any other source. We even begin to worship the source rather than focusing on the wisdom itself.

That reminds me of another incident, when I spoke to 250 senior managers from a leading investment bank in Mumbai, India. This was the second time I'd been invited to speak to them. I decided to go even deeper into the oneness paradigm and how to increase our efficiency in everything we do. It was presented in simple, accessible language. At the end of the presentation, people gathered around me to continue with their questions.

One executive in his mid-forties told me, "Sir, I have a personal question for you. Your lecture was very enlightening, and it was clear to me that you have a very thorough understanding of the Bible. In fact, I have never heard the Bible explained so fundamentally. Obviously, your study of the Bible is very thorough, and thus your knowledge comes from the Bible. But then, sir, why did you not acknowledge that fact and offer credit to the Bible?"

Another gentleman standing right next to him immediately responded before I had a chance to say anything. "No, no. Sir's lecture was based on the five-thousand-year-old Hindu Upanishads and not the Bible. But I am really disappointed that you, sir, did not even mention anything about the Upanishads."

Before I could say a word, a Sikh gentleman jumped in and said, "You both are wrong. Just look at him; he is wearing a turban. Obviously, he is a Sikh, and I know what he is talking about. It is all in our Sri Guru Granth Sahib, and he should be proud to acknowledge that all his knowledge comes from our Guru Granth Sahib. Sir, please tell me if I am wrong."

I smiled and responded, "Gentlemen, before you kill me, let me share a real-life incident with you that happened just a few days ago. Hopefully, it may address some of the issues you wise people have raised."

All three of them stepped forward, curious and anxious to hear what I was going to say. "On this trip, I met one of my old college classmates, who is a very successful businessman in Mumbai. He invited me and my family for dinner at his beautiful penthouse in the posh area of Khar. It so happened that his daughter and her thirteen-month-old baby were visiting him that night. The little baby was fascinated with me and did not hesitate to play in my arms. There was a full moon that night, and I was trying to draw her attention to the moon by pointing a finger at it. But every time I pointed to the moon with my finger, she would catch hold of my finger instead of looking at the moon."

The three gentlemen gave me looks as though asking how my story was possibly addressing their concerns. Then I asked, "Now, my friends, aren't you doing the same thing that little girl did? All the various scriptures (equal to my finger) are pointing you toward a path (the moon, so to speak), but you all simply want to hold on to my finger (your religious scriptures). Furthermore, you want to own it, worship it, and fight over it as to who has a superior finger (religion), but you are not at all persuaded to go where the religious scriptures (fingers) are asking you to go. And now you are upset that I, too, am not holding on to the finger (acknowledging the scriptures).

> **The real mission is to go to the moon or, in other words, practice spirituality and not hold on to the finger (the scriptures). Spirituality is basically an absence of duality.)**

"My friends, the real mission is to go to the moon or, in other words, practice spirituality and not hold on to the finger (the scriptures). Spirituality is basically an absence of duality. These scriptures are merely instruments to guide us on our journey to reach the moon—that is, reach nirvana through losing our egos and practicing oneness."

I continued, "By the way, the same thing holds true for your avatars or gurus or your revered gods in human form. They were here to show us a path. It is their teachings, their messages we need to follow. But what we do, unfortunately, is worship them or fight over them, and we never try to fully comprehend and follow the path they have shown us. Please think: Would you ever be cured of a disease if you simply worshipped your doctor, but never took the medicine your doctor prescribed for you?"

The most amazing part of this incident was the ending. One of the listeners jumped forward and fell on my feet. So you see, the worshipping of the messenger continues regardless of all the sincere efforts of the messenger to prevent it.

As time went by, I began running into people who had heard me on the radio, seen me on television, or read my book *Secret of Success*. Even though I was gaining an audience and notoriety, I knew that I must continue focusing on delivering the message coming through me, as I was benefitting from the message as much as my listeners were.

> **"The world is screaming for a book like this!"**
> —Richard Mayes

Throughout 2005, I recorded programs for Aashta TV. Usually, before each recording, I would have a cup of tea and empty my mind of any worldly thoughts so that I could allow this universal wisdom to come through me.

One day, Ray Jr., who had been busy making adjustments before we started, announced that we were going to be behind schedule, so, with a cup of tea in hand, I asked him to go ahead and begin recording.

I said, "To remove all our stress and frustration, all we need is a cup of tea, and with the right recipe of tea, all our stress and frustration will simply go away. The recipe of that right tea is hidden in each letter of the word *tea*. The first letter, *t*, stands for 'truth,' the real truth and not the pseudo-truths we have been mistaking as real truths, and hence the source of all our frustrations and stresses. The second letter, *e*, stands for our erroneous 'expectations,' and when these expectations do not come through, we get frustrated and stressed. We literary mortgage our life to these unrealistic, wishful, and self-centered expectations. The third letter, *a*, of the word *tea* stands for 'acceptance.' The secret to living stress free is to accept life as it unfolds and then take advantage of the new opportunities presented in that moment by living in the present."

The entire half-hour show was based on understanding the wisdom in each letter and then how to use this wisdom in real-life situations. It was a powerful show, and we received lots of e-mails and comments from our viewers. This show also gave me the concept for the book *TEA: The Recipe for Stress-Free Living.* Ray Jr. kept saying that I needed to write a book on this idea. I made several attempts over the next couple months to write something, but it wasn't coming together. Although the core concepts were there, nothing rang as engaging and empowering.

Then, one day, I was sitting in my study once again, and a thought process came bubbling up through me. I began writing. It only took me a week to write the entire book. The stories came flying through me as though someone were dictating. It was an amazing experience of being in the flow that so many people have talked about. Numerous aha moments occurred, bringing tears to my eyes. It was an incredible week and literal proof of the oneness paradigm in action.

"I will return to TEA periodically to remind me of what is important. THANK YOU!"
—Paul Malchesky, DEng

Ray Jr. was tremendously instrumental in making the book a reality. He handled all the aspects of publishing, finding a printer and cover designer, and formatting the book's interior. Many times, he worked well into the night. His father, Ray Sr., helped me for several weeks with polishing and finishing the book in its current version. He also wrote a poem at my request, which I used as the acknowledgment for the book.

TEA has sold thousands of copies around the world, and thousands have been given away as gifts at conferences and various gatherings. The role of the book is to spread the message of oneness. In 2009, the largest publishing company in India, Rupa & Company, published it with a newly designed cover. Rupa published *The Secret of Our Ultimate Success* at the same time in paperback, also with a new cover design.

> Your book couldn't have come at a better time for me.
> I consumed it … perhaps too hungrily the first time.
> Now I want to go back to it, slowly, and from time to time,
> and drink of your *TEA*.
>
> —Sherrod Brown
> US Senator

> In a very simple dialogue, *TEA* provides a life-changing recipe
> that frees us from the pains associated with worldly living
> and gives us the power to understand our purpose in this world!
>
> —Dr. R. Chowdhury
> Kent State University

In 2006, I received a call from a *Times of India* journalist, Khushwant Singh, who was writing a book on successful Sikhs around the world, focusing mainly on the U.S and UK. He was looking for unusual success stories. The following is from his book, *Sikhs Unlimited*.

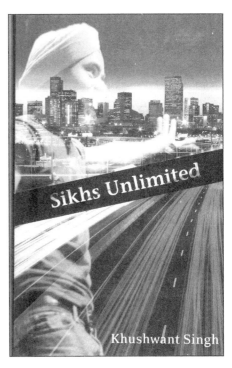

Written primarily to celebrate the huge success of the Sikh diaspora in these two countries [the US and UK], the book also intends to inspire Indian youth by presenting them with unique roles models from different fields.

And lastly, the book celebrates "western" Sikhs as having a mainstream identity.

Emigrating to the west from the beginning of the twentieth century, the enterprising Sikhs have carved out an exclusive place for themselves in the world, not only as a unique cultural identity, but also through their eminence in various spheres. *Sikhs Unlimited* showcases the inimitable success of Sikhs in the UK and the US; and there could be no better time for this commemorative book, when the Sikh diaspora is set to complete a century of its existence in the west.

Through sheer hard work and sharp vision, Sikhs have been able to excel in a foreign and mostly hostile cultural environment.

Khushwant, in his interview with me, brought up the subject of my expanding notoriety and how I was beginning to be perceived by the public.

> And as I sipped my coffee and Ratanjit his tea, I asked him the question that had bothered me ever since we met. "You have a publishing house under the name Discoverhelp Publishing and it happens to be the same publishing house that has published your book *TEA and Other Realignment Tools*. Raymond II is your manager and Raymond I hosts "Visions." Aren't you just a product who is being marketed with huge financial backing? It seems your team is constantly engaged in branding you as some sort of a guru. There appears to be a lot of "I" in the whole affair; the very word that you propagate should be discarded."

"I'm not a marketing person; I am a polymer chem-ist. People who understand marketing have come into my life, and I trust them that they are trying to help me share this thought process and add value to others. They are marketing this entity Ratanjit that is not me. Ratanjit is not me, but simply a vehicle to convey the message. For example, *Guru Granth Sahib* [the Sikh spiritual scriptures handwritten by the founding gurus] is a vehicle to convey the message, though we have started worshipping it. Marketing is my door, similar to one that is required to enter a building. How do you enter otherwise?

"With regard to your story of this 'Ratanjit,' please keep in mind that this story is not at all about him, but what comes through him when he is absent. Otherwise, it will remain just another story about a guy who made money and wore a turban."

Because of the interview process, I began to realize more and more what my true mission was. As a polymer scientist, I was trained to un-derstand the gelling process of polymers, but little did I know that to understand the true gelling process, I needed to understand and apply the oneness process in every facet of my life.

Keeping this in mind, I put more and more time into Discoverhelp activities via television, radio, books, speaking engagements, and presentations. That meant I was becoming less and less involved with POLY-CARB. In my mind, I'd made the decision that I needed to create an exit strategy to minimize my responsibilities with POLY-CARB.

There were two possibilities: (1) the company became self-man-aged, but in order for the value system of the company to be sustained, I remained an anchor; or (2) I took the wisdom I was being gifted and shared it with the world to make many POLY-CARBs come alive. In my heart, it was clear which direction I should go.

I remembered a quote from the book *TEA*, found on page 95: "All of our worldly successes are only given to us in order to create a platform for us to add higher value to society."

I had to ask, "Am I adding the highest value to the bigger One by staying at POLY-CARB, as it is consuming an incredible amount of my time and energy, or should I move on by selling POLY-CARB and using the success as a platform to add higher value to the bigger One?" This debate reminded me that nothing is ever owned. In truth, I had never owned POLY-CARB. It was simply a resource with which to create a platform to add higher value.

Obviously, the answer was to let go of POLY-CARB and go out into the world, make many POLY-CARBs come alive, orient as many people as possible to this thought process, eliminate their stress, and make a difference in people's lives.

I had faith in the people running POLY-CARB, and I wanted to give them a stable platform upon which they could flourish and continue growing.

I brought in a professional manager who had experience with Fortune 500 companies to handle the day-to-day duties of running the business. I decided the company needed to be positioned for sale, and I needed to get on with my mission of the bigger message and pass on the running of POLY-CARB. Some of our older members began to move on to start their own companies, so the company began to change.

The company continued to expand, and we opened a large facility on twenty-six acres in the town of Roberta, near Macon, Georgia. We started manufacturing some of our own raw materials under GNS Technologies, a division of GNS Enterprises, two separate companies initiated by POLY-CARB.

Toward the end of 2006, Dolly came into my office one day, a little frustrated with me. She complained that I needed to pay more attention to the chemical business rather than becoming more and more engrossed with Discoverhelp activities. We sat in my office and talked. I said, "We are growing so fast, and we're extremely successful and highly profitable. Why don't the DOW Chemical companies of the world acquire us? We have unlimited growth potential, and our business is almost unaffected by economic ups and downs."

Dolly asked, "Why did DOW come to your mind of all the companies?"

My response was that from what I had seen in my visits and in reading about the company, I had developed a high degree of respect and admiration for them. Therefore, I thought the POLY-CARB team members would have fertile ground to practice their values and operating principles, helping them to continue their growth, working for DOW.

As if the universe were listening to me, exactly one month later, we got a call from DOW's senior management, saying they wanted to meet with me. At the meeting, they disclosed that in their research, they had determined that POLY-CARB fell right into their sphere of growth plans. They wanted to incorporate a business that added high value and had an unblemished, high-quality name.

We explained that we weren't really for sale, but if they met certain critical conditions for us, both financially and philosophically and without subjecting us to all their evaluations, etc., we would proceed forward. We came to an agreement concerning price before they did their due diligence. In October of 2007, POLY-CARB was acquired by DOW, the world's second-largest chemical company. Although they asked me to serve for five years, my condition was to not continue with POLY-CARB. I stayed for a year and then concluded my journey with POLY-CARB.

That October, I sent out the following e-mail to friends and business associates, informing them of the sale of POLY-CARB to DOW Epoxy Systems:

We have some good news to share. As you all know, Dolly and I have two daughters, Nisha and POLY-CARB. You will be glad to know that our second daughter, POLY-CARB Inc., has been engaged and is getting married to DOW Chemical Co. Yes, you heard it right. POLY-CARB, the company that Dolly and I founded 34 years ago, will now belong to DOW. DOW has also purchased our second company, GNS Technologies, located in Roberta, GA.

GNS Technologies specializes in providing high-performance products and customized systems to thermoset polymer markets with a focus on cross-linking polymers, such as epoxies, polyurethanes, polyureas, etc., used for civil engineering, industrial maintenance, and steel-structure coating applications.

DOW is planning to expand the POLY-CARB brand and has offered me a job ... yes. After forty years of my playing around, I landed a real job. I had always assured Dolly that one day I would have a real job.

We must confess that this would have never happened without your support and good wishes. Dolly, Nisha, and I are extremely grateful for your precious and continuous friendship.

With warmest regards,

Ratanjit and Dolly Sondhe

Dow Chemical had this to say about the acquisition of POLY-CARB and our other two companies, GNS Technology and GNS Enterprises, as well as UPPCAG, a business located in Germany:

"We are pleased to complete the acquisitions and add such high-performing businesses to our Epoxy Systems portfolio," said Pepe Carnevale, Global Business Director for DOW Epoxy Systems. "All three companies are leading players in their respective markets and their vast experience in systems fits well with our rich technology. Bringing those two elements together will enable us to deliver more value to customers, including enhancements to products and services and the development of unique material solutions.

"We are pleased to welcome UPPC, GNS, and POLY-CARB employees onto the DOW Epoxy Systems team and look forward to the success we will achieve together," said Carnevale. "Our immediate goal is to ensure continued excellence in customer service and to begin accelerating product development and other growth activities."

Dolly, me and Nisha, 2008

So now it was official. For thirty-four years, I had been the CEO of POLY-CARB, instituting an entirely new business paradigm that had brought POLY-CARB onto Dow's radar screen. I wondered if DOW realized or would ever realize that POLY-CARB's market position, profitability, quality image, and technology and product line, which had initially attracted DOW, were merely consequences of implementing and practicing our values and operating principles, guided by POLY-CARB's vision and mission.

It was almost inevitable that sooner or later, DOW would bring POLY-CARB under its standard corporate practices, and the values and operating principles that had brought POLY-CARB to its distinct level of uniqueness and glory would be lost in the shuffle. There was a remote possibility that POLY-CARB's values and operating principles might draw some attention from DOW's senior management and, in some form or another, get subsumed into the bigger umbrella of DOW.

Fundamentally, I have always believed that whenever and wherever human beings dig deeply into their souls, they will find similar, if not the same, values and operating principles. Oneness is omnipresent and inescapable. Sooner or later, we all will land there if we are not hopelessly drowning in our insecurities, fears, greed, and egos.

What concerned Dolly most about POLY-CARB being acquired by DOW was the well-being of our team members. I explained that I was comfortable in regard to the consequences of following our value system. I was sure that our values and principles, as followed by our team members, would always distinguish and enhance them, even in the vast corporate ocean. To my mind, values and principles are followed and practiced only by people and not by companies, although companies are known by the values and principles practiced by its people.

POLY-CARB was now moving into a new chapter of its life, and it would be without me. We each needed to move on with our lives, such as they were, to discover new horizons for ourselves. Whatever POLY-CARB's outcome was going to be did not include me anymore. I was now free to pursue my other burgeoning interests. I would certainly be interested in observing POLY-CARB's continuing journey—and my hope was that the values and operating principles would influence the larger company, DOW, in ways that would elevate their stature in the world. Time would tell. Meanwhile, I needed to look forward, not backward, and greet life's next opportunities where I could implement my own values and operating principles to continuously make a difference and add value.

Chapter 19

Life after POLY-CARB

I t was Monday morning, and I had no business meetings or appointments scheduled all day. Friday had been my final day with POLY-CARB, now a part of DOW Chemical Co. I had a ton of things lined up to do, yet I didn't know where to begin. I sort of felt as if I were on my first day of vacation from work; it hadn't fully sunk in that I was no longer employed with a mountain of tasks in front of me. That reminded me of an incident that occurred in 2005. It concerned something I wanted to pursue once I retired, whenever that occurred.

My cell phone rang. It was my daughter, Nisha, calling from New York.

"Hello, Nisha. How are things with you? What are you up to today?"

"Hi, Dad. How are you? I was just cleaning the pictures I shot last night."

After a well-timed pause, I said, "Cleaning your pictures? Why would you shoot dirty pictures? Don't you know better?"

Nisha, who is a professional photographer in New York, did not expect this response and laughingly yelled at me, "*Daaad*, I don't take dirty pictures!"

After a gap of a few seconds, she continued, "Dad, you have to find something to do since this DOW thing or else you are going to drive me and Mom crazy!" Again there was a pause, and then, in all seriousness, Nisha asked, "What are you going to do now, Dad—now that you're retired?"

Smiling, I replied, "I was thinking of becoming the rock star of classical Indian music."

She laughed and said, "Mom has already revoked your license for all musical activities. I think you better stick to your books, radio, TV broadcast, and leadership training." We both laughed.

I had always been fascinated by Indian classical music, especially vocal music. I'd never gotten a chance to learn it, as I'd thought it was a natural gift of voice with which one was born. This belief was challenged by an amazing master of Indian classical music, Ms. Hasu Patel, whom I met in Cleveland in 2005, before DOW appeared on the scene. She assured me that anyone could learn to sing like a professional as long as he or she was prepared to put in hard work and practice under the guidance of a proper teacher or guru. She offered to be both.

I started my music lessons with a dream of one day performing on-stage in front of a live audience. With great enthusiasm, I started taking lessons every Sunday morning from 8:00 to 9:00 a.m. at her residence, located on the west side of Cleveland. It would take me at least an hour to travel from Chagrin Falls, where I lived. I would digitally record all of my lessons so that I could practice at home.

I sat in my study every Sunday afternoon with headphones on, listening to my recorded lessons and practicing. I had no idea of my progress or my inherent musical talents until I was already into my exercises and had practiced for over a month.

One Sunday afternoon, when I was engrossed in my practice and singing with the recorded voice of my teacher feeding into my ears through my headphones, our home phone suddenly started ringing. Dolly answered the phone, but in the midst of my melodious singing, she could not hear a word. She came into my room to ask me to put my practice on hold for a moment so that she could carry on her phone conversation. My eyes were closed, and I was into my exercises, singing with all that my lungs could pump out. She had to shake me and pull my headphones off to make me stop.

As she went back to the phone in her hand, she found she'd been disconnected. The call had been from POLY-CARB's technical director, Dr. Hemant Naik, from his home. Dolly called back, and Hemant's wife, Deepti, answered informing Dolly that Hemant had rushed out of their house and was on his way to our house after hearing the loud, terrifying howling coming through his phone. He was sure that someone had broken into our home and was choking Dolly.

When Dolly shared Deepti's husband's unsolicited evaluation of my musical talents and honest reaction to it, my dream of performing at the famous Carnegie Hall in New York City was shattered, and I had no choice but to give up my dream of becoming a rock star of Indian classical music. Good thing I'd not booked an agency and PR firm to launch my budding career. Although, I was able to bribe Nisha to take some high-resolution pictures of me just in case a newspaper or magazine wanted to do a feature on me. Painfully and with a heavy heart, I had to rethink my recent career shift to music and had to pursue something a little less noisy—and less frightening.

Isn't it amazing how, when we have a great idea about a new direction we'd like to take in our lives, our best-laid plans suddenly go awry and we find the door closed on us? I was disappointed when a simple phone call exposed my true musical talent and the door was closed on my rock-star dreams.

Here it was, 2007, and I was on my own, with everyone thinking I was going to become a man of leisure. But what I truly needed to be focusing on was right in front of me—and it wasn't retirement.

Here's how I view life's progression: life, as so many of us know it, is a series of cycles (e.g., youth & old age, school & graduation, work & retirement, and birth & death). We can't seem to escape any of them, yet within the oneness paradigm, our vision and mission for our life becomes integrated with our journey of making a difference and adding the highest value in all that we think, do, and undertake. Thus, retirement gets re-defined as merely a change of venue and not a change of our life-long mission—a journey of adding value.

Therefore, in the oneness paradigm, there is no such thing as retirement.

As law number nine, the The Law of Grace, states, *"The gift of life in its full integrated glory is only granted to us as we continue to add the highest value to the bigger One by completely and gratefully engaging all of our creative capacities until our last breath."* This is done on a daily basis—moment to moment—in all of our interactions and endeavors until our last breath.

> **#9: The Law of Grace**
> "The gift of life in its full integrated glory is only granted to us as we continue to add the highest value to the bigger One by completely and gratefully engaging all of our creative capacities until our last breath."

What I've discovered for myself is that essentially, school isn't out until I've taken my last breath—and even then, my consciousness will continue on into unimaginable explorations of worlds and planes of existence beyond my ken. This means that I am a learning machine meant to continually evolve, change, grow, and become more than I can imagine. Therefore, the concept of retirement appears to be a choice. In the oneness paradigm, though, it isn't a choice at all. For me to retire would be to stop living and just subsist or mentally and creatively die before my actual death. Is that the real purpose of living, and is it truly living?

When I looked up the word *retire*, I found some interesting synonyms: *shut down, give up, withdraw, hibernate, retreat, lose ground, ebb, resign, be shelved*, and *exit*. These words are pretty negative and strongly imply just the opposite of being engaged with life.

I needed to engage all of my faculties after DOW's acquisition of POLY-CARB, to engage with the true purpose of the oneness principle of adding the highest value at all times and in all that I did.

The idea of retiring really is a misconception, a misnomer, and a misdirection. So what was I to do if I was not retiring—continue working at some job? The answer was this: add value. There are a million ways for me to add value, from volunteering to part-time and full-time engagements. Life is not just about getting a job and making myself a useful and paying member of society. It's far more than that, as it pertains to giving of my expertise, time, and energy to whatever speaks to my soul and also adds value to others. Essentially, it's integrating the laws of the oneness paradigm into every facet of my life and applying them at all times.

Introducing the oneness thought process can be the turning point for any individual or organization no matter how small or large, young or old.

I have found that introducing the oneness thought process can be the turning point for any individual or organization no matter how small or large, young or old. As a mind-set, it challenges the prevailing one-dimensional paradigms of "king of the hill," "dog eat dog," and the "What's in it for me?" attitude. Oneness applies to every facet of life. If our attitude in any relationship of any type is that of being top dog and attaining a greater share of the relationship's benefits, then we're living in an unbalanced state of being.

It's all about our egos completely running the show and attaining what fits our personal agendas.

It is this short-sighted mind-set that imprisons us in a stress-filled, insecure, and empty life completely void of oneness. Without oneness, we are living against the way nature designed us. It is like driving a car in reverse on the highway at full speed—an accident just waiting to happen. Isn't this chaos much of what we're seeing displayed around the world?

Our world is at one of the most important junctures in its history. Do we use the same thinking that got us into this state to also get us out of our current predicament—Einstein's definition of insanity—or do we reach for a higher perspective and level of consciousness? Innately, my heart yearns to do what is right, honest, and ethical. I believe we are all designed to operate in this mode. It is in this mode that our lives become stress free, harmonious, and fulfilling. Do we live per our inborn design or contrary to this design? The choice is ours.

> Innately, our hearts yearn to do what is right, honest, and ethical. We are designed to operate in this mode. It is in this mode that our lives become stress free, harmonious, and fulfilling.

As I look around me, I see that ever-greater numbers of people are realizing the need for something better, something borne of our greater being—inclusive, empowering, deeply meaningful, life affirming, and unconditionally adding the highest value in all things. It is ironic that a line of thinking five centuries old can help us move forward into our future.

Even in the so-called real world, my sustainable and true happiness is gifted to me only when I am able to make someone else happy, and my happiness is further enhanced when it is unconditional. The formula is rather simple: to be happy, make others happy; to be rich, design a system that adds maximum value to others and makes everyone involved in the process share in the riches.

Right now, people are chafing, as they are not feeling a sense of freedom, of having uplifting options, or even having a great deal of hope. Yet, conversely, I see beautiful examples of people loving, serving, and giving unconditionally in response to events like tsunamis, earthquakes, and tornados. It would be truly extraordinary for us to live every day at this level instead of being prompted to do so during moments of crises. What an amazingly different world we would be living in if we invested every communication, relationship, and action with the wisdom of oneness.

Adding the highest value and oneness are, without a doubt, two extraordinary and life-changing imperatives. They can transform any situation, challenge, difficulty, conflict, and relationship. They are un-complicated—simplicity itself—yet they tear down old, stultifying systems while conversely raising us to greater heights of self and expression. The sky is the limit. So when I think of retirement, it's really time to re-assess what I'd like to do next with my life.

I see retirement as the time to truly let go of any strictures, conventions, and systems by which I've been living and to think big, let my creative juices flow, and soar. No longer am I earthbound; I am traveling the airwaves of invention, enterprise, and innovation. I'm no longer impeded by thoughts of mistakes or failure; instead, I perceive everything as a means to create greater value in the world—and if I am truly adding greater value, the universe will move needed resources to me.

Having said that, when I "retired" upon DOW's acquisition of POLY-CARB, I thought deeply about what I wanted to do with my time and energy that would add greater value to my community and the world at large. I observed with keen interest the events and goings-on in the world and determined that there were four major areas in which I could provide insight and creative innovation.

The four projects are large and have many tentacles, so they keep me busy and take every ounce of my energy and time.

One area involves education. I'm working with universities and institutions to eventually give birth to The International Institute of True Leadership. At this institution, education wouldn't be parked in silos, and the curriculum would be considered merely a tool. The real education would be about what we do with these tools, which is to connect to our overall purpose for being here on this earth—adding the highest value. We'd teach leadership—from the perspective and understanding of oneness and the nine oneness laws illustrated in this book—and students would learn to lead themselves first before attempting to lead others. This would crystallize their purpose and mission in life: to add value in all endeavors.

The second major focus for me is entrepreneurialism. I want to make entrepreneurship not about oneself, but about putting a team together to add the highest value. I have a center I've designed that focuses not only on entrepreneurs, but on getting entire communities involved in the mind-set of oneness and entrepreneurialism. Community involvement enhances the potential of buying into this process, thereby increasing its chances of succeeding and expanding.

The third incentive involves health care. Wellness, as we understand it today, only relates to our physical body, but doesn't address an wholistic approach of mind, body, and spirit. Furthermore, the business model of health care is heavily skewed toward making money on sickness rather than making money on wellness. Therefore, I'm currently working on a way to revise the health-care industry from a system of managing illness and addressing symptoms to one of capitalizing on prevention; we need to re-organize the entire health-care impetus and

Oneness is the fundamental spark within all of us. It enlivens all that we think, say, and do; it is the originator, the instigator, and the exponent; it is the prime directive by which we can order our lives.)

scenario so that the industry is rewarded for promoting and sustaining wellness.

The fourth project impacts us in our pocketbooks, livelihoods, and national and global economies. As our society matures, I find the paradigm of job creation obsolete. What we've seen historically is job creation as a Band-Aid that only addresses economic issues and crises in the short term. The project I'm working on focuses on wealth creation rather than job creation, which enriches our entire society, enhancing its buying power and long-term sustainability.

Now is the time to take on the meaningful projects and ideas that will benefit all of mankind. It's time to stretch beyond who we've always felt ourselves to be. As Sherman Finesilver put it, "... greatness is a measure of one's spirit." And that spirit—oneness—is the fundamental spark within all of us. It enlivens all that we think, say, and do; it is the originator, the instigator, and the exponent; it is the prime directive by which we can order our lives.

So what does that mean for you? What are you going to do in the next moment that will add value to your family, community, country, or world? What have you always wanted to do, but never done that would shed new light on something, open doors of perception and understanding, invite others to explore and discover or re-discover, or uplift humanity? Is it something that means starting at the top or taking small steps that build momentum toward critical mass?

What will you discover about yourself?

You know what it is—don't be afraid to let it out, to let it fill you, to share it. Enlist others in your vision; see who's already doing something similar, and collaborate with him or her to see just how you can create ever-greater value together. What will it be—the environment, politics, our tax system, potable drinking water, renewable energy sources, health and well-being, social enterprise, entrepreneurship, education, aging and elder care, the human genome, history, the arts, population issues, the sciences, astrophysics?

There are a million possibilities, and one of them is waiting just for you. Now is the time.

Just as in 1968, when I embarked on my journey to the US, I had no idea what lay in store for me. Yet here I am, over four decades later, having trekked across an amazing terrain of experiences, challenges, and opportunities—and life is still an adventure full of possibilities. The key is oneness. Oneness integrates all, encompasses all, and brings the much sought-after harmony each of us seeks in all aspects of life. Oneness is truly humanity's destiny.

> True joy comes from focusing on the journey of life
> rather than the destination.
> Journeys bring joy, as they are tied to exploration and discovery,
> which inspire gratefulness and acceptance of whatever comes.
> If we put all of our focus on making a positive difference
> throughout each step of our journey,
> the destination will take care of itself.

And so it is with each of our journeys—with your journey. How will you give of your gifts today? What collaborations can you initiate that will encompass and uplift the hearts and engage the minds and imaginations of everyone involved? Let go of the noise and distractions of the world by integrating into oneness. Stop and consider the following: "In what ways can I become a pure, value-adding entity enabling me to live a successful, joy-filled, and stress-free life?"

The world is waiting for you!

Appendix A

Life's Intrinsic Wisdom

Life is an extraordinary, ever-shifting journey shaped and modulated by the people in our lives, events and experiences, our relationships, our talents and skills, and the energy and creativity we put toward all of our undertakings. Absolutely everything is a stepping stone that aids us in understanding ourselves and the world around us and in not only surviving, but thriving.

Life is also an ongoing challenge, one fraught with myriad highs and lows. Many life maps have been created over the years, giving people pathways to resolving and solving conflicts and issues in their lives. Each has its methodology and system for attaining greater understanding and equanimity in one's world. Yet, challenges still abound day in and day out, and we're left searching for yet another means for engendering lasting well-being at home, at work, in our communities, and in the world at large.

I have found in my life experience that many people are seeking the indefinable, all-encompassing connection to the fundamental core of their being—the one that answers all needs, assuages all fears, that provides the insight and wisdom to navigate life's gauntlet of surprises and tests and fills one's heart with unending and immeasurable love, peace, and joy. The question many have asked me over the years is: "What is the thing that will save me, that will give me the freedom I seek?"

I've always answered, "Oneness." I've written about oneness throughout this book, which I hope has given you an understanding of what oneness is and the intrinsic laws by which we can live it. To provide a recap, I've arranged these laws into what I call the nine Laws of Wisdom. They are, in a word, universal: unchallengeable, absolute, incontrovertible, and cannot be denied. They are like the universal principles of gravity and light.

> The nine laws are the supporting structure upon which you can build a whole new life, not just for yourself, but for all of humankind.

These nine Laws of Wisdom change lives. Just as ripples spread from a stone dropped into a still pond, the effect of these indisputable laws radiates out into the world, transforming those it touches. Change occurs: perceptions change, motivations change, lives change.

Mahatma Gandhi said, "Be the change you want to see in the world." Yes, *you* can be the change. It's simple, and the nine Laws of Wisdom are the supporting structure upon which you can build a whole new life, not just for yourself, but also for all of humankind. In review, you'll see how each law builds upon and supports the others, creating a latticework scaffolding of enduring steps to freedom.

#1 – The Law of Purpose:

"Our sole purpose in life is to add the highest value we can in all our endeavors unconditionally and continuously."

This includes all of humanity, life, and the environment—the bigger One.

This is the prime directive for life and covers every facet of our daily interactions both in our own minds and in working with others. It truly is a mind-set, a radical departure from the current paradigm within which the world operates.

Once you know who you are, then you know who everyone else is. That recognition automatically establishes your interconnection with everyone, and you begin to think as one. Just as the parts of our human bodies work to keep us alive, each person has his or her role to play, yet works with others as an ensemble to sustain the bigger body unconditionally. Once our understanding of who we are becomes clear, our purpose in life becomes clear: adding the highest value to whomever comes in front of us.

Oprah Winfrey, for example, started in television as the co-anchor of a local Tennessee evening news show when she was nineteen. From there, she was transferred to the daytime talk-show format, went on to form her own production company, and her talk show became the highest-rated program of its type in television history. Her show was at first considered tabloid television, so Oprah sought to broaden the show's format, draw, and significance and thus focused more on literature, self-improvement, and spirituality. She has now taken that format to an even higher level with her show *Oprah's Lifeclass*, which her web site states elucidates her "lessons, revelations and aha moments over the past 25 years broken down to help make your life better, happier, bigger, richer—more fulfilling."

Additionally, Oprah formed Oprah's Angel Network, a public charity, in 1998. The network "… was established to encourage people around the world to make a difference in the lives of others. Oprah's vision is to inspire individuals to create opportunities that enable underserved women and children to rise to their potential. Oprah's Angel Network initiates and supports charitable projects and provides grants to not-for-profit organizations around the globe that share in this vision." The network has done the following:

- Built over fifty-five schools in twelve countries, providing education for thousands of children in rural areas
- Provided more than $1 million in school supplies to eighteen thousand impoverished African children
- Had nearly three hundred homes built or restored in Texas, Mississippi, Louisiana, and Alabama following Hurricane Katrina
- Along with Free the Children, launched the O Ambassadors school-based program that inspires young people to become active, compassionate, and knowledgeable global citizens
- Given grants to organizations that provide life-changing assistance for women and girls
- Provided scholarships and grants to individuals, organizations, and charities

Though the Angel Network is no longer operating, in its many years, it managed to garner over $80 million in donations, and Oprah plans to continue her philanthropy with her new cable network.

#2 – The Law of Acceptance:

"Accept life as it comes to us with gratefulness and without conditions."

To enable ourselves to stay on the path of adding the highest value, we must first accept life as it comes to us—with utter gratefulness and unconditionally—without prejudice, fear, judgment, or regret. As a consequence, we will operate in the present and will then be in a position to explore the hidden opportunities—in both our failures and successes—to add the highest value.

Life is full of rich experiences; what we take from those experiences depends on how we choose to perceive life: it is either happening to us or for us. If we determine that all of our experiences are happening *for*

> Everything happens for a reason, and it's all about our evolvement to a greater understanding of who we are, our place in the world, and how we can add to life in brilliant and immeasurable ways.

us, then life takes on greater meaning and depth. Truly, there is nothing to fear then. Everything happens for a reason, and it's all about our evolvement to a greater understanding of who we are, our place in the world, and how we can add to life in brilliant and immeasurable ways.

Accepting life as it comes to us is about living in the present and not living in a mind-set of what might have been or could be. It's not about focusing on regrets derived from our past or fear of what the future might hold for us. All action and the capitalization on our opportunities can only take place in the present. We can only operate in the present when we accept our current situation and creatively figure out a way to add the highest value.

In 1982 in Brisbane, Australia, Nicholas Vujicic (Vooy-cheek) was born without arms or legs. What could he ever do or become while living with such a massive disability? Little did he, his parents, or anyone else know, this limbless baby would one day become someone who could inspire, motivate, and touch the hearts and minds of people from all walks of life around the world.

Growing up, Nick dealt with the same issues many kids do, from bullying to self-esteem issues. He struggled with depression and loneliness, wondering, *Why me?* He questioned what possible purpose he could have, having been born the way he was.

Over time, he adapted to his physical challenges and discovered ways to do many of the things most people do, from everyday care of his body to swimming and diving to surfing and golf. By age nineteen, Nick found his calling: motivating people to be more than they could imagine, no matter what life served them. He firmly believes that every single person on Earth has a purpose in life and that one's attitude will determine his or her ability to overcome any kind of obstacle.

Nick, now living in California, has become the president of Life Without Limbs, an organization focused on the message of "freedom to love without limits" and the "freedom to overcome without limits" (www.lifewithoutlimbs.org). He has traveled around the world, speaking to people of all ages, including students and teachers, businesspeople, entrepreneurs, and church congregations. He encourages audiences to have a vision, to dream big, to examine their perspectives and see beyond their situations no matter what they are. Everything to him is an opportunity to grow. He believes that the decisions we make affect not only us, but the world around us. Therefore, we must face our fears head-on, have no regrets, and make the changes that will create the fulfilling life we envision.

#3 – The Law of Abundance:

"Abundance comes from the realization that resources do not belong to us, but are merely allocated to us to add the highest value."

In order to operate in an abundance mentality, it is important to understand that it is not possible to own anything, as all resources belong to the bigger One and are merely allocated to us. Their allocation is either enhanced or depleted based on whether we are adding the highest value to the bigger One or not.

Many of the world's problems are based on a "this is mine, and you can't have it" mind-set. This territorial thinking has been with us since day one. It sets up a system of haves and have-nots and competition at any cost. Adding

Adding the highest value dispenses with egocentric, possessive thinking and seeks only to uplift the world around us. In the process, we also uplift ourselves.

the highest value dispenses with egocentric, possessive thinking and seeks only to uplift the world around us. In the process, we also uplift ourselves, though that is not our primary focus, just an additional benefit. Once we leave the selfish words *I, me, my*, and *mine* out of our communication and interactions and seek only to add the highest value, the universe will take notice. Then watch and see what happens.

We must all understand that all the resources of the universe are merely gifted to us, and if we add the highest value, those resources will continue to increase. If someone else adds higher value, these resources will surely migrate to the entity adding the higher value. Fundamentally, we do not own anything.

For any business to remain sustainable, they must position themselves on the path of continuous improvement, making sure that these improvements add the highest value to our society, an integral part of the bigger One.

In today's global situation, the US thinks that its competition is Brazil, Russia, India, and China with their low labor costs and government subsidies. But the fact is that US companies are not able to clearly distinguish what they produce as the highest-value-adding products, so the only denominator left is pricing. The US can't win that war.

For the US to compete with these countries, it has to produce products that are far superior, that add the highest value and sustain the path of continuous improvement.

In this amazing paradox of letting go of ownership, we begin to operate in unconditional and limitless abundance. We realize that all the resources of the universe are at our disposal as long as our focus remains on unconditionally adding the highest value at all times and serving the bigger One. The oneness paradigm is flawless in that there is no "I, me, my, mine," and there's no beginning or end, as in itself, it is a complete process of being.

The truth is, even when people with the greatest egos are in the middle of creating something great, their egos don't exist.

The trap in all of this is, of course, the ego. Ego rises up when we take ownership. In life, we are given awards and rewards for the things we do. This feeds and inflates our egos, as we think we are the ones who have done great things and are special beyond others. The truth is, even when people with the greatest egos are in the middle of creating something great, their egos don't exist.

When you go to concerts at Carnegie Hall and artists are at the peak of their performances, they don't exist. Only the music exists. They have become completely one with their art and performance. Ego only comes in at the end, when there is resounding applause. Their egos stand and take the bows, not the art or the artists.

In general, the egocentric happiness we experience is fleeting, as what we have accomplished is external to our being and quickly becomes nothing but a memory and disappears into the vast abyss of human history. Happiness is therefore tied to the journey, not the destination—and the journey is continually and unconditionally staying on the path of adding the highest value at all times.

#4 – The Law of Integrity:

"For true, sustainable, and stress-free success and happiness, every thought, word, action, and decision must be completely immersed in and integrated into oneness."

This is the key to true, sustainable, and stress-free success in all aspects of life.

The big question is this: What is oneness?

Oneness is that common omnipresent power, energy, and link running through everyone and everything, giving us life itself. Oneness unifies us into a bigger One. Essentially, we're vehicles consciously enlivened and physically powered by that common superpower—oneness.

That means we are all a single, unified One and not separate entities in spite of the apparent fact that we are physically individuals with our own minds and bodies. We can think and do whatever we desire and without anyone's interference or permission or knowledge. We can call that omnipresent force or power whatever we please: the Universal Power, the Supreme Soul, the Divine Power, or even God. It is this power or force that unifies us into a bigger One. And that bigger One is what brings us into alignment with unconditionally loving, serving, and giving in all our endeavors.

Oneness encapsulates every aspect of our lives and living. In the absence of this truth, all of our choices, decisions, efforts, and even best-thought-out plans coupled with persistence and hard work supported by the most sophisticated technology and data will only lead us to unsustainable, short-term, and partial successes that are full of stress and uncertainties.

To not live and operate within the oneness paradigm is to see the world through a glass darkly: we're basing our actions and decisions upon a partial picture of reality and are therefore subject to the vagaries of life. We're easily pulled off course by all of life's stimulating distractions.

In oneness, we become a catalyst for bringing about a positive change that benefits all the components of the bigger One—all of humanity, all living creatures, and the planet itself.

Oneness sweeps aside all distractions and illusions and dives right into the very core of life: the bigger One. In oneness, we become a catalyst for bringing about a positive change that benefits all the components of the bigger One—all of humanity, all living creatures, and the planet itself. Most amazingly, all the needed resources we seek will gravitate to us to support the bigger common purpose. We are then serving the bigger One, the Divine that permeates and enlivens everything.

The only way to serve this collective, omnipresent power is to serve that same power present in everyone we come across. The only way to do that is to first experience and feel the presence of that power—oneness—within ourselves, which is done by continuously adding the highest value through our specific gifts, talents, skills, resources, and our continuous yearning for knowledge.

In simple and practical terms, the dynamic of oneness is that whatever happens to one person or being affects everyone. A good analogy for this mind-set is our own human body. It consists of numerous parts and organs with clearly defined functions. Yet the entire body works in unison. If one part goes bad or gets injured, the pain and suffering will be felt by the entire body. Failure of a single organ can kill the entire human form.

The most extraordinary part of operating in oneness is that we are automatically supported by the wisdom and power of the universe. It's like rowing a boat in the same direction as a flowing river—there's no stress, and there's no getting exhausted. We get help from natural forces. Our decisions are not burdened by or entrenched in our worries, fear, greed, false hopes, prejudices, or egocentric insecurities and confidence. We're not even confined to the limits of our conceived assets, including our knowledge, experience, wealth, intelligence, and education.

We are now positioned for true success in all of our endeavors, which are not limited to our businesses or careers, but also include our relationships and personal and social successes. We can enjoy success that is inclusive and complete, ever growing and expanding as we seek to add the highest value in all that we do.

#5 – The Law of Leadership:

"We cannot lead others until we lead ourselves first. In order to lead ourselves first, we must know who we truly are through comprehending the oneness paradigm."

The irony is that many of us think we are leading ourselves, when instead, our egos, insecurities, and greed end up leading us. The essential prerequisite for leading ourselves is to discover who in us should lead what in us.

Shakespeare's "To thine own self be true" is a wonderful admonition to us all. We get so caught up in this frenetic world that we lose sight of who we truly are. In life, we want to be accepted and included by our families, friends, jobs, and communities—so much so that we begin to behave according to the dictates and demands of those relationships. Consequently, the person we show the world is a facsimile, a mask, a role—not the real us. Acting as a facsimile, we find ourselves lost in a sea of external

To find that true, genuine self, we have to begin the process of rediscovering our authentic being by reviewing how we got off track, peeling away the layers of our life experiences, and learning to lead ourselves once more rather than being led.

influences, and one day, we begin to feel dissatisfied and unfulfilled with life and work, with who we've become—we are no longer true to ourselves.

To find that true, genuine self, we have to begin the process of re-discovering our authentic being by reviewing how we got off track, peeling away the layers of our life experiences, and learning to lead ourselves once more rather than being led. It starts with remembering and understanding the fundamental core of our being: oneness and our intrinsic interconnection with all of life. We are now set to lead ourselves, no longer buffeted about by life and the wants, needs, agendas, opinions, and judgments of others. Now we can practice and live the qualities of leadership, which are not according to the shifting intrigues of a fickle world. This is the wellspring of true leadership.

Each of us inherently has a leader residing within us, yet for various reasons, we either hide from it and let others lead or we take on the characteristics of socio-cultural definitions of leadership and end up getting waylaid by the misunderstandings and distractions of leadership. True leadership is borne from within, directly connected to the greater source/power residing within all of us—the bigger One. It's there within *you*. It's not about ego, fame, wealth, power, or control. It's about your direct and infinite connection to the bigger One, however you define it.

You already have residing within you all the skills of a true leader. Mahatma Gandhi did not see himself as a leader, and he never strove to be a leader. He did understand, though, that a true leader's principles and values are not for sale, displayed only when others are watching, or adhered to when convenient. He lived his principles and values every day without wavering. Others gravitated to him, the resources of the universe gravitated to him, and he was no more special than anyone else.

> A woman brought her son to see Gandhi because her son was eating too much sugar. Since her son was so captivated by Gandhi, she thought her son would listen

to him. The two undertook a long journey, traveling by foot under a hot sun in order to visit Gandhi. When they arrived at his compound, they waited a long time to see him, and when seated with him, the mother explained the situation with her son and sugar. Gandhi's only reply was to ask her and her son to return in two weeks. The mother was perplexed, but did as she was asked. Once again, they made the long, tiring, and hot journey on foot. This time, when seated with Gandhi, he simply told her son to stop eating sugar, saying that it wasn't good for him. The mother was rather perturbed with Gandhi, wondering why he hadn't told her son this the first time they'd visited, especially since the trip had been so arduous. Gandhi explained that since he himself had been eating too much sugar at the time, then he couldn't in all integrity ask someone else to stop eating sugar until he had himself quit.

That leader resides within you. All you need to do is unveil your true self. And remember, you can't lead others until you lead yourself first—and you can't do that until you unveil your true self.

#6 –The Law of Freedom:

"We create real freedom through the discipline of oneness, which guides us in choosing and living our values unconditionally."

It is only the wisdom of oneness that gives us our core value system, and we are then able to practice those values even when no one is watching. It is through living these values that we create our true freedom.

Discipline is one of those words from which most people shy away or even run away. We think in terms of strict teachers and intractable prison wardens watching and judging our every move. True discipline has nothing to do with that type of oversight. It's about first determining what our values are and then following through at all times in practicing and living them. It has nothing to do with other people. If we're practicing values for other people's benefit, then we've missed out on the central theme of this immutable wisdom: to thine own self be true—period.

> An integrated value system grounded in oneness empowers and supports our willpower. In its absence, our willpower is merely a wish list.

Once our values and discipline are firmly integrated into the fabric of our being, we have discovered true freedom, and nothing can deter us. Our total being unconditionally accepts the discipline to follow our values, and thus, discipline happens without resistance or thought; it's an organic initiative and response all at the same time. Therefore, true discipline has less to do with willpower and more to do with a well-integrated value system. An integrated value system grounded in oneness empowers and supports our willpower. In its absence, our willpower is merely a wish list.

When Nelson Mandela was on trial in 1964 at the Pretoria Supreme Court in South Africa, he stated, "During my lifetime I have dedicated myself to the struggle of the African people. I have fought against white domination, and I have fought against black domination. I have cherished the ideal of a democratic and free society in which all persons live together in harmony and with equal opportunities. It is an ideal which I hope to live for and to achieve. But if needs be, it is an ideal for which I am prepared to die." The outcome of the trial was life imprisonment. In 1990, Mandela was released after serving twenty-seven years of his sentence.

During his incarceration, the treatment by the warders was often brutal and rested upon a system of rules and punitive responses to infractions aimed at breaking a prisoner's spirit. Throughout Mandela's imprisonment, he maintained his dignity, giving the rest of the political prisoners a model to follow. Additionally, through his exemplary deportment in all communications and assiduous maintenance of his daily schedule of prison routines, he presented a means to break down the walls of racism and power exhibited by the prison staff. With young revolutionaries, he remained a serious, calm, focused, and fatherly figure of disciplined composure.

From the beginning of his trial, to his twenty-seven years in prison, to the day he was freed to the day he was elected president of South Africa, Nelson never wavered from his values, personal and political, which brought about an end to apartheid and racialism in his country and launched the movement toward equanimity for all South African citizens. He remained true to himself and his purpose in life, which was to create a world of equality not just for South Africa but for all peoples of the world.

#7 – The Law of Change:

"Living in the reality of constant motion and change, we must remain in a student mode of learning and making our best better."

By making our best better, we are bettering ourselves. Remaining in student mode gives us unprecedented freedom, as we don't limit ourselves in any way; we become a constant state of motion and change as we seek new solutions and more creative and productive processes to uplift everyone, not just ourselves or a select group.

Did you know that you acquire a whole new body every two to three years? Literally, the you of today didn't exist two or three years ago because each molecule has been replaced by a new molecule. So you see, change is happening right within each of us, just as the solar system and universe are not static, but moving at incredible speeds. Once we accept the inevitability of change, we can then plan everything based on change, which is going to come about either through technology, circumstances, or events. All changes offer opportunities to add the highest value in everything we do.

Walt Disney strove tirelessly to improve on his work. He began by making commercials based on cutout animations and then became interested in animation and started producing Laugh-O-Grams. After moving to Hollywood, he began Alice Comedies, which morphed into the first Disney studio, and the Disney entertainment empire has now become a $35 billion industry.

When Disney first began planning Disneyland, team members dubbed themselves "Imagineers," a term first coined by Alcoa in the 1940s as a combination of *imagination* and *engineers*. Imagineers are tasked with ongoing creativity and technological innovation in all aspects of the Disney Company and its affiliates. To date, the Disney Imagineers have been granted over 115 patents in various areas, such as ride systems, special effects, interactive technology, live entertainment, fiber optics, and advanced audio systems. Essentially, the Imagineers never stop seeking ways to improve, expand upon, and add greater value in all they do. And all of us get to benefit from their efforts in ways of which we aren't even aware.

> By being open and not being afraid to explore and take information in without judgment, we are more apt to discover life's continuing wonders.

The world is in constant motion, and what we call reality is always changing. By being open and not being afraid to explore and take information in without judgment, we are more apt to discover life's continuing wonders. And who knows what areas will pique our interest, where we can contribute in some way that will benefit all of humanity and the environment? We can all become Imagineers in every area of life. Who knows what wonders the universe has in store for us? It's time to step out of our gravity boots of safety and security, trust the universe, and soar.

#8 – The Law of Values:

"We can only live our inherent, true values, true integrity, when we are completely integrated with and immersed in the one Divine Power—oneness."

Oneness results in the removal of our illusionary egos, and we become truth and trustworthiness—essentially, integrity itself.

Integrity is one of those words, unlike *discipline*, that engages us in a positive and grounded way. We feel good when we display integrity. The thing about integrity, though, is that it is a 24-7 scenario, not a once-in-a-while opportunity to show off in front of others. Living our values 24-7 creates a clear pathway for us to follow, undeterred by life's distractions and our egocentric desires. The outcome, integrity, will radiate outwardly to those around us. Combined with the other immutable Laws of Wisdom, we're now in a position to truly lead ourselves, which will translate into providing true leadership for others.

"I'm not an American hero. I'm a person who loves children." Clara McBride Hale said this when she attended former president Ronald Reagan's State of the Union address in1985. In his address, he said of her, "Harlem and all of New York needs a local hero. Mother Hale, you are the one ... an American hero, whose life tells us that the oldest American saying is new again: Anything is possible in America if we have the faith, the will, and the heart."

Ms. Hale accepted this national recognition with the deep humility and reserve for which she was known. Though she received over 370 awards and 15 honorary degrees in her lifetime for working tirelessly with the children of poverty, addiction and AIDS, her sole focus was on providing care for at-risk children and their families.

Starting in 1940, Ms. Hale, a single mother of two, began caring for children short term and long term in her small home in Harlem, New

York City. During this period, she became known as Mother Hale, named so by those who benefitted from her loving care.

Beginning in 1969, when she intended to retire at age sixty-four, she instead began caring for the babies born exposed to alcohol and/or drugs because the need was so evident, yet non-existent. At that time, Hale House was opened in a Harlem brownstone. As children became healthy beyond the addictions with which they were born, Hale House then worked to have the children adopted into suitable homes.

Then, as AIDS appeared in the early '80s, Hale House became the first institution to create visibility around the innocent victims of the AIDS crisis—babies who had lost their parents to AIDS and/or were born HIV positive.

Ms. Hale was cognizant of the social and ethnic disparities in the US and was vigilant in ensuring young people had access to the highest levels of education. Hale House's key operational words are *empower, educate*, and *excel*.

It was said of Ms. Hale's contributions: "Well, Mother Hale didn't have a PhD, MD or any other kind of D, but she just took in that first drug baby back in 1969. All she had was a rocking chair."

Throughout her years working with children in Harlem, Ms. Hale was grounded in the values instilled in her by her mother's example and those of her church. She continued living and working in Hale House until her passing in 1992 at the age of eighty-seven.

She was a living example of someone who practiced oneness without labeling it as oneness. She never judged the children she took care of or called them addicts or orphans. She merely saw the presence of the same one Divine power in them and served them as her own. She became integrated with them through oneness and thus was able to practice integrity.

The operating title for Hale House today is the Center for the Promotion of Human Potential. Ms. Hale, through her values and unconditional giving and inclusiveness, was an exemplar of this every day of her life.

We only activate or invoke our integrity, which otherwise lies dormant within us, when we first become one and completely integrate with the oneness process and see the omnipresent one Divine power within everyone. This integrity empowers us beyond our wildest imagination to undertake unprecedented missions and objectives to add the highest value to our families, communities, businesses, and to all of humanity and the environment unconditionally.

> Integrity empowers us beyond our wildest imagination to undertake unprecedented missions and objectives to add the highest value to our families, communities, businesses, and to all of humanity and the environment unconditionally.

It is important to realize that all our other values—honesty, trustworthiness, loyalty, ethicalness, self-control, discipline, kindness, respect, gratefulness, lack of ego, selflessness, humility, dependability, honoring our promises, courage, fearlessness, loyalty, cleanliness, vision, fairness, a sense of humor, good communication and listening skills, the ability to be a team player, confidence, the ability to function at a high level—all organically come out of the seed of integrity, which originates from oneness.

#9 – Law of Grace:

"The gift of life in its full integrated glory is only granted to us as we continue to add the highest value to the bigger One by completely and gratefully engaging all of our creative capacities until our last breath."

In the oneness paradigm, there is no such thing as retirement. We must engage our creative capacities on a daily basis—moment to moment—in all of our interactions and endeavors until our last breath.

The founder and longtime chairman of Apple, Inc., Steve Jobs, was the epitome of this immutable wisdom. He didn't retire even though he knew he had only a few days left to live. He worked until the last day his human body allowed him in order to deliver his innovations, vision, guidance, persona, and the empowering glue that inspired his team to consistently operate in its highest mode. Making money and achieving fame were distractions for him. His fulfillment came from adding the highest value through breakthrough technology infused with intuitive, easy-to-use products, innovative concepts, and customer-focused services.

His greatly touted financial success was merely a by-product. Anything he would put Apple's name on had to be the best in its category. In fact, he even redefined "the best" over and over again by making his best better. The world kept wondering what he would do next. He kept his team's focus on adding the highest value. The world called him gifted, a genius, and visionary. He merely kept his focus on paying his dues for the gift of life and the creative energy granted to him by the bigger One—and he kept on paying his dues until his last breath.

Immutable and Intrinsic Wisdom for Success in Life

#1 – The Law of Purpose

"Our sole purpose in life is to add the highest value we can in all our endeavors unconditionally and continuously."

Our sole purpose in life is to add the highest value we can in all our endeavors—to the bigger One—including for all of humanity, life, and the environment unconditionally and continuously.

#2 – The Law of Acceptance

"Accept life as it comes to us with gratefulness and without conditions."

To enable ourselves to stay on the path of adding the highest value, we must first accept life as it comes to us—with utter gratefulness and unconditionally—without prejudice, fear, judgment, or regret. As a consequence, we will operate in the present and will then be in a position to explore the hidden opportunities—in both our failures and successes—to add the highest value.

#3 – The Law of Abundance
"Abundance comes from the realization that resources do not belong to us, but are merely allocated to us to add the highest value."
In order to operate in an abundance mentality, it is important to understand that it is not possible to own anything, as all resources belong to the bigger One and are merely allocated to us. Their allocation is either enhanced or depleted based on whether we are adding the highest value to the bigger One or not.

#4 – The Law of Integrity
"For true, sustainable, and stress-free success and happiness, every thought, word, action, and decision must be completely immersed in and integrated into oneness."
This is the key to true, sustainable, and stress-free success in all aspects of life.

#5 – The Law of Leadership
"We cannot lead others until we lead ourselves first. In order to lead ourselves first, we must know who we truly are through comprehending the oneness paradigm."
The irony is that many of us think we are leading ourselves, when instead, our egos, insecurities, and greed end up leading us. The essential prerequisite for leading ourselves is to discover who in us should lead what in us.

#6 – The Law of Freedom
"We create real freedom through the discipline of oneness, which guides us in choosing and living our values unconditionally."
It is only the wisdom of oneness that gives us our core value system, and we are then able to practice those values even when no one is watching. It is through living these values that we create our true freedom.

#7 – The Law of Change
"Living in the reality of constant motion and change, we must remain in a student mode of learning and making our best better."

#8 – The Law of Values

"We can only live our inherent, true values, true integrity, when we are completely integrated with and immersed in the one Divine Power—oneness."

Oneness results in the removal of our illusionary egos, and we become truth and trustworthiness—essentially, integrity itself.

#9 – Law of Grace

"The gift of life in its full integrated glory is only granted to us as we continue to add the highest value to the bigger One by completely and gratefully engaging all of our creative capacities until our last breath."

In the oneness paradigm, there is no such thing as retirement. We must engage our creative capacities on a daily basis—moment to moment—in all of our interactions and endeavors until our last breath.

Appendix B

A Little Indian History

In 1968, when I was to fly to America to begin my PhD program at The University of Akron, I realized that per restrictions imposed by the Reserve Bank of India, I could only get eight dollars in American exchange to come to the United States.

Fortunately, I had a close friend, Dr. Rao, who had just returned from the US and could lend me $500 to start my life in America.

The story behind this exchange restriction is etched in Indian history. In the 1960s, India was still in the early decades of nation building. After almost three hundred years of Muslim rule and two hundred years of British colonial domination, India was freed and became an independent nation in 1947.

India is the birthplace of four religions—Hinduism, Sikhism, Jainism, and Buddhism—and is also home to Muslims, Christians, and

Jews. Its diversity and natural resources are immense, but in 1947, it was a country recovering from the aftermath of colonial policies that had stifled manufacturing and drained it of its natural resources to serve an imperial economy.

India's early national leaders—Mahatma Gandhi and Jawaharlal Nehru (India's first prime minister)—stressed the importance of building an indigenous economy to generate self-reliance and kept imports to a minimum. Generating employment for the millions of poor, uneducated men and women of India was crucial.

Within this socialist model of the state being the "big player," meaning that the biggest industries were state owned, another key aspect was education. By the 1960s, as a result of Nehru's vision for an educated India, there were several premiere institutions educating engineers, medical doctors, and scientists while charging a fee of only five to ten dollars a month. The competition to be accepted into these institutions was tough, but students didn't have to be rich.

Interestingly, even though such education was heavily funded by the state, no one was expected to serve the state in return. It was argued that in a democratic state, an Indian could choose to work where he or she wanted to. By the late 1960s, Indian engineers and scientists ready to enter the market were ahead of the pace of India's industrialization, and many began seeking new pastures overseas in the UK, the US, and Canada. The newly changed immigration laws of 1965, wherein the US began a preferential immigration quota for professionals in science, provided a perfect fit for someone like me.

While as an Indian citizen I was free to relocate overseas, my government maintained stringent policies concerning foreign exchange in order to discourage the transfer of wealth out of India. So, eight dollars was the ceiling allowed for carrying cash. However, we could take personal belongings, and I could buy tickets for traveling to the US, which my travel agent arranged. Thus, on September 23, 1968, I entered the US via Boston with eight dollars in my pocket.

Before I flew to Akron, I spent my first two weeks with Amrik Singh Pabley in Boston, an engineer and my cousin from India, who was my introduction to America—a country that was to be my home for decades to come.

About the Author

Ratanjit Singh Sondhe emigrated from India to the United States in 1968 with no more than a few dollars in his pocket and the belief that our purpose in life is to add value to the lives of those around us. Over the past forty years, this purpose has brought Ratanjit great success. He was the founder and CEO of the international materials science company POLY-CARB, Inc., which was acquired by The DOW Chemical Company in 2007. Ratanjit is also an educator, lecturer, author, radio and television host, well-respected member of the community, father, and husband.

To help others achieve stress-free success and true joy, Ratanjit wrote *TEA: The Recipe for Stress-Free Living, The Secret of Our Ultimate Success*, and numerous award-winning papers; has hosted more than five hundred international radio and television programs; and has traveled the world, delivering captivating words of wisdom to help others succeed, realize their true freedom, maximize their potential, take full control of their lives, unveil their true passions, and live stress free.

More information about Ratanjit S. Sondhe can be found online at www.discoverhelp.com and www.ratanjit.com.